The Living City

THE LIVING CITY

Towards a sustainable future

EDITED BY
DAVID CADMAN AND GEOFFREY PAYNE

Routledge
London and New York

First published 1990
by Routledge
11 New Fetter Lane, London EC4P 4EE

Simultaneously published in the USA and Canada
by Routledge
a division of Routledge, Chapman and Hall, Inc.
29 West 35th Street, New York, NY 10001

© 1990 David Cadman and Geoffrey Payne
Typeset by Gilfillan Limited, Mitcham, Surrey.
Printed in Great Britain by
Richard Clay Ltd, Bungay, Suffolk

British Library Cataloguing in Publication Data
The Living City: towards a sustainable future.
1. Cities
I. Cadman, David II. Payne, Geoffrey
307.7'64

Library of Congress Cataloguing in Publication Data
The Living city.
Papers presented at the Seminar on Future Cities held at Oxford Polytechnic in 1987.
Includes index.
1. Cities and towns – Congresses. I. Cadman, David. II. Payne, Geoffrey K. III. Seminar on Future Cities (1987: Oxford Polytechnic)
TH107.L58 1989   307.76   89-10416
ISBN 0-415-01250-3

Contents

Preface   vii
Acknowledgements   x
Introduction: **Towards another city**   1
    David Cadman and Geoffrey Payne

About Part I   35

    1 **On the development of cities**   37
    Dennis Hay

    2 **The future economic role of urban systems**   54
    Iain Begg and Barry Moore

    3 **Urban change in the Third World: are recent trends a useful pointer to the urban future?**
    Jorge E. Hardoy and David Satterthwaite   75

    4 **Can Third World cities be managed?**
    Carole Rakodi   111

About Part II   125

    5 **Alternative futures for cities**
    James Robertson   127

    6 **Town and country**
    John Holmes and Geoffrey Steeley   136

    7 **Mad Maurice III: metropolitans in the making**
    Joe Cullen   152

    8 **The metabolism of cities**
    Herbert Girardet   170

9 **Barriers, channels and community control**
John F.C. Turner   181

10 **The politics of sustainable Third World urban development**
Tade Akin Aina   192

11 **Increasing technological choice in Third World settlements**
George McRobie   206

12 **Controlled Third World decentralization: a tale of two countries**
Charles L. Choguill   212

13 **Development through partnership: the Orangi project in Karachi**
Arif Hasan   221

Conclusions and new beginnings
David Cadman and Geoffrey Payne   227

Index   236

Preface

If you were trying to rank ventures in their order of danger, you would probably put hang-gliding or crossing the Atlantic in a hot-air balloon fairly high on the list and organizing a seminar on the future of the city fairly low. However, even seminar organizing has its risks. The safest thing to do is to gather together people of like minds and then let everybody, 'say their piece'. The result? - a general sense of well-being and the agreeable confirmation of one's own prejudices. So, if you want to discuss the future of the city in Europe, America, and the Third World,[1] you may *either* gather together a number of mainstream urban and regional economists *or* invite a similar number of people committed to an alternative, ecological vision of appropriate development. *Do not* on any account mix the two together. The trouble with this approach is that none of us have a monopoly on truth and perception; and unless future scenarios are to be no more than fantasy they have to start here, now, with the world as it is – like it or not.

The Seminar on Future Cities held at Oxford Polytechnic in April 1987 was not for those who prefer the safe if rather dull world of the converted. It was intended to bring together people that were known to have different views, not only about the nature of the city but also about the factors that have to be taken into account in even beginning to think about its future. Broadly speaking, these people fell into two groups – academics who specialize in mainstream research of urban problems in the First and Third Worlds, and academics, writers, and others who come from the broad church of the 'alternative' movement but, in particular, have been associated with the work of The Other Economic Summit and the recently established New Economics Foundation.

In the European Year of the Environment and the International Year of Shelter for the Homeless, which took place in 1987, it seemed appropriate to be thinking about the future of the city and to begin the process of preparing an agenda of relevant issues as part of the work of the New Economics Foundation. To do this we had to decide: where do we start from; what are the most important social and economic factors shaping future cities; how much of the present do we have to take for granted; what can and should be changed?

This book is an attempt to begin that process by publishing a series of essays based largely upon the papers presented at the Oxford Seminar. The book is in two main parts. The first part presents mainstream ideas about recent trends and current conditions in First and Third World cities, giving an indication of the present direction of change and the issues of policy that arise there from. The second part presents some alternative views about the city from those that would wish to question the assumptions that lie beneath the 'neutral' analysis of the economist. If the first part is supposed to be value-free, the second part is unashamedly value-laden.

The theme that draws these essays together is a deep-seated dissatisfaction with current orthodoxy. We believe that by allowing a narrow economic imperative to dominate our thinking about the future of the city we exclude other perspectives which are not only of equal importance but which, in the longer term, are likely to be of greater significance. These include notions of participation, ecological balance, local self-reliance, economic sustainability and technological choice. We recognize that these terms are often used without sufficient care and that there is a danger that such abuse will debase their currency. Much work needs to be done to refine them before we can apply them with confidence. None the less, a start has to be made and this book offers a number of views which both examine the current orthodoxy and begin to refine ideas relating the 'new economics' to the future of the city.

As an introduction to both parts of the book, we have prepared an essay entitled 'Towards another city' in which we lay bare our own prejudices and hopefully set something of a context for the essays that follow. It deliberately invites the reader to challenge the imperative of economic determinism and to consider the relationship between the city and the lives of the people that live and work there.

Although the essays that follow are intended be relatively self-contained, the main parts of the book and each essay are preceded by a brief introduction. We hope that this will help the reader to follow the common themes that connect the separate essays.

At the end, under the title 'Conclusions and new beginnings', we attempt to draw together some of the main themes and issues of the collection of essays to provide the basis for an 'agenda' which may be of assistance in developing new perspectives of the city and, in turn, lead to alternative forms of action which not only retain economic dynamism but also make future cities better places in which to live.

David Cadman and Geoffrey Payne
London

Preface

Note

1 The terms 'First' and 'Third' Worlds originated to distinguish between countries with high levels of industrialization, urbanization, and per capital incomes (the First World), and those in which these indices were at a low level (the Third World). With the economic rise of several 'Third World' countries, such as South Korea, Taiwan, and Brazil, etc., the terms have been widely criticized for oversimplifying a complex situation.

With regard to cities, however, the terms still have some validity. First World cities tend to be declining in population in favour of metropolitan regions, as a result of increased affluence and residential mobility. In Third World cities, rapid population growth continues as a result of high natural increase and rural – urban migration levels, both of which create cities with predominantly low-income populations. This pattern appears to continue even in countries which may otherwise no longer be considered 'Third World', and it is in this sense that the terms are used in this book.

Acknowledgements

We would like to acknowledge all those who helped to organize the original conference on 'The Future of the City' from which these papers were developed. This includes the Centre for Development and Environmental Planning and the Joint Centre for Urban Design at Oxford Polytechnic, particularly David Weston, and those that sponsored the conference, that is Christian Aid, the World Association for Christian Connection and the New Economics Foundation. We would also like to acknowledge those organizations that helped to fund the New Economics Foundation during 1987. These are the Allen Lane Foundation, the Network Foundation, the Scott Bader Commonwealth, the Konrad Zweig Trust and the Quaker (Peace and Service) One Per Cent Fund. We were most grateful to Paul Ekins and Harford Thomas for reading the final draft of the papers and making very useful comments and in the course of preparing the work, we would like to thank both Francoise Hausermann and Claire Feeney for typing and re-typing endless scripts.

Introduction:

Towards another city

David Cadman and Geoffrey Payne

The city in crisis?

On the corner of a drab street in Hackney, one of London's poorest inner-city areas, two young men lean against a police barrier left over from some disturbance or other and discuss what they will do for the rest of the day. They are unemployed. The have no work, very little money and too much time. Two or three streets away, in the City with a capital 'C', two young men are facing a bank of screens and telephones. Half sitting and half standing, they are all noise, energy and 'buzz'. They are money brokers. They have too much work, a lot of money and not enough time. Worlds apart or part of the same world? That is the question.

Concern for the inner areas of British cities began to emerge in the 1960s, gaining force in the 1970s as the true extent of the collapse of the economy began to be revealed.[1] Between 1972 and 1977, as the reality of the loss of population and employment was revealed, a number of reports, the 'Inner Area Studies', were published – concerning the social and economic problems of the inner areas of Britain's largest cities. Conferences were called to discuss the findings of these reports and the government produced its White Paper 'Policy for the Inner Cities',[2] and then, in 1978, the Inner Urban Areas Act. While the problems that were identified were clearly a matter of concern for those most affected and, indeed, were discussed at length both by the professionals concerned and in the columns of the serious press, they did not very often reach the front pages of the popular tabloids.

Then, on 10th April 1981, in the Railton Road area of Brixton, London, there was a riot in which property was set afire, shops were looted, 400 people were injured and 350 arrested. On 5th July 1981, in the Toxteth area of Liverpool, it happened again and 'The Inner City Problem' was headline news. Politicians and public reacted with shock and fear. One MP, called the riots 'urban savagery' and claimed that scenes like this can never have been seen in a British City under the rule of law this century.[3]

Although they remained front page news for a relatively short time, Brixton and Toxteth heightened the concern of both the public and government, and a series of new initiatives to increase investment and reduce social unrest were both discussed and, to some extent, put into practice. For four years the discontent of the inner-city areas was to remain in some sort of tenuous equilibrium, but on 9th September 1985, in the Handsworth area of Birmingham, another confrontation between young people and the police led again to riot, arson, and looting. This time two Asians died when their sub-post office was set on fire. On 28th–29th September, riots again broke out in Brixton after the accidental shooting of a woman during a police search of her house and then, on 5th–6th October 1985, erupted on Broadwater Farm Estate, Tottenham (strictly speaking a suburban rather than an inner-city area), following the death of a woman from a heart attack as police searched her home. Again, amidst rising anger, there was riot, violence, arson, and looting; and, on this occasion, a policeman was stabbed to death. 'The Inner City Problem', with all its confusion and tragedy, was back on the front page.

Many different causes of the riots were identified, some pointing to poverty and unemployment and others to drugs or racial and political agitation. However, most commentators accepted the significance of the fragile relationship between the police and the local communities, and all seemed to reveal a state of tension that was vulnerable to anger, frustration and, perhaps, exploitation. The remedies proposed fell into two main categories – 'law and order' and 'environmental improvement' – both, in a sense, a reaction to the most visually apparent characteristics of the riots 'as seen on TV'. The first stressed the need for firmer or, in some instances, more sensitive, policing. The second recommended a mixture of physical renewal and support for small-scale local initiatives to encourage enterprise. In either case, the remedies were presented as if the conditions of the inner city were in some way isolated from the larger social and economic forces affecting not only the rest of the city but all cities. It was as if the problems of the inner cities and their solutions were supposed to be found and resolved within the confines of the areas themselves.

In London, in contrast to the dereliction and dismay of the inner city, is another kind of city – the City of London (generally known as the City). Here, now expanding beyond its traditional 'square mile', is one of the world's three most important financial markets. It is a world of brokers, with screens and telephones moving money fast between currencies, gambling on shifts in price and exchange rates. It is a brash world of high towers and high rents, an energetic world of deals, risk, and speculation. Strangely enough, the inner city and the City are closer than you might think. They are not separate places, remote and apart. They stem from the same root. They are part of the same process of change – the life and death of the city, its growth, decline and transformation. The shift and concentration in economic function that creates euphoria in the City also creates despair and dereliction just round the corner in the inner-city areas. The contrast between the two, and the way in which they are presented separately as representing success and failure, is evidence of the real crisis of the city, evidence of the extent to which one perception of the city has come to obscure our vision.

Cities have, of course, always served an economic function but the best have offered something more, something that appealed to the spirit as much as to the pocket, and this chapter is an attempt to challenge the dominance of the view of the city as no more than a market place, a place to be determined only by a narrow form of financial accounting. It is a plea for a broader vision of what might be regarded as possible, and for a new definition of 'viability'. In seeking such a new vision, it must be understood that no part of the city can be considered other than in the context of the future of the city as a whole, and the search must take account, at least in part, of three factors: the ancient process of life and death common to all cities; the history of the city; and the more recent phenomenon of urban growth, sprawl, and disintegration. There must also be a willingness to see the city as something more than its physical form – something more than its concrete shell and architecture. It is necessary to get beneath the skin and investigate, and come to terms with, the physiology of the city – the functions and processes, the essential forces that give life and bring death.

The proposition that we need to redress the balance of forces that are given sway to shape us and our cities is not new. Indeed, it has been a constant theme of the history of the city and civilization. Nevertheless, there are times of crisis, times when the danger signals multiply and there is a whiff of decadence and unreality. When City 'yuppies' cut up their cocaine with their American Express Gold Cards and sniff it through £50 notes,[4] whilst on the corners of less glamorous streets in the inner city the same drugs are traded with more desperation than daring; when the highest rents, the highest wages, and the highest buildings are dedicated to an activity which, beneath its 'glitz' and moneyspeak jargon is no more than the activity of the bazaar; then, there must be reason to suppose that this may be such a time.

In his book *The City in History*,[5] Lewis Mumford strikingly sets out the lessons to be learned from the rise and fall of the great city of Rome:

Its history presents a series of classic danger signals to warn one when life is moving in the wrong direction. Whenever crowds gather in suffocating numbers, wherever rents rise steeply and housing conditions deteriorate, wherever a one-sided exploitation of distant territories removes the pressure to achieve balance and harmony nearer at hand, there the precedents of Roman building almost automatically revive as they have come back today: the arena, the tall tenement, the mass contests, the football matches, the international beauty contests, the striptease made ubiquitous by titillation of the senses by sex, liquor and violence – all in the Roman style. So, too, the multiplication of bathrooms and the over-expenditure on broadly paved motor roads, and above all, the massive concentration of glib ephemeralities of all kinds, performed with supreme technical audacity. These are the symptoms of the end; magnification of demoralised power, minification of life. When these signs multiply, Necropolis is near, though not a stone has yet crumbled. For the barbarian has already captured the city from within. Come hangman! Come vulture![6]

Suffocating crowds, steeply rising rents, poor housing conditions, mass sporting contests, glib ephemeralities performed with technical audacity – if these are indeed the danger signals perhaps we should take heed for they seem unnervingly familiar!

There is a further aspect of the present crisis that we need to take note of, and that is not so much the phenomenon of change itself but rather the pace and scale of contemporary change, and our capacity or otherwise to cope with it. Caught in the fortunes of disparate national and local economies and in the rise and fall of those that govern them, the city is always moving away from or towards equilibrium but is never at rest. It proceeds through the cycle of life, death and transformation, through periods of 'disruptive transition'.[7]

Coming to terms with the inevitability of this process of change is an essential pre-condition of trying to understand it but, in contemporary terms, it is a problem made all the more difficult by a lack of adequate experience. For most of the post-war period, the professionals that plan, design, and build cities in countries like Britain have been taken up with the problems of growth, of expanding populations, of overspill and rising land prices. Until recently, few have had to cope with the problems of decline. If they have experience of 'growing pains', they have little experience of the problems of transformation that take place when a city is dying, or at least finding a new and less extensive form and function. And yet the lessons are there. Indeed, Lewis Mumford goes as far as to suggest that 'the very structure of the city itself ... has made physical disintegration – through war, fire, or economic coercion and blight – the only way of opening the city up to the fresh demands of life'.[8]

Perhaps the problem is one of the scale and pace of change. In his book *Beyond the Stable State*, Donald Schon argues that, as part of our mechanism for survival, as 'a bulwark against the threat of uncertainty', and in order to protect ourselves from 'apprehension of the threats inherent in change', we need to be able to believe in stability.[9] Given an unprecedented and accelerating rate of contemporary change, this need is increasingly difficult to satisfy. In human societies of the past, generational change has often been the vehicle through which major cultural changes have occurred, but, 'as diffusion times have shrunk steadily from 120 to 60 to 30 to 15 years, problems of adaptation which could once have been handled ... through the conflict of generations and the replacement of one generation by another must now be handled within a single generation'.[10] Such a phenomenon is made manifest in the ever-increasing pace and scale of interconnected currency transactions effected in centres around the world leading to the cycles of euphoria and despair witnessed in world financial markets in 1987. It may be, suggests Schon, that as we try to absorb ever greater levels of technological activity and performance we may 'pass beyond certain social thresholds' of adaptation.[11] Superimpose this upon the rigidity of a 'concrete', physical environment and some of the problems become apparent.

Although the process of urban renewal and change is not new, what is new, at least in historical terms, is the massive growth of cities in Europe and North America from about 1800 to the first half of the twentieth century and their subsequent and more recent disintegration. In the First World, therefore, this has left professionals and the public at large with a legacy that no generation before has had to inherit.

In the Third World, where extremes of wealth and poverty are even greater, and the public resources to bridge that gap are trivial by comparison, cities are still experiencing historically unprecedented population growth rates. In the metropolitan conurbations such as Mexico City and Cairo, this can involve increases of over 1,000 people every day, and even smaller cities commonly double in population every 10 years. As national populations increase, so does the proportion unable or unwilling to remain in rural areas, leading inexorably to urbanization and urban growth. Much of this growth is, however, due to natural increase rather than in-migration, so that simplistic attempts to restrict it by discouraging in-migration are not likely, in themselves, to achieve success. Of even greater concern to policy makers, urban administrators, and concerned professionals, however, is that, of these expanding city populations, a large and increasing proportion are living at or below subsistence levels. Given the extent of poverty and the tendency to conspicuous consumption frequently adopted by the affluent minority, it is perhaps remarkable that riots of the sort experienced recently in Britain are not routine events. The fact that they are not is, of course, due to a number of complex factors – such as levels of awareness and education, forms of social organization, and the practical pressures of survival on a day-to-day basis – which leave little scope for alternative considerations. It may also, in part, be a reflection of surviving rural patterns of social cohesion and mutual support. What is clear is that the perceptions and behaviour regarding urban life are only partially affected by economic criteria and that other factors are at least as important. In other words, the economic imperative is only a partial explanation.

The problem of understanding is considerable, the task of action is daunting, but an attempt at both is essential. Can we, as Lewis Mumford says we must, 'restore to the city the maternal, life nurturing functions'?[12] To answer that question we will have to look at ourselves and to the values that we espouse, for we build cities in our own likeness. We have the technical skills, but do we have the necessary imagination and will? It is the answer to this question that will, in the end, determine our future cities.

The city in history

The life cycle

The story of the city spans more than 5,000 years and is the starting point for an understanding of the phenomenon of urban change and the future of the city itself. The history begins in the fourth millennium BC as the first civilizations start to emerge in the fertile plains and valleys of the Nile, the Indus, and the Tigris and Euphrates. The 'city' was a common characteristic of these developing communities and increasingly it became the dominant social form, spreading its influence into the surrounding countryside. Warka, lying in the potentially rich farmland of the lower Tigris and Euphrates, was probably the first such city – 'the earliest city in the earliest civilisation'.[13] Established some 3,000 years BC, it grew rapidly, and by 2,500 BC had a population of 50,000 people protected by a great wall enclosing a site of some 160 acres. Warka was a temple city, providing a stronghold for defence, and a centre for the storage and distribution of the agricultural, pottery, and textile products of its region. The temple was the dominant feature and represented the focus of power, for the priesthood governed the economic as well as the religious functions of the city. Setting a pattern for the future, the growth of Warka was based upon the need for the concentration of social and economic organization, in this case the need to manage the complex system of dykes and canals required to make the best of the highly fertile lowland environment, and to support the initial colonization of southern Mesopotamia. Like all the cities that were to follow, Warka was to grow, develop, and then decline. For the history of the city reveals a process of growth, decline, and transformation – a cycle of life, death and, sometimes, re-birth – a process that in some cases, such as Athens and Rome, has been dramatic.

By the latter part of the fourth century BC, following a bitter and bloody war with Sparta, Athens had become the cultural centre of the Greek world, the 'school of Greece'. Here, philosophy and learning flourished as never before, the Parthenon had been built as a shelter for the goddess Athena, and the population rose to some 155,000.[14] In these times it would have been difficult, perhaps, to suppose that the life of the city could be threatened, but over time the very attitudes that had created the love of learning were to lead to its downfall. Regarded as ignoble, trade and commerce were left to the Metics who were 'outsiders', and increasingly, as the city became reliant on foreign merchants, it became economically insecure. For a while, and throughout the third century BC, the equilibrium was maintained, but during the second century the influence of Rome began to be felt. Slowly at first and then with gathering force, as the framework of Greek civilization began to break down, Rome increased its grip and, in 86 BC, Athens was captured by the Romans. At first, and for some time, it was favoured, but later the schools of philosophy were closed and power and wealth were transferred to Constantinople, which began to grow as the new centre of the Greek world. By contrast, Athens sank to the level of a small provincial town and even in 1850 only had a population of 25-30,000 people – less than a fifth of its size 2,300 years before.[15]

Rome provides another example of the life, death, and re-birth of a city, rising and declining with the Roman Empire in the first half of the first millennium AD and then rising again in the seventeenth and eighteenth centuries as the centre of papal influence. Following the reorganization of the city of Rome by Emperor Augustus in 7 BC, the first century AD saw the beginnings of a period of stable government and relative tranquillity. Rome prospered and, despite the Great Fire of AD 64 after which Nero rebuilt the city, it had, by AD 100, reached its peak population of 650,000.[16] Rome was now at the height of its influence and grandeur, its population being swollen by the immigration of slaves and freemen from the provinces of the now far-flung empire. However, during the second century AD, the strains of maintaining this empire began to tell, and Rome began to lose its political and economic power. The decline of Rome reflected its form of growth. The impetus for growth lay with the growth of the empire, but, as the empire developed, Rome itself became increasingly dependent on its extended territories. The city was not the centre of production but rather the centre of consumption, failing to develop the skills and technology to exploit the natural resources of its empire and devoting its energies to trying to maintain control, eventually relying upon an ever more powerful and costly army. During the second century AD, Rome became increasingly politically and economically insecure. Corruption and debauchery were rife and, as the city began to give way to the power of Constantinople, the population began to decline. As external pressures increased on the northern and eastern frontiers, the civilian government collapsed and the armies in the different provinces tried to set up their own commanders as emperors. They proclaimed them and deposed them at will. Within a period of 50 years, from AD 235 to 285, there were twenty-six emperors, only one of whom died of natural causes – what is more, economic life was shattered. According to Mumford: 'The disintegration of Rome was the ultimate result of the over-growth, which resulted in a lapse of function, and a loss of control over the economic factors and human agents that were essential to its existence'.[17] The military triumphed over the civilian, the empire was divided, and the centre of gravity shifted eastward. In AD 330 Constantine established a new capital city at Byzantium, which he renamed Constantinople. The empire broke into an eastern and a western half and during the fifth century AD Rome was sacked and taken by the Goths. By AD 600 the population of Rome had fallen to a mere 50,000, less than 8 per cent of its peak 500 years earlier.[18] It was to remain at this level until the end of the sixteenth century before growing again in the seventeenth and eighteenth centuries, reaching 170,000 by 1850;[19] even then, however, little more than one-quarter of its size at the height of its power.

Similar processes of the growth and decay of cities have occurred elsewhere and at other times. High levels of urbanization and urban growth were experienced in the Middle and Near East, for example, well before they accelerated in Britain. Revenue from excise taxes on overland trade routes between Asia and Europe had fed the treasuries of states throughout the region and generated a network of affluent trading and administrative cities. The Ottoman Empire, in particular, derived vast sums from such trade. But, then, the opening up of quicker and safer sea routes led to the expansion of maritime trade and turned the region into an economic back-water. Deprived of their economic base, cities throughout the region suffered a steady decline which has only been reversed since oil was discovered. Further afield, the decline of overland trade or the spatial impacts of colonialism wrought similar changes. Lahore, for example, is estimated to have shrunk to one seventh of its size as a result of changing trade patterns, whilst Dhaka's population declined from 150,000 in 1824 to only 20,000 in 1837.

The life cycle and transformation of cities can also be seen in the rapid growth of Florence as a centre for trade at the beginning of the fourteenth century or, in the same century, in the rise and fall of the city of Norwich which became the second largest city in England and a centre for the wool trade. In 1300, Norwich had a population almost two-thirds the size of London. By 1600 its population was less than 10 per cent that of London and by 1800 less than 5 per cent. The same process was at work in the nineteenth century, in cities such as Manchester and Bradford which grew as centres for the textile industry only to decline as that industry itself declined in the face of foreign imports. In more recent times, too, cities such as Middlesbrough and Coventry have seen the disintegration caused by the failure of the industries that had caused their growth and upon which they had come to depend. Again and again, history provides examples of the rise and fall of population, the expansion and contraction of the city.

Contraction is less common among contemporary cities in the Third World. However, many cities tend to fluctuate in their growth rates, due to such factors as changes in regional economic parameters or public policy. Even Calcutta, once considered to be the harbinger of urban social and economic collapse, has experienced a reduction of its growth as migrants have discovered other options. In India, Turkey, and many other countries, the dominance of a few metropolitan centres has shown signs of receding as a number secondary cities achieve self-sustaining economic and population growth. Such processes are extremely complex and are still not fully understood, though it is clear that they are far stronger than public policy or investment strategies alone could hope to control. Cities have always reflected such subtle and yet dynamic external pressures and will, no doubt, continue to defy the most sophisticated projections.

Making a living

Throughout their 5,000 years of development, cities have been built to serve a great variety of functions – as temples, forts, market places, and centres of administration, industry, and entertainment. All these functions have had their impact on the physical form of cities and have determined their growth and decline. However, perhaps the most fundamental, the most compelling and continuous force has been the need to make a living – the need to eat, drink and find shelter, the need to survive. Thus, we have seen that the first city, Warka, was built to serve a trading function, the exploitation of the fertile farmland of the plains and valleys of the Tigris and Euphrates, and the collection and distribution of the produce of its region. We have noted how both Florence and Norwich grew as centres of trade in the fourteenth century and have referred to the forces of trade and industry that caused the growth and the decline of cities such as Manchester, Bradford, Middlesbrough, and Coventry. In all this, as Lewis Mumford explains, the city has acted as a centre for economic and administrative organization:

> While the city brought together and welded into a visible unity village, shrine, stronghold, workplace and market, its character altered from region to region, from age to age, as one or another component dominated and coloured the rest. But always, as a living cell, the organising nucleus was essential to direct the growth and the organic differentiation of the whole.[20]

From the beginning, the city acted as a magnet, drawing people to it for work and trade, but the nineteenth century was to unleash a force that would transform the scale and pace of urbanization. That force was the Industrial Revolution, and the new form of production was to change beyond recognition the countryside and the lives of citizens and villagers. Throughout the nineteenth century, both Britain and Europe experienced massive urbanization as industrialization gathered momentum. Increasingly, men and women came to the towns and cities in search of employment and economic advancement. For many, of course, there was little choice; in his novel *Tess of the d'Urbervilles*, Thomas Hardy accurately describes the process of rural depopulation as 'the tendency of water to flow uphill when forced by machinery'.[21] The forces underlying this massive urbanization were the same forces driving the process of industrialization. Coal, cotton, manufacture, and trade, these were the forces that shaped London, Manchester, and Liverpool in the nineteenth century, transforming the country from a rural to an urban state in less than 100 years. In 1800 London was the only large British city. Some 80 per cent of the population of England and Wales lived in villages or towns of less than 20,000 people, and both Manchester and Liverpool still had populations of only 80,000 or so. By the end of the nineteenth century, Britain had twenty-three large cities of more than 100,000 people, the population of London had grown from under 1 million to over 4.5 million, and the populations of Manchester and Liverpool had grown to some 545,000 and 685,000 respectively. A rapidly increasing population had been both industrialized and urbanized. In fact, during that single period of 100 years, there had been a complete reversal of population in England and Wales, with those classified as 'urban' growing from 23 per cent in 1801 to 44 per cent in 1851, and then to 77 per cent in 1901.

The reverse side of the same coin was reported during the nineteenth century by several writers, including Karl Marx. They showed how the growth of cities such as Bombay was a direct outcome of British colonial policy, which sought supplies of raw cotton for the mills of Lancashire to replace those cut off from America by the Civil War. The export of raw cotton from India through Bombay and other ports fed the urbanization of Britain and enabled the processed articles to be re-exported to India at prices which undercut the local market. The growth of cities in India and many other parts of the Third World was related to similar processes initiated in Britain and other European colonial powers, creating what became known as 'dependent urbanization'.

Economic forces have continued to dominate urban form in the twentieth century. During the first half of the century, and particularly as the period progressed and the form of industrialization changed to more modern industries based on the new technologies, such as electric power, automobiles, and chemicals manufacture,[22] the trend in already industrialized countries was for decentralization from the core of the city to the suburbs and then to the satellite towns around the main conurbations. More dramatically, as industrialization has given way to a new 'service economy' in the last 30 or so years, the populations of the major cities have begun to decline and the populations and economies of the more rural areas of the country have begun to grow. Newly emerging industries, no longer dependent on traditional industrial locations, have been drawn to the rural market towns to find the appropriate space for their production and an environment that meets the new standards set by their workforce. Since the 1960s this migration has continued apace, and recent studies[23] show population and employment moving out beyond the metropolitan areas and the free-standing cities, and even out of the larger towns, to the smaller market towns of the rural counties. A population once dependent upon manufacturing industry has become increasingly employed within the service sector. Such an economy is much less constrained in terms of the locations of its activities than the traditional industrial economy, but it is as powerful in determining the shape of town and countryside. It leaves its mark both on the cities that have been abandoned and the smaller towns that have been invaded.

It would, of course, be wrong to give the impression of a population returning to some kind of medieval village life with merry maids and yokels dancing around the maypole. Indeed, while the largest cities have been losing population, the same social and economic forces have also led to the depopulation of the most remote rural areas. Furthermore, far from there being a renaissance of rural like and self-sufficiency, with the countryside encroaching on the town, it is rather the other way about. It is the city and the town that are spreading their people, their values, and their way of life into the countryside. Britain today remains a largely urban nation dependent on its towns and cities for employment and services. Indeed, there is some evidence that the populations of cities such as London and Manchester may be stabilizing, and perhaps even beginning to grow, as they move towards the end of the twentieth century and new kinds of economic activity are once again attracted to them. Elsewhere in the world, the concentration of urban population is still continuing, although even some of the Third World cities are occasionally witnessing major internal population shifts from the centre to the periphery, creating urban regions many miles across and urbanizing villages in the process.

Love me, love me not

This ancient process then, this 'life cycle', seems to be the natural, or at least the historic, pattern for the city, its 'historic essence and continuous life',[24] and its most compelling masters would seem to be business, commerce, trade, making a living, and trying to survive in a material world. This chapter does not seek to suggest that this is likely to change. Indeed, all the evidence seems to indicate that it will intensify. It does, however, insist that the debate about the nature and purpose of the city be re-opened. This debate, which is as ancient as the city itself, is dealt with at length in Andrew Lees' *Cities Perceived*.[25] Here is rehearsed the case both for and against the city in general, and the cities of the nineteenth century in particular, describing how they have been 'celebrated and condemned, reprobated and praised, loved and hated by writers who discerned in them the worst and the best that life had to offer'.[26] Even before the period of the early Christians, Babylon had been 'singled out as *the* city, incorporating and synthesising the evils of all the cities in the world'.[27] However, while St Augustine depicted the city as the scene of supreme sin and folly, the alternative view of ancient cities is also expressed in the literature of classical antiquity. According to Thucydides' version of the funeral oration delivered by Pericles in 431 BC, the Athenian polis constituted a model of civilised morality, embodying both liberty and community and displaying both 'daring and deliberation'.[28]

In the eighteenth century, the men of the 'Enlightenment' regarded the city as the embodiment of civilized virtue. Voltaire 'lauded London as the "rival of Athens" because of the respect it displayed for talent'.[29] Samuel Johnson, writing in 1777, declared in a letter to his friend Boswell: 'No, Sir, when a man is tired of London, he is tired of life; for there is in London all that life can afford.' Both Johnson and Boswell were devoted to the city life, the latter comparing the variety of the metropolis 'to a museum, a garden, to endless musical combinations'.[30] But there were those who took a markedly opposite view. Rousseau described Paris as 'a city of noise, of smoke, and of mud ... a "moloch" that fed greedily on blood supplied by the provinces and corrupted those it did not kill', and in England similar sentiments were expressed by Daniel Defoe, Alexander Pope, and Henry Fielding.[31]

Nevertheless, it was the nineteenth century that brought the strongest, the loudest, protestations. At the turn of the century both Blake and Wordsworth described the city with a 'sense of gloomy foreboding and alienation',[32] and this tone was picked up and expressed again and again by writers such as Dickens and social investigators such as Booth. William Cobbett proclaimed a deep hostility and, writing about London in his 'Rural Rides', published in 1821, posed the question: 'But what is to become of the great wen of all? The monster, called ... "the metropolis of the empire"?'. However, not all nineteenth century commentators spoke with an unreservedly harsh voice. The poet and historian Robert Southey, for example, writing in the early part of the century, expressed both the pessimistic and the more optimistic view. Although he saw London as 'a wilderness wherein they, who live like wild beasts upon their fellow creatures, find prey and cover', a city 'animated by the pursuit of material gain and the spirit of greed', he also regarded it as 'the seat of intellect'.[33] Indeed, many observers, such as the historian Thomas Macaulay, saw in the city 'forces for moral uplift and social progress', lifting the city-dweller above 'the retrograde status of the countryman'.[34] Others pointed to its role as a centre for music, painting, and drama; the congregationalist Robert Vaughan claiming that 'the successful patronage of the fine arts depends less upon the existence of noble families, than upon the existence of prosperous cities'.[35] In contrast to Rousseau's view of eighteenth-century Paris, Zola, writing in the late 1890s, affirmed the city unequivocally 'as a place and an agent of human betterment'.[36]

By the turn of the century, some were prepared to go even further. The German architect, Auguste Endell, declared:

> The big city despite all the ugly buildings, despite the noise, despite everything in it that one can criticise, is a marvel of beauty and poetry to anyone who is willing to look, a fairy tale, brighter and more colourful, more diverse than anything ever invented by a poet, a home, a mother, who daily bestows new happiness in great abundance upon her children.[37]

Others stressed the great variety of city life, the stimulus that it gave to artistic and commercial innovation and to radical thought. The liberal American, Brand Whitlock, wrote:

> Thus the cities have ever been in advance. In them the great battles of liberty on the intellectual and political, the social and the

industrial field have been fought ... [The city] is the expression of man's determination to free himself from the slavery of obdurate isolation, and from the thralldom of primitive fears ... to release the spirit to higher flights.[38]

The debate has continued throughout the twentieth century, and perhaps the best celebration of the contemporary city, indeed of a city in decline, can be read in Adrian Henri's poems of Liverpool. Describing his work, Margaret Drabble says:

Henri's city is a good-hearted, swarming, jostling jumble, of brown ale, take-away curry, pie and chips, Beatles records, double-decker buses, butcher's shops, electric clocks, nylon panties, cream-painted bedsteads, PVC shopping baskets and cats waiting for their Kit-e-Kat all thrown together in an ideal (and idealized) harmony – the kind of city that ought to be possible, but which people have to assemble for themselves, from unpromising materials – a collage city, for those who can love what is there, rather than yearn for what is gone.[39]

You may make a choice between the protagonists or accept that both visions reveal a part of the complex and contradictory character of the city. Nevertheless, whichever side you take, whether you applaud or feel appalled, the debate remains and must continue.

In summary then, the story so far reveals the city as a focus for economic organization, the management of which has, throughout history, given power to a ruling elite, be they priests, kings, landowners, industrialists, or financiers. Following the period of massive industrialization and urbanization of the nineteenth century, cities are now in a period of unprecedented transformation, which in industrialized countries reflects a process of decentralization that has been taking place for the greater part of the twentieth century but which has become especially pronounced during the last 25 or so years. People and work have been moving out of and away from cities, first into the larger satellite towns and, more recently, into the smaller market towns of the countryside. This abandonment of the city can be seen as part of an ancient process that enables a new city to emerge in response to fresh demands. It has to be recognized, however, that this change is driven by an economic/functional motor as new kinds of economic activity and patterns of consumption find their place.

The decentralization of social and economic activity that has been taking place for the last 30 or so years, has, for the time being at least, diverted creativity and innovation away from the cities – leaving a residue of negative forces, particularly felt in the inner-city areas, that inhibit the rebirth of the city and compound its decline. The historic debate about the virtues of the city may now be moving away from those that praise to those that condemn it but, at the same time, as the smaller towns of the countryside are seen as areas of opportunity, rural areas are becoming increasingly influenced by urban commercial values which begin to impose themselves upon, and to some extent disrupt and destroy, the village communities that they invade. for the force that causes the growth is the very same force that in time causes the decline – the force of economic determinism. It has always been the case that cities have been formed and reformed by economic change. Now, that transformation again reaches deep into the countryside, carrying with it a new but universal set of values and assumptions that constitute a virulent, acquisitive, economic ethos. This time, the television, the car, and the concentration of economic control into large conglomerates and multiple traders, have produced an urban form that is instantly recognizable wherever you are – if only you could recognize where it was. Personality has given way to style: the 'shopping experience' and the designer's label are more important than the products that are purchased; and the 'themed leisure park' has come to represent adventure – the image has become the reality. In its new form, the ancient economic imperative may now be more alluring and seem more accessible, but it is as powerful as it has ever been – and probably more so.

Other perspectives

So far, the story of the city has been driven by two particular perceptions – the historical and the functional. The historical perception reveals a life cycle for the city, a cycle of growth and decline, of formation and reformation, and a city that has been both adored and condemned. The functional perception sees the city as an 'organising nucleus', most often serving an economic and/or an administrative function. However, while such analysis may be necessary it is not sufficient. It is no more than the analysis of the external observer. It is the city seen from the outside and not from within. To really understand the city, to feel what it is like and to know its meaning, we must move into the streets and enter its houses, its restaurants, and its places of work. Here, the literature seems to suggest three particular perspectives: the physical; the social; and the personal. The first is concerned with the effect upon us of the physical environment (architectural and environmental determinism). The second is concerned with the concept of 'neighbourhood', and the third sees the city through the eyes and experience of the individual person.

David Cadman and Geoffrey Payne

The physical city

The general belief that the behaviour of people is affected by their surroundings has a respectable pedigree, for we have already seen that the city has been both applauded and decried for at least 2,000 years. In turn, it has been seen as the centre of virtue or of corruption. But in particular, as the growth of industrial cities took place during the nineteenth century and then declined in the twentieth, concern has been expressed about the living conditions of the poorest citizens, trapped by their poverty and, more recently, by their unemployment and lack of marketable skills. Throughout this period of 200 or so years, it has been supposed that there was a direct relationship between the physical conditions of the environment and people's social and personal behaviour, and in the nineteenth century a great variety of more or less practical 'utopias' were planned and in some cases built,[40] their physical form reflecting the social ideology of their promoters. This crusade for a better, or at least alternative, physical environment was carried into the twentieth century by visionaries such as Le Corbusier and Ebenezer Howard and, indeed, directly influenced the new town development programme in post-war Britain.

As it happens, the term 'architectural determinism' was first adopted[41] not to describe the squalor of city life but to examine the friendship patterns of American students living in a housing project known as 'Westgate'.[42] This project seemed to show that the physical environment in which the students lived, and the particular configuration and design of their housing, 'exerted heavy directives on group formation, and the dynamics of its processes'.[43] It suggested that architectural design had a direct and determinate affect on the way people behave, and that people could be moulded by the environment provided for them by architects and planners.[44] Although the concept had its critics, it gained considerable acceptance during the 1960s, particularly amongst professional architects and planners, and was reinforced by the work of Oscar Newman, in particular in his book *Defensible Space*,[45] which was concerned with the relationship of petty crime and housing conditions, and which included quite specific design solutions to reduce levels of vandalism and crime.

While few would now deny that the character and quality of the physical environment influence social conditions and, therefore, personal experience and behaviour, the nature of this relationship is more subtle and convoluted than is often supposed. In his book *Living Cities*,[46] Charles Mercer refines the ideas of architectural and environmental determinism and draws attention to two particular aspects of this relationship. The first is termed 'expectation' and the second 'adaptability'. We start with the concept of expectant man – who 'compares what he has with what he has a reasonable right to expect, and is satisfied if the comparison is favourable and otherwise complains'.[47] In a culture of rising and deliberately titillated expectations, the significance of the aspirations of 'expectant man' would seem to be of great importance in understanding the way in which the differential environment of the city impacts upon its citizens. It can be seen that the assessment of the physical environment can not be made only in absolute terms but must reflect relative advantages and disadvantages. The greater the difference, or, more importantly, the greater the perceived difference, between those that have and those that have not, the greater is the potential for individual dissatisfaction with, social disruption within, and damage to, the built environment.

Moving on from 'expectation' to 'adaptability', Mercer suggest, that we are not simply passive recipients of environmental conditions. We are proactive as well as reactive. We survive both by adapting to our habitat and by shaping it to our needs, and this ability to adapt comes from a strong and primordial sense of survival. The way in which we react to our environment is related to the way in which we have had to acquire knowledge and process information through 'millenia of hardship and danger'.[48] Referring to the concept of 'man the stimulus seeker',[49] Mercer continues to develop this idea of the proactive response by looking at the way in which we both seek and at times avoid, the environmental stimuli that shape our habitat. Man is a 'territorial' animal,[50] with 'a need for territory, its acquisition, maintenance and defence'.[51] And man is an animal whose behaviour is greatly influenced by his social, cultural, and emotional inheritance in the broadest sense – a sense close to Jung's notion of the 'collective unconscious'.[52]

Again, Mercer summarizes thus:

> we have seen that it is useful to view man as a territorial animal, that identity and social communication are both inextricably involved with the physical environment. We have seen that people's treatment of space is a language in its own right and although displaying enormous cultural variations is perhaps a very primitive communication channel, a system which is heavily utilized when the veneer of sophisticated social interchange loses its lustre.[53]

We seek out, therefore, as well as respond to environmental signals in an attempt to make sense of our habitat and then to fashion it to a form that we can sustain and that will sustain us. We thus both determine and are determined by our environment, and defend our territory with a tenacity that is more instinctive than rational.

So much, then, for the conventional notions of architectural and environmental determinism, but before leaving the influence of architecture upon people's lives, reference must be made to a rather unconventional architect with a particular philosophy of design, an architect who sees the relationship between people and their buildings and towns rather differently than most. In his remarkable book, *The Timeless Way of Building*,[54] Christopher Alexander puts forward the notion that 'every place is given its character by certain patterns of events that keep on happening there'.[55] These patterns may be 'alive or dead'[56] and will affect buildings or places accordingly. The design of buildings or indeed of towns should reflect those patterns which are alive and emerge from a natural language of place that exists within each one of us. It is called 'the timeless way of building' and here is how Alexander describes it:

> There is one timeless way of building.
> It is thousands of years old, and the same today as it has always been.
> The great traditional buildings of the past, the villages and the tents and temples in which man feels at home, have always been made by people who were very close to the center of this way. It is not possible to make great buildings, or great towns, beautiful places, places where you feel yourself, places where you feel alive, except by following this way. And, as you will see, this way will lead anyone who looks for it to buildings which are themselves as ancient in their form, as the trees and hills, and as our faces are.
> It is a process through which the order of a building or a town grows out directly from the inner nature of the people, and the animals, and plants, and matter which are in it.
> It is a process which allows the life inside a person, or a family, or a town, to flourish, openly, in freedom, so vividly that it gives birth, of its own accord, to the natural order which is needed to sustain life.[57]

This is a language, a way of expressing ideas, that may excite you or leave you cold, but it is certainly philosophy of design that raises new questions about the extent to which cities determine the lives of those that live in them. It turns the proposition on its head and argues that it is the lives of the people that determine the nature of the city. We shall return to this idea again.

The social city

The concerns of the urban sociologist are wide ranging and far too extensive to encompass here. One particular concept, however, does merit attention and this is the concept of the 'neighbourhood' and its relationship with notions of 'community'. There is a question as to whether or not the words 'neighbourhood' and 'community' mean anything at all or whether they are 'so vague as to be nonsense'.[58] Nevertheless, the debate is important, not least because much modern town planning is based upon the concept that it is possible to create 'communities' through physical design.[59]

The term 'neighbourhood' was first defined in 1929 by the American, Clarence Perry, as: 'that area which embraces all the public facilities and conditions required by the average family for its comfort and proper development within the vicinity of its dwelling.'[60] Six principles were proposed to define the size and extent of such a neighbourhood. These related to an optimal size of community, the need for defined boundaries, parks, the provision of communal services at the centre of the neighbourhood, shopping provision at the periphery, and an adequate network of streets proportionate to their traffic load.[61] Such ideas, heavily dependent as they are on notions of the physical characteristics of the neighbourhood, were enshrined with some modification in the UK in the Dawdle Report of 1944.[62] This report maintained that 'a feeling of neighbourhood or community' was 'one of the fundamentals of social well being'.[63]

Thus the notion of 'neighbourhood' developed and was discussed and debated by sociologists, architects, and town planners who increasingly used the concept in the design and layout of post-war new town development. In 1954, Lewis Mumford, who supported the notion of the neighbourhood unit, expressed the idea thus:

> In the neighbourhood, if anywhere, it is necessary to recover the sense of intimacy and innerness that has been disrupted by the increased scale of the city and the speed of transportation.[64]

However, the notion has not gone unchallenged. Herbert, for example, claims that there is no evidence of an optimum size of community, nor is there evidence to suggest that neighbourhoods as such create 'community'. As he puts it:

> The neighbourhood unit concept is at best neutral and at worst antipathetic to the development of an integrated community life...basically because people are not contained or constrained in their behaviour by the planner's imposition of a territory based community and because the deliniation in territorial terms is neither desired nor perceived.[65]

Nevertheless, the concept of 'neighbourhood' has remained important to many urban sociologists and town planners. Studies have been undertaken to try and identify the way in which individuals define their neighbourhood both physically and socially by looking, for example, at the mental maps that people have of the places that they live in and the importance that they attach to physical boundaries (such as a river or railway line) or to key features (such as a particular building, monument, or park).[66]

There is much too much in all this to capture in the space of a paragraph or two, but a great deal of it turns upon the way in which we come to recognize and understand the places that we live in (what Mercer refers to as 'spatial cognition'), and the way in which we understand and relate to our own environment. Mercer's remarks on this point lead us into the next section:

> As our physical environment becomes increasingly man-made and as our cities continue to grow and become increasingly difficult to navigate, the understanding of such mental activity becomes paramount. If urban man is ever going to understand his own urban behaviour, he must know how he cognizes his self-created urban scene.[67]

The personal city

At last we come to ourselves, to those of us that live and work in cities or simply visit them from time to time. We have abandoned the impersonal historical and economic view of the city, in which the city is seen as an entity; we have lowered our gaze from the buildings that make up its concrete form; and we have detached ourselves from notions of neighbourhood and community.

The nature of the conceptual systems that we use to make sense of the places that we live in appears to be an area of great uncertainty. In his book *The Psychology of Place*,[68] David Canter traces the development of environmental psychology over the last 50 or so years.[69] Much attention is given to the work of Kevin Lynch and his book, *The Image of the City*.[70] Using sketch maps as a means of exploring the conceptual systems associated with particular people and particular cities, Lynch 'attempted to identify some of the features of the townscape which contribute to the ability to form an accurate image' of a place.[71] Using a language that follows our earlier discussion of the concept of 'neighbourhood', he suggests that the mental maps of the city that we carry in our heads gave five principle elements – paths, edges, districts, nodes, and landmarks[72] – and that, together, these provide 'a vocabulary for examining city forms'.[73] The form that these maps take and the image of the city that they represent vary, and constitute evidence of the range of perspectives of a city that may exist at any one time. The range and variation reflect not only the differences of the people that inhabit the city, and in particular the different roles that they perform, but also the changes in perception for each person that take place over time. The map of the city that you carry in your head as a student will be different from the map that you carry when at work, and different again from the map that you have when in retirement.[74]

This perspective is one that has become of increasing interest to those who study the city, a reaction to the positive approach, the quantitative revolution of the late 1950s and 1960s with its preoccupation with measurable phenomena and 'technique'. Moving away from the environmental determinists, some human geographers are now advocating a return to the late nineteenth and early twentieth century Vidalian tradition with its notions of place representing both an objective location and an idea.[75] Referring to the 'sense of place', these writers seek to integrate the meanings that individuals give to a place through their conscious experience of that place – an existential phenomenological approach, concerned with the meaning and structure of human existence in space. Drawing a contrast with earlier studies of 'place', such as Von Thunen's central space theory of place as a location within a hierarchy, writers such as Tuan[76] and Relph[77] see place as a repository or focus of meaning.

It would seem that, however much cities are made for people, people will make their own city, and each person will make a different city for themselves. As Jonathan Raban says in his book, *Soft City*:

> Cities are plastic by nature. We mould them in our own image: they, in their turn, shape us by the resistance they offer when we try to impose our own personal form on them ... The city as we imagine it, the soft city of illusion, myth, aspiration, nightmare, is as real, maybe more real, than the hard city one can locate on maps, in statistics, in monographs on urban sociology and demography and architecture.[78]

The very nature of the city, its size and complexity, its pace and the insistent, intrusive proximity of so many strangers, means that each citizen needs to acquire the protection of a set of well-known personal 'routes', extended territories between fixed points such as home and work. 'one man's city, says Raban, 'is the sum of all the routes he takes through it, a spoor as unique as a fingerprint'.[79] He goes on to suggest that 'we map the city by private benchmarks which are meaningful only to us',[80] first establishing our personal territories and then reinforcing them by usage.

It is its 'intrinsic illegibility'[81] that forces us to create our own image of the city. This perspective's importance, in contrast to more conventional and impersonal perspectives, is again captured by Raban, thus:

We need – more urgently than architectural utopias, ingenious traffic disposal systems and ecological programmes – to comprehend the nature of citizenship, to make a serious imaginative assessment of the special relationship between self and the city; its unique plasticity, its privacy and freedom.[82]

Now we begin to enter the most fascinating realm of all – the symbolism of the city and its meaning at the most essential and personal level, the relationship of city and self. This is deep water indeed and water that, at least for the present, we must leave unexplored. Those that cannot resist the temptation might like to try Clare Cooper's *The House as Symbol of Self*.[83] For the rest, we have probably already gone too far.

Nevertheless, in celebration of the importance that we attach to places, and to the fact that in reality they mean more to us than the economist can ever understand or at least describe, we end this section with the following passage from Hermann Hesse's *Knulp*, in which he describes the return of his dying hero to the city of his childhood:

Once again the homecomer savoured the light and air, the sounds and smell of his native town, and the exciting, appeasing feeling of being at home: the crush of peasants and townspeople at the cattle market, the sun-drenched shadows of brown chestnut trees, the dark autumn butterflies in funeral flight by the city wall, the sound of the market fountain with its four streams of water, the smell of wine and the hollow wooden hammering that issued from the cooper's vaulted doorway, the familiar street names, each one shrouded in a dense and restless swarm of memories. With his whole being the wanderer drank in the enchantment of home, of recognition, of memory, of comradeship with every street corner and every kerbstone. All afternoon he roamed tirelessly from street to street, he listened to the knife grinders by the river, watched the turner through the windows of his workshop, read old familiar names on freshly painted signs. He dipped his hand into the market fountain, but to quench his thirst he waited till he had come to the little Abbot's Spring, which still gushed mysteriously, as in years gone by, from the lower storey of an old house and gurgled between the stone flags in the strangely clear half-light of its springhouse. He stood for a long while by the river, leaning on the wooden rail and looking down at the dark, long-haired water weeds and the slim black fishes that hovered motionless over the floor of trembling pebbles. He stepped out on the old footbridge and when he came to the middle flexed his knees as he had done as a boy, in order to feel the gentle elastic counterthrust of the wooden structure.

Without haste he went on, forgetting nothing, neither the linden tree and the small grass plot by the church nor the upper millpond, which had once been his favourite bathing place. He stopped outside the little house where his father had lived long ago, and for a time leaned his back gently against the old door ... This bit of world belonged to him, he had known every inch of it and loved it.[84]

This section started with the claim that the historical and functional view of the city, and in particular the analysis of the mainstream economist, was necessary but not sufficient. Now, three additional perspectives of the city have been introduced – the physical, the social, and the personal. We have brought to the surface of our attention the built environment of the city, its communities and, at last, its people. The first two perspectives are well documented in the literature of architecture and sociology, with their notions of 'architectural determinism' and 'neighbourhood'. But the third and most personal perspective leads us into areas that are much less well defined. Nevertheless, it is here, at the personal level, that the life of the city exists. In the next section of this chapter, therefore, we examine ideas about a New Economy that begin to incorporate into the analysis of the city some of those needs and values that have now begun to emerge.

Another economy

Having deliberately looked beyond the realms of historic and economic determinism to take account of other views of the city, the physical, the social and personal, we must return again to the economy. For however much we may wish to question the form of that economy, we can not deny its force in shaping the city. Indeed, it is because we recognize the power of the economy, and of those that control it, that we must be concerned with its direction and the values that underlie it.

One step towards 'another city', therefore, is to consider 'another economy'. Such an alternative perspective is provided in *The Living Economy*.[85] Subtitled 'a new economics in the making', this volume of essays edited by Paul Ekins and dedicated to Fritz Schumacher was constructed from fifty or so papers presented at two conferences organized under the title of 'The Other Economic Summit (TOES)' in 1984 and 1985. The object of the conferences, and the book, was to seek to 'develop and promote a New Economics, based on personal development and social justice, the satisfaction of the whole range of human needs, sustainable use of resources and conservation of the environments'.[86]

The Living Economy covers many issues arising from experience in both the First and the Third Worlds, but there are, perhaps, three that merit our particular attention. They are:

1. The development of a new set of principles and measures for assessing the performance of the economy and for establishing the context of values within which the economy should operate.
2. The examination of current and likely future patterns of work.
3. The re-examination of ideas about investment.

Changing the rules

Much discussion of economics in conventional terms is based upon the implicit assumption that the working of the economy is neutral or value-free. In a theoretical sense this may be true, but in practice economics can be no more than a means to an end within a context of values. Nevertheless, these 'rules' are often treated as if they were of the same order as natural laws, so that the acceptance of the primacy of 'market forces', for example, has the same significance as acceptance of the force of gravity and as such has come to be implicit in discussions that in reality involve considerations that extend well beyond the realm of economics. Notions of wealth have come to usurp more ancient notions of well-being, and economics has come to determine our behaviour rather than serve our needs.

In an attempt to put economics in its place, some writers and activists have begun to look for a New Economics.[87] One of the key texts of this emerging body of thought, and included in *The Living Economy*, is Manfred Max Neef's essay on 'Human-scale economics',[88] and one of the most revealing parts of that essay is his concept of human needs and his distinction between 'needs' and 'satisfiers'.[89] According to Max Neef, fundamental human needs are finite, few and classifiable, and they are the same in all countries and historic periods. It is only the form in which those needs are satisfied that changes over time. Nine fundamental human needs are identified: permanence (or subsistence); protection; affection; understanding; leisure; creation; identity (or meaning); and freedom. Max Neef declares that:

> From such a classification ... it follows, for example, that housing, food, income are not to be considered as needs, but rather as satisfiers of the fundamental human need of permanence (or subsistence). By the same token, education is a satisfier of the human need of understanding.[90]

And no doubt wearing the right make of jeans or using the right brand of shampoo are not the only ways of satisfying the basic need for 'identity' or 'meaning'.

Given this useful distinction between needs and satisfiers, it is possible to begin to think about alternative forms of economy, about alternative ways beyond shampoo in which human needs might be met.

By not confusing ends with means, by concentrating on the extent to which needs are satisfied rather than on the products that purport to satisfy them, it is possible to contemplate a reversal of the process of economic determinism. The emphasis shifts from the implicit economic 'rules' that must be accepted to the explicit human needs that must be satisfied. The values now precede the 'rules', not follow them. They are central, not peripheral.

Another key issue of the New Economics, and one that very much affects the form of economy, concerns the measurement of economic performance. At present, such performance is measured by changes in Gross National Product (GNP), it being assumed that increases in GNP (i.e. 'economic growth') are always to be regarded as desirable. This practice has become so established as to be beyond question. However, if we look to see what GNP measures, or more importantly what it fails to measure, we find that it is no more than a partial measure of human activity.[91] It only measures those forms of activity caught up in formal market transactions – the formal economy. So that if, for example, a woman stays at home to look after her family, her activity does not feature in GNP. If, by contrast, she takes a job and employs a housekeeper, her activity and that of the housekeeper add to GNP. Her activity has moved from the informal/household sector of the economy (ignored by GNP as making no contribution to economic performance) and into the mainstream formal sector, at which point it is recognized as having come within conventional measurement. So this most important characteristic of conventional economic appraisal and assessment of progress appears to be not so much a fundamental law of life but rather a special and somewhat limited kind of measure. For, while GNP measures all that monetized activity taking place in the formal economy (comprising both private and public sector production), it excludes activity taking place in the informal economy (comprising the black economy, the voluntary economy, and the household economy – which, together, may account for at least half of all human activity).[92]

Furthermore, even for that part of the economy that it covers, GNP in its present form fails to take proper account of the 'externalities', or costs, of economic growth – the negative side-effects of, for example, environmental pollution or the general wear and tear on both the urban fabric and people. Indeed, the expenditure that is incurred in counteracting these negative side-effects is added to GNP as part of the calculation of economic progress.[93] So that, for example, the cost of disposing of the waste materials of increased consumption or the costs of health care associated with problems of over-work and stress, increase total GNP and give a false impression of 'growth'. In an attempt to confront this issue, Christian Leipert has put forward the notion of Adjusted National Product (ANP), in which the product arising from economic activity is reduced by the 'defensive expenditure' necessary to protect living, environmental, and working conditions.[94] The ANP then provides a more realistic measure of positive or negative economic change.

Such ideas, and the associated notions of 'resource accounting' and 'social' and 'health indicators',[95] when added to the greater awareness of the informal as well as the formal economy (to which we have already referred), are likely to suggest a quite different kind of economy, with different choices being made about the utilization, pricing, and distribution of resources. And if history is to guide us, this new economy, designed to a different purpose, will in turn shape and change the form of the city with as much force as earlier or present economies.

The future of work

In his paper in *The Living Economy*,[96] and at greater length in his book *Future Work*,[97] James Robertson examines present and likely future changes in patterns of work and life-style, which are themselves associated with new ideas about the economy. He puts forward three views about the future of work. The first, which he describes as 'business as usual', is a future based upon conventional notions of employment and unemployment. The second, which he calls 'hyperexpansionist (HE)', is a vision of a high-technology future of decreasing work and increasing leisure. The third, which he terms 'sane, humane and ecological (SHE)', is a world in which the keyword is 'ownwork', a merging of work and leisure in which increasing numbers of people will take more control of their work and other aspects of their lives. Such a future, making the best use of the new technology, 'will help to bring productive work back into the home and the neighbourthood, and enable local work to meet a greater proportion of local needs'.[98]

Having described each of these possible futures, Robertson suggests that 'the real answer must be that the actual future of work is almost certain to contain elements of all three'.[99] A 'four-sector economy' is then forecast. The first two sectors – capital-intensive, large-scale production and large-scale services in both the public and private sectors – are likely to see falling levels of employment. The two sectors with the greatest potential for employment or 'ownwork' are local, small-scale enterprises and the household/neighbourhood sector. As Robertson puts it:

> New work in these sectors will include some expansion of
> conventional forms of employment in small local businesses and

some expansion of home-based self-employment in professions and trades. But it will also include an expansion of work in a whole range of local activities and enterprises such as community businesses and community associations which, although they will have to be economically viable, will not be exclusively economic in the normal sense of the word. Similarly it will include expanded production of goods and services for direct consumption by household and family members and close neighbours – in other words, an expansion of the informal economy.[100]

Much of this already exists in Third World cities, not as a result of public policy but as a basic necessity, given the absence of formal-sector investment or of jobs in sufficient quantity. In many such cities, the informal economy is actually larger in terms of population employed than the public and formal private sectors combined. It is more adaptable, less capital-intensive and less wasteful of scarce resources. Thus a Pakistani garage can produce an AK-47 rifle as well as maintain a car, and both for a fraction of the cost of the large-scale manufacturers. The ability of the informal sector to absorb semi-skilled labour and put limited capital to effective use has always given it an advantage under conditions of rapid urbanization or social change, and it may well be that Third World experience in this respect could offer valuable lessons to economic planners in Britain and other First World countries.

These new patterns of work, and the implications that they carry for the location of places of work, for the relationship of workplace and home, and for patterns of work travel, will in turn require new urban forms. They suggest changes in function for the city and the possibility of more decentralized, locally-based, and perhaps self-reliant communities.

Forms of investment

At the 1984 TOES Conference, a paper was presented entitled 'Financial Futures or Money "as if people mattered"'.[101] The main thrust of this paper is that post-war investment in the UK has been marked by a separation of saving and investment – personal saving and institutional investment. Rising disposable incomes, relative prosperity and, at times, concern about inflation, have enabled and encouraged a growing number of people to set aside a part of their income as 'savings'. However, for the greater part of this period, this increase in personal saving has not led to an increase in personal investment. On the contrary, such investment has decreased in the post-war period. In the period 1940–80 the proportion of ordinary share capital owned by private individuals fell from some 80 per cent to less than 40 per cent, and then to little more than 20 per cent in 1984.[102] And whilst the recent cult of 'popular capitalism', the privatization bonanza, with its media hype to 'Tell Sid' and 'Be a Part of It', has increased the number of people who now own shares, it has not done much to reduce the institutional hold on the ownership of share capital. Increasingly, either voluntarily or as part of their contracts of employment, private individuals have passed their savings to financial institutions to be invested on their behalf by professional fund managers, and the principal beneficiaries of this transfer of funds have been the building societies, the insurance companies, and the pension funds.

Whilst there are, no doubt, advantages in this institutional model, there are disadvantages too. The concentration of funds into the hands of relatively few institutions causes a 'lumpiness' in investment flows, with some loss of investment diversity and a preference for projects of a certain type and size. Large financial institutions have large sums of money to invest and, given that a small project may well require as much if not more analysis, appraisal, and subsequent management as a large one, it is not surprising to find that fund managers prefer a few large investments to many small ones. Furthermore, the essential personality of saving and enterprise are inevitably separated by the impersonality of large, centralized institutions.

However, although this institutionalization of investment is the dominant trend in mainstream financial markets, there is evidence, not only in the UK but throughout the western world and, indeed, in some parts of the Third World as well, of a countervailing force at work. Sometimes referred to as 'social investment', it represents a growth of small-scale financial initiatives, often locally based and almost invariably designed to achieve both a financial and a social rate of return.[103] In part this reflects the inadequacy of existing forms of both public and private sector funding, but it also represents a growing financial awareness and concern by individuals for the way in which their savings are invested.

At the 1984 TOES Conference, several papers were presented describing new financial initiatives and the growth of 'social investment'.[104] In the discussion that followed, there emerged an explanation of post-war trends in saver/investor behaviour in terms of the development of what was termed 'saver sovereignty'.[105] According to this explanation, there are three main phases of development. These are: dependency; awareness; and saver sovereignty. At first, in the phase of dependency, individuals, unfamiliar with the world of finance, are content to hand over their savings to professional fund managers for them to invest on their behalf. Secondly, as savers become more familiar with investment and as they are bombarded with information from competing institutions quoting different rates and terms, they come to understand that they have some choice in the allocation of what, after all, is their money. They begin to ask questions and become more financially aware. Finally, as individuals become better informed and begin to make the connection between their savings/investment and the social and economic conditions of their community, they begin to demand that their money be used in a particular way. This is the phase of 'saver sovereignty'.

In 1984, the third and final phase seemed some way off, but since then the growth of what is now called 'ethical investment' has been remarkable. In less than three years, at least four major ethical investment funds have been established and together they have invested some £82 million. At the same time the Ethical Investment Research and Information Service, which was established in 1983 to give advice on ethical investment, has attracted a regular but revolving list of 200 customers seeking to invest a proportion of their savings ethically.[106] So far, most of this activity is 'negative' ethical investment, that is to say that it is invested against criteria that exclude certain kinds of activity such as the manufacturing of cigarettes, alcohol, weapons and trade with South Africa. But emerging from this is a growth in 'positive' ethical investment in which investors choose those activities or companies that they wish to support.

In absolute numbers and as a proportion of total investment funds, the impact is at present small – although it should be noted that in the summer of 1987 it was estimated that ethical investment accounted for 10 per cent of all the funds invested on Wall Street. Nevertheless, there is the possibility that such a change in saver/investor behaviour, together with a growing acceptance of the relevance of 'social investment' as a third sector of investment alongside the more conventional public and private sectors, might, if it continued to grow, make possible a more broadly based and perhaps more diverse form of city development, responding not only to the normal 'rules' of finance but also reflecting more personal and locally based needs.

The above discussion has deliberately looked at an alternative view of the economy in the knowledge that the form of the economy and the values that underlie it substantially determine the shape of the city. The ideas put forward in *The Living Economy* provide a basis for beginning to describe another economy. Let us suppose, then, that we have such an economy: an economy based upon Max Neef's concept of 'human needs'; encompassing the formal and the informal sectors; and measured and assessed to take account of Leipert's 'defensive expenditure'. Let us also suppose that new patterns of work and investment emerge, with more emphasis upon local self-reliance within the context of global interdependence and an ethos of sustenance rather than growth. Can we now begin to formulate ideas about the kinds of cities that might evolve? This is the task to which this book is directed.

So far, we find ourselves confronted with different views about the city – historical, functional, physical, social, and personal. Each of these has its advocates, those that lay greatest emphasis on some part of the collection – an inevitable cycle of growth and decline, a city determined by its economy, the imprint of architectural determinism, the importance of 'community', the primacy of unconscious and primordial needs and fears represented in questions about the relationship between city and self and, finally, a city shaped by a new economy. Each of these may be a necessary part of an understanding of the nature of cities and of their likely future, but no one view is sufficient on its own. A proper understanding requires an acceptance of the relevance of each view to the vision of the city as a whole. Nevertheless, even within such an understanding, there are questions about the primacy of one view over another, about the ranking of importance and the selection of those parts of the whole that predetermine the rest. At present, the economic/financial/functional view and the associated notion of 'economic growth' are given the highest position in the hierarchy. They preach competition but seem too often to produce, at all levels, dependency within a context of conflict. The New Economics suggests that primacy be given to the notion of human need, ecological balance and, most important, the concept of human well-being not only in a material but also in an emotional and spiritual sense. If it is at present no more than a vision, it would seem to be a vision worth working for.

Notes and references

1. Hall, p. (1981) *The Inner City in Context*, p.114, London: Heinemann.
2. DoE (1977) *Policy for the Inner Cities*, London: HMSO.
3. *The Times*, 7th July 1981.
4. See also Chapter 7 of this book.
5. Mumford, L. (1961) *The City in History*, Harmondsworth: Penguin.
6. ibid., p.280.
7. Schon, D. (1973) *Beyond the Stable State*, p.23, London and New York: Norton.
8. Mumford, op. cit., n. 5.
9. Schon, op. cit., n. 7,
10. ibid., p.27.
11. ibid., p.25.
12. Mumford, op. cit., n. 5, p.655.
13. Redman, C.L. (1978) *The Rise of Civilisation*, p.263, San Francisco: W.H. Freeman & Co.
14. Chandler, T. and Fox, G. (1974) *3000 Years of Urban Growth*, London: Academic Press.

15. ibid.
16. ibid.
17. Mumford, op. cit., n.5, p.277.
18. Chandler and Fox, op. cit., n. 14.
19. ibid.
20. Mumford, op. cit., n. 5, p.113.
21. Drabble, M. (1984) *A Writer's Landscape*, London: Thames & Hudson, p.94.
22. Barras, R. (1985) Pending, p.3.
23. Fothergill, S., Kitson, M., and Monk, S. (1983) *Changes in Industrial Floorspace and Employment in Cities, Towns and Rural Areas*, University of Cambridge Department of Land Economy, Working Paper no. 4.
24. Geddes, P. (1968) (first published 1915) *Cities in Evolution*, Tonbridge: Ernest Benn.
25. Lees, A. (1974) *Cities Perceived*, Manchester University Press.
26. ibid., p.6.
27. ibid.
28. ibid., p.7.
29. ibid., p.8.
30. ibid.
31. ibid., p.9.
32. ibid.
33. ibid., p.35.
34. ibid., pp.41 – 42.
35. ibid., p.45.
36. ibid., p.212.
37. ibid., p.207.
38. ibid., p.214.
39. Drabble, op. cit., n. 21, p.242.
40. Hardy, D. (1979) *Alternative Communities in Nineteenth Century England*, London: Longman.
41. Brady, M. (1966) *The Territorial Imperative*, New York: Atheneum.
42. Mercer, C. (1975) *Living Cities*, pp.74 – 9 (referring to Fetinger *et al.*, 1950), Harmondsworth: Penguin.
43. ibid., p.79.
44. ibid., p.71.
45. Newman, O. (1972) *Defensible Space*, New York: Macmillan.
46. Mercer, op. cit., n. 42.
47. ibid., p.54 (referring to Jay, 1968).
48. ibid., p.55 (referring to Kaplan, 1972).
49. ibid., p.63.
50. ibid., p.123.
51. Ibid, pp.125 – 6 (referring to Ardrey, 1966).
52. Jacobi, J. (1973) *The Psychology of C.G. Jung*, Newhaven and London: Yale University Press, pp.34 – 5.
53. Mercer, op. cit., n. 42, p.147.
54. Alexander, C. (1979) *The Timeless Way of building*, New York: Oxford University Press.

55. ibid., p.x.
56. ibid.
57. ibid., p.7.
58. Mercer, op. cit., n. 42, p.151.
59. ibid.
60. ibid.
61. ibid., pp.151 – 3.
62. Dawdle Report (1944) *The Design of Buildings*, London: HMSO.
63. Mercer, op. cit., n. 42, p.154.
64. Mumford, L. (1954) 'In defence of neighbourhood', *Town Planning Review* 24:256-70.
65. Herbert, G. (1963-4), 'The neighbourhood unit principle and organic theory', *Sociological Review* pp.11 – 12.
66. Mercer, op. cit., n. 42
67. ibid., p.173.
68. Canter, D. (1977) *The Psychology of Place,* Architectural Press.
69. ibid., ch. 2.
70. Lynch, K. (1960), *The Image of the City*, Cambridge, Mass: MIT Press.
71. Canter, op. cit., n. 68, p.24.
72. Lynch, op. cit., n. 70, p.47.
73. Canter, op. cit., n. 71, p.24.
74. ibid., ch. 7.
75. Espinet, M. (1986) 'The reassertion of man in geographic thought', Unpublished essay.
76. Tuan, Yi Fu (1974) 'Space and Place: Humanistic Perspective', *Progress in Geography* 6:212–52.
77. Relph, E.C. (1973) 'The phenomenon of place: an investigation of the experience and identity of places', Unpublished doctoral thesis, University of Toronto.
78. Raban, J. (1975) *Soft City*, London: Fontana/Collins, p. 10.
79. ibid., p.94.
80. ibid., p.166.
81. ibid., p.242.
82. ibid., p.250.
83. Cooper, C. (1974) *'The House as Symbol of Self'*, in Long *et al.* (eds) *Designing For Human Behaviour,* Strasbourg: Dowden Hutchinson and Ross, pp.130 – 46.
84. Hesse, H. (1986) *Knulp*, London: Triad/Grafton, pp.110–12.
85. Ekins, P. (ed) (1986) *The Living Economy – a new economics in the making*, London and New York: Routledge & Kegan Paul
86. ibid., Preface.
87. New Economics Foundation, 89 – 94 Wentworth Street, London E1 7 SE.
88. Max Neef, M. (1986) 'Human-scale economics: the challenge ahead', in P. Ekins (ed.), op. cit., n. 85.
89. ibid., p.49.
90. ibid.
91. Henderson. H., and also Lintott, J. *et al.* in Parts I and II of P. Ekins (ed.) op. cit., n. 85

92. See p.34 of P. Ekins (ed.), op. cit., n. 85.
93. See ch. 6 of P. Ekins (ed.), op. cit., n. 85. See also: Hueting, R. (1987) 'Economic Aspects of Environmental accounting, *Journal of Interdisciplinary Economics* 2 (1): 55–70.
94. See P. Ekins (ed.) op. cit., n. 85 pp.132–139
95. See Part II, ch. 6 of P. Ekins (ed) op. cit., n. 85.
96. Robertson, J. (1986) *'What comes after full employment?'*, in part II of P. Ekin (ed.), op. cit., n. 85.
97. Robertson, J. (1985) *Future Work*, Aldershot: Gower/Maurice Temple Smith.
98. Robertson, p.87 of op. cit., n. 96.
99. ibid., p.88.
100. ibid., pp.89 – 90.
101. Cadman, D. (1984) 'Financial futures or money "as if people mattered"', Paper delivered to the 1984 TOES Conference.
102. Wolmuth. P. (1981) 'Big fish grab sell-off shares', *Labour Research* 76 (9): 7–8.
103. Robertson, J. and Cadman, D. (1985) 'Finance for local employment initiatives', a report prepared for the Commission of the European Communities, DGV Study 84/2.
104. See pp.194 – 209 of Ekins, op. cit., n. 85.
105. Developed by David Cadman, based on the discussion at the 1984 TOES Conference and, in particular, the comments of Herman Daly who suggested the term 'saver sovereignty'.
106. EIRIS can be contacted at 401 Bondway Business Centre, 71 Bondway, London SW8 1SQ.

About Part I

In our Introduction we argued that the present preoccupation with the economic imperative restricts our understanding of the city in its entirety. Nevertheless, in trying to develop a new perspective we need to understand the key assumptions that underlie mainstream views. Here, in Part I, we begin that process by examining some of these ideas and assumptions. Given the enormous differences in context between cities in different parts of the world, Part I looks separately at cities in the First and Third Worlds. Indeed, even within these two broad categories, major differences exist and the essays draw attention to some of them.

In Chapters 1 and 2 the authors describe the forces and events that have shaped the cities of Europe and North America during the nineteenth and twentieth centuries, pointing to the role of technology in both their growth and decline, before going on to give an impression of the direction in which these forces are taking us. The emphasis is upon the economic rationale of the city and its need to meet the demands of new forms of industrial and commercial activity. Rather ominously, at the end, we are warned that 'casualties are to be expected'.

Chapters 3 and 4 examine two central concerns relating to Third World cities. Chapter 3 questions the extent to which forecasts of mushrooming mega-cities are justified and suggests that the growth rates of many metropolitan centres are being overtaken by secondary cities whose needs have not yet attracted similar attention. Chapter 4 questions widespread assumptions regarding the breakdown of urban administration under conditions of rapid growth and examines current thinking on management options relating to the private sector and community groups.

This examination of mainstream views provides a basis for the development of new perspectives that place the economic imperative into a wider context of concerns. The essays in Part II begin this process by exploring some of the social, political, ecological and technological issues which must be considered if we are to take a more comprehensive and balanced view of the city.

Chapter 1

On the development of cities[1]

Dennis Hay

*In this Chapter, Dennis Hay begins the examination of current
orthodoxy by describing the forces and events that have shaped the
cities of Europe and North America during the nineteenth and twentieth
centuries, pointing to the role of technology in both their growth and
decline. He draws attention to Knight's distinction between 'traditional'
and 'industrial' cities and suggests that the dilemma lies in the way in
which these different kinds of city can pass through the transition to
'advanced industrial cities'. Focusing upon the concept of the
Functional Urban Region, and describing eight stages of centralization
and decentralization, Hay finally identifies four broad trends that, in
the eye of the urban and regional economist are seen to affect the future
of cities in the First World – a continuing decline of the heavy
manufacturing sector, a continuing trend towards suburbanization and
exurbanization for the most mobile sections of the population, the
emergence of new forms of manufacturing and communications
industries with new locational preferences, and, for the 'traditional
cities' a new role as centres for office, finance and knowledge based
activities.*

*Dennis Hay is currently Research Manager for the College of Estate
Management in Reading. Former positions include Research Officer to
Peter Hall in the Department of Geography, University of Reading;
Research Assistant at the International Institute for Applied Systems
Analysis, Laxenburg, Austria; Visiting Research Fellow at the Institut
fur Raumplanung, Universitat Dortmund; and senior Research Fellow
in the Joint Centre for Land development Studies and in the department
of Economics at the University of Reading. Earlier research covered
the comparative analysis of urban systems in Europe with Peter Hall
and the evaluation of urban problems in the European Community, the
latter commissioned by EEC. He has a continuing interest in urban
regeneration projects and the alternative use of industrial land and
redundant property for recreation and tourism.*

Until relatively recently in western Europe, the predominant dynamic characteristic of cities was growth of population and economic activity competing with each other for urban space, whilst the primary concern for policymakers was how to contain that growth and at the same time stimulate the lagging peripheral and rural regions. Today the positions are almost reversed. The trend is away from agglomeration and towards dispersal, whilst a malignant disease of decline and decay spreads through once proud cities. But not all cities are similarly affected. There seem to be differences between the performances of cities in terms of their patterns of growth and change and their economic success. But there are cities which have done very well in the past and are now in deep trouble and others which have lain dormant for centuries and have now erupted into feverish activity.

Most cities want to be successful, not only for the improvement and maintenance of the standards and quality of life for their present inhabitants, but also for those of their descendents. There are obviously a multiplicity of complexly interrelated forces which determine this state of satisfaction, and it is partly the evolution and partly the regulation and manipulation of these forces which condition how well cities perform. In order to understand the picture more clearly, it is useful to first divide cities into Richard Knight's simple classification of cities.[2] In this classification, 'traditional cities' are taken generally to mean the older, historic cities which have evolved over many centuries through their role as major or subsidiary central places. These are cities which generally survive because of the range of activities they perform and the durability of some of those activities – such as administration or as centres of communication. They are not, however, without their periodic problems, but these are seen as relatively transitory and reflect a city's adjustment process to changing global and market conditions. 'Industrial cities', on the other hand, are those which for reasons of siting of raw materials, or of raw-materials processing, grew through their industrial role. These are the cities which have seen the most spectacular turnaround from explosive economic success into seemingly irreversible decline. It is the means of transition of these industrial cities into the third category, the 'advanced industrial city', which is the current dilemma.

Urban and regional economists and urban geographers have tried to find some order or pattern from the apparent randomness and complexity of city development and to assess the impacts of the different forces which are operating. This can be done, for example, by analysis of population and economic changes in the geographical areas which make up cities and their regions,[3] and can be correlated with periods of major technological advances or innovations. In essence, the argument here is that at each stage of economic development, the dominant technology that is available to society (be it coal and steam power, electricity or micro-electronics) determines its prevailing pattern of production across the main sectors of the economy (such as agriculture, industry and commerce). The requirements of production and the capability of technology determine the scale, concentration, and location of economic activity, which in turn influence the pattern of human settlement and the flows of trade. Technology can therefore be said to influence where people live and work, the nature of the work they undertake as producers and the means by which they are able to travel. The totality of these influences is a crucial determinant of the pattern of urbanization at each stage of economic development.

Economic historians have identified a series of 'long waves' or 'growth cycles' of development, whereby the emergence of fundamental new technologies leads to a major new wave of economic growth, which is accompanied by a corresponding wave of new building investment. For each new technology, there is thus a distinctive pattern of urban development, and a shift in the type and location of buildings which make up the physical fabric of towns and cities.

This process can be identified over a long period. The most easily recognizable upswing in the cycle began between about 1740 and 1780 in the United Kingdom, when the large-scale shift of employment from agriculture to industry heralded the onset of the Industrial Revolution. The combined effects of advances in agriculture (which reduced demand for labour) and the developments of technology led to the 'take-off into self-sustained growth',[4] including the growth of new cities linked to the sources of raw materials.

This upswing lasted for well over 100 years. The nineteenth century was both the age of industrialization and the age of urbanization. In the United Kingdom during most of the period, the real national product nearly doubled every two decades, increasing fifteen-fold over the century as a whole. The proportion of the national product accounted for by agriculture declined from 33 per cent to 6 per cent; the share of services remained fairly constant at 35–40 per cent, while the share of industrial production nearly doubled from 23 per cent to 40 per cent. The population as a whole grew nearly four-fold, from 10 million in 1801 to 37 million in 1901, and the proportion of people in cities leapt from around 30 per cent to nearly 80 per cent. London's population increased from 1 million to 5 million, and the great industrial cities of the North and Midlands grew out of small pre-industrial towns – there being no towns over 100,000 outside London in 1801, but there were twenty-three by 1891.

Underlying this dramatic transformation of the British economy and society lay the revolution in methods of industrial production based on steam-power, and iron and steel manufacture. First, between 1780 and

1840, there was the application of steam-power to textile manufacture, leading to the growth of the factory towns centred on Manchester. Later, between 1840 and 1895, iron and steel production and the building of the railway networks created the conditions for massive expansion of heavy engineering, based in cities such as Birmingham and Glasgow. The corresponding wave of building which took place in these industrial towns in the second half of the nineteenth century created the physical fabric of what constitutes today's inner city areas.

The twentieth century brought an ever increasing pace to fluctuations in the economic cycle, with depression and recession and two major wars interspersed with periods of growth and new technological change – and with changing patterns of urbanization. The broad mix of activities within the economy changed little, however, in the first half of the twentieth century, with the share of manufacturing industries in the national product remaining fairly stable at around 40 per cent. But this concealed a major shift from already declining heavy engineering industries based on nineteenth century technology to more modern industries based on new technologies such as electric power, assembly line techniques, and motor vehicles. In particular, the transport and communications revolution (represented by electric trains, the telephone, and wider use of automobiles) stimulated a shift in emphasis in established towns from urbanization to suburbanization. Increased opportunities for commuting led to a reduction in the density, and improvement in the quality, of urban development, while new, clean factories were built along arterial roads radiating from the major cities. Rather than being largely determined by the needs of production, the pattern of urban development was now as much influenced by the residential preferences of households.

In the post-war period, this shift in the balance of forces between the needs of production and the locational choices of households has been further strengthened, to such an extent that the predominant characteristic of urban development has now changed from suburbanization to decentralization or de-urbanization. The most important factors underlying this trend have been the further increase in household mobility, due to mass ownership of motor cars and the construction of the motorway network, and the locational flexibility of the new consumer industries based on new technologies such as electronics, synthetic materials, and pharmaceuticals. Unlike the declining heavy industries of the last century, these new industries are not constrained to locations close to ports or sources of raw materials, but rather are free to move where their managers and workforce choose and where the motorway network or airport locations allow convenient access.

Consequently, the search for good housing and social facilities such as schools, plus a pleasant living and working environment, is now pulling urban development away from the industrial cities and back into smaller market towns, particularly those in the south of the country which had apparently been left behind by the Industrial Revolution 150 years earlier. This out-migration from the cities, which has been reinforced by planning policies such as new-town development and green belts, also reflects a rejection by large segments of the population of the congestion, dereliction, and the fear of crime which they perceive within established cities. The result is a vicious circle of decline within the inner city, as the most mobile social groups move out (particularly the younger skilled middle-class families), leaving the most disadvantaged and immobile social groups (such as unemployed manual workers, the elderly, and the racial minorities) to cope with shrinking job opportunities, declining social services, and a decaying physical fabric of nineteenth-century housing and infrastructure.

The process of de-urbanization in Britain is still in its early stages, and it is likely to be greatly influenced by the current transformation or latest upswing which is taking place within the structure of the economy, involving the change from an industrial to a post-industrial 'information economy'. It should be remembered that Britain has been a 'service economy' throughout most of this century, in the sense that total services have accounted for a greater proportion of the national product, at around 50 per cent, than all production industries (including manufacturing with a share of no more than 40 per cent). These relative shares reflect both the continued strength of the country's commercial and financial services when heavy industry has been in decline, and the large investment in social services (particularly health and education) in the post-war welfare state. Since these service industries in general enjoy the same locational mobility as the new consumer goods industries, they have also tended to follow the out-migration of population from the cities, thereby assisting the de-urbanization trend.

Nevertheless, despite the growth of the service sector, manufacturing industry in Britain was maintaining its share of the national product right up to the mid-1960s. Thereafter, the story has been one of accelerating decline, particularly since 1979. In the 20 years between 1964 and 1984, the share of manufacturing industry in the national product has declined from 34 per cent to 24 per cent, while manufacturing employment has declined from 37 per cent to 26 per cent of the total. Over the same period, services output has increased from 48 per cent to 56 per cent of the national total, and service employment from 48 per cent to as much as 65 per cent. Declining international competitiveness in industry, as is dramatically illustrated by the deteriorating balance of trade in manufacturing industry within the economy, has been paralleled by the first stage of a technological revolution in services, based on the application of service activities. With information as its basic commodity, this technological revolution is increasing the importance of information-based services, such as financial and business services, and laying the foundations for a radically new type of 'information economy'.

Similar patterns of industrial and urban development have taken place or are now taking place in North America and Europe but at different points in time and at varying speeds and intensities. The time taken for the spread of an innovation and the relative advantages of different locations at different times all have a bearing on the type and rate of urbanization. But if the global urban system is taken as a whole, then it is clear that cities are all at greatly varying stages of development – suggesting that the nature and extent of the response to technological change is determined as much by location and the capability of taking new innovations on board.

From work done in the UK and in The Netherlands on comparisons of European cities over the last thirty years,[5] It was found that a significant proportion of cities and their regions do indeed experience similar patterns of development (albeit at different rates, different intensities, and at different points in time): of centralization, followed by suburbanization and exurbanization, and then often by decline. Additionally, similar types of problems are present at each of these stages (albeit, again, at different levels of intensity). Thus, for example, in growing cities, both strong centralization of population and economic activity produce congestion for which they are not equipped to cope; whereas, in declining cities, out-migration of the more mobile sections of the population, for whatever reason, engenders increased polarization within society, and produces remainders of disadvantaged groups in those cities with attendant social and economic problems. Here it is not a question of a deficiency of facilities within the older parts of cities, but more a problem of maintaining those that are already there.

Any analysis of demographic, social, or economic patterns (both across and within international boundaries) is hampered by the very different statistical systems and types of territorial areas used for comparison. It is not merely sufficient to compare existing local or regional administrative areas, for they can be very dissimilar in their definition, composition, status, or size. Many are historical accidents of political and administrative evolution and if the policymaker is concerned with the objective relative measurement of disadvantage, then more comparable units have to be used. Following the work of Brian Berry for the United States,[6] the analyses for Europe used Functional Urban Regions (FURs) for comparisons. The logic of these

FURs is to apply the same rules to define the boundaries of medium-sized and large cities along with their respective daily activity spheres, so that similarly defined cities and their regions (here defined as commuter fields) can be compared. This requires aggregation of the smallest feasible spatial building blocks for which sufficient statistics are available, both for definition and for the data base. This is not without its difficulties. For instance, major administrative reform in some European countries (Sweden, Norway, Denmark, the UK, Belgium, and the Federal Republic of Germany) presents problems of maintaining time-series data: more recent statistics are not always obtainable for the exact pre-reform areas. Some countries change the concepts and definitions of their data through time (witness the constant manipulation of unemployment statistics). Others choose to take their censuses at dates that are incompatible with those of other countries (France), and some have not even been able to take a recent census at all (Denmark, The Netherlands, the FRG has since had a census (1987) but did not take one in 1981).

By comparing the relative changes of city and hinterland population between each census, it is possible to identify eight permutations or 'stages' of centralization and decentralization of population (see Table 1.1). Furthermore, a significant proportion of FURs in each country progress at varying rates from stage to stage, partly in response to conditions that develop at the previous stage, partly to national and local policies, and partly to the introduction of new technologies.

The first stage shows cores growing and hinterlands declining within the context of overall FUR growth, characteristic of regions experiencing the strong rural-to-urban migration common in more agrarian economies. At the last measurement point (1981) within the EEC, the group of cities at this stage mainly consists of the smaller Spanish cities. By the third stage, population suburbanizes beyond the city boundary faster than the rate of in-migration to the city, and by the seventh stage (typical of declining industrial regions), the whole region loses population, but faster from the hinterland than from the core. Many of the FURs in this group – including Charleroi, Essen, Nancy, Valenciennes, Sunderland, Glasgow, Doncaster, and Halifax – are amongst those where the greatest problems of urban decline combined with industrial decline are perceived. In the eighth stage, population grows in the core while both hinterland and FUR lose population. At present in Europe there are only a few small, lagging agricultural regions in this group – which are more reminiscent of the first stage in the sequence than of the last.

But if the recent trend described by Ganz[7] (of a return to core growth amidst continuing regional decline in some US industrial regions) persists, then perhaps it is signalling the beginnings in existing large towns of the 'reurbanization' phase proposed by van den Berg *et al.*[8]

43

Table 1.1 Stages of urban growth: population change

	1 Centralization during loss (LC)		2 Centralization absolute (AC)	3 Centralization relative (RC)	4 Decentralization relative (RD)	5 Decentralization absolute (AD)	6 Decentralization during loss (LD)	
	A	B					A	B
	1	2	3	4	5	6	7	8
Core(C)	–	+	+	+	+	–	–	–
Hinterland (H)	–	–	–	+	+	+	+	–
Region (C+H)	–	–	+	+	+	+	–	–
	–ΔC < –ΔH			ΔC > ΔH	ΔC < ΔH		–ΔC > –ΔH	
(van den Berg et al.)	(8)		(1)	(2)	(3)	(4)	(5)	(6)
(Equivalent)	(7)							

Note: ΔC = rate of change of core population; ΔH = rate of change of hinterland population.

This is certainly relevant to Europe, and to the older industrial nations in particular, since the American urban system has already had similar experiences of the trends and problems currently afflicting Europe's declining cities.

By 1981, 68 per cent of the 390 largest FURs in the European Community were still growing; but if the urban cores of these FURs are taken separately, then only 43 per cent (147) were actually still increasing in population. Of these, it is small and medium-sized ones which have the greatest number growing (79 per cent). At urban core level, decline is greatest in the largest cities, with 86 (66 per cent) out of 130 losing population between 1975 and 1981.[9]

Total population change, however, is the result of the relative contributions of births and deaths and of net in- and out-migration. With the exception of Ireland, birth rates in EEC countries began to fall universally from about 1965 onwards, from peaks of around 19.0 per thousand to roughly 11.5 per thousand by 1983. Death rates have also declined, resulting in a significant ageing of the population. This has implications for future service provision for the elderly and means that there will be far more dependent people if present trends continue. The picture is further complicated by migration patterns. In the more developed urban systems of northern Europe and North America, it is the more mobile middle classes who tend to migrate or to suburbanize in search of employment opportunities or lower-density living. These also tend to be some of the more fertile age groups which, in turn, again means changes in demand for services and housing. On the other hand, the less mobile sectors of society who are left behind in the inner areas (the elderly, the unskilled and unemployed, the immigrants, and the single parent families) represent a totally different type of demand for housing or services.

European cities, then, are undergoing very different types of population development which appears to vary according to the stage of growth of the city and to its function, but all under the same conditions of changing global economic trends. Industrial regions are losing population from the whole metropolitan area, while the longer established, 'traditional' cities appear to be more healthily decentralizing. In the Mediterranean areas most cities are still gaining population, though the largest are beginning to decentralize. Migration patterns between and within FURs have accelerated differences in the age and social composition of regions and, importantly, of different parts of regions. In turn, this is continually forcing a redistribution of the requirements of particular sections of the population. Urban systems are in a state of constant flux, throwing up new problems as the old ones diminish.

Manufacturing employment, as would be expected, has declined everywhere but, significantly, in the older industrial regions it is not being replaced by corresponding increases in service employment. Copenhagen, Liverpool, and Belfast lost almost half of their jobs in the manufacturing sectors in the 1971 to 1981 period, Liverpool being the hardest hit overall because many service jobs which were linked to the port were also lost. Employment in services outside the 'worst' cases of industrial decline has, however, generally tended to grow rapidly. In percentage terms this has been at higher rates than the percentage losses in manufacturing; but in absolute terms, service jobs have not increased fast enough to compensate for these manufacturing job losses. Added to this are job losses in other sectors, such as component manufacture in the car industry, the construction sector, or certain service types which are sensitive to the performances in the lead sectors.

At such coarse sectors of activity some trends are missed. New types of manufacturing jobs are being created in the UK and mainland Europe, with the fastest increases in activity taking place furthest from urban centres. Thus, UK cities at least are losing their function of production and, as in the United States, there appear to be definite anti-urban factors operating in the location decision process for new manufacturing. This may be due to lower operating costs in out-of-town areas with lower rents, taxes, and labour costs. Cities may now better fulfil the function of the development of a product, whilst its manufacture and distribution are more cheaply performed elsewhere; the shift from labour-intensive to capital-intensive production appears to have awarded greater flexibility. There may also be a greater need for less cramped locations, for access to trunk networks, or for a more attractive working and living environment. In many European countries there is also a southwards shift of economic activity – another parallel to the American experience with its move away from the 'rustbelt', or 'frostbelt', and towards the 'sunbelt'.

In Europe the tendency to decentralize employment has not occurred on anything like the same scale as in the US, whilst in some countries there are still some large, growing cities which are gaining jobs. In Spain, Portugal, and Greece, however, many cities have missed much of the heavy manufacturing stage and have progressed directly from an agrarian market/regional capital function to a predominantly service-based economy. Despite this, the recession has provoked a return migration of workers, both from abroad and from the older industrial regions, to the growing Mediterranean cities – resulting, especially in Spain, in massive unemployment.

Whilst recession and restructuring policies have contributed to high levels of unemployment, it must not be forgotten that these coincided with the arrival in the labour market of the 'baby bulges' of the late 1950s and early 1960s, and growing female participation. For example, female activity rates increased from 31.6 per cent in 1968 to 40.1 per cent in 1984 in the Federal Republic of Germany, and from 40 per cent in 1973 to 46.3 per cent in the UK (activity rate of persons of working age).[10] Unemployment, however, has generally risen less since 1980 in cities than in their hinterlands, and less in those FURs which had the worst/longest established cases of urban decline for the main reason of out-migration.

It is apparent that very different problems are manifest in different types of cities: those that are growing; those which are suburbanizing and ex-urbanizing; and those which are experiencing seemingly secular economic and urban decline. For growing cities, the mere fact of growth is a problem in itself. The result is congestion and deficiencies in infrastructure and public services. For example, traffic congestion in Athens is so serious that car owners may only drive in the city on alternate days. As agriculture becomes more marginal, or is reformed or becomes more efficient, surplus labour migrates to the cities where greater employment opportunities or scope for participating in the black economy exist. But these rural in-migrants cannot initially afford the relatively higher rents and costs of living. The result is rapid growth of minimal, illegal housing on the periphery of the city. Here the problems are of the almost total absence of opportunity and amenities: of proper housing, water, sanitation, electricity, schools, hospitals, roads and public transport, retailing, or jobs themselves. The population are trapped in ghettos on the edge of the city, although some of the luckier ones will find their way into the city to live at ever increasing densities. Meanwhile the urban rich remain in the central city, house and land values rise and remain highest near the centre. But as the spiral of growth continues and the congestion and pollution and quality of the city environment continue to deteriorate, then it is this group that first starts to decentralize. Underemployment and the black economy co-exist with unemployment and much needed local income for improvements fails to materialize.

The onset of decentralization brings its own new set of problems. As local government invests in attempting to solve some of the problems of growth – by re-designing street layouts, providing parking facilities, improving public transport, and building schools and hospitals – then the population and some of the jobs begin to move to the suburbs and beyond, creating a further demand for services in new locations. Increasing segregation in society emerges – of rich versus poor, skilled versus unskilled, of foreign versus local, of young versus old – with each group having their own specific needs. Central city employment declines, some retailing moves to out-of-town locations, the core loses much of its residential function, and ghettos of deprivation are now the fate of those left in the inner city. Overstretching of public transport and declining user charges necessitate increasing subsidies for running and maintenance costs. The historical, architectural, and environmental qualities of the city become degraded along with much of the considerable capital stock and infrastructure. At the same time as people and jobs move beyond the city boundary, income from local taxation declines, resulting in fiscal stress and an inability of the local government authorities either to pay for maintenance of services themselves or to maintain services at existing levels. But the suburban dwellers still make use of city public services for which they themselves may not have paid. Some European city authorities have borrowed extensively to finance grandiose schemes and now find them unneeded along with a sizeable debt to service at the taxpayers expense. In the UK, to counter spending limits imposed by central government, this borrowing is now used simply to prevent further deterioration of the services and stock already there.

If the city is of the traditional kind with an ongoing market and nodal function, then these problems may be merely problems of transition to a new role. But if the city is of the industrial kind, susceptible to losing its competitive advantage, the problems are of a much more serious nature. Within this latter group of cities could be included: Cleveland, Akron, Detroit, or Pittsburgh in the United States; Liverpool, Glasgow, Belfast, or Sunderland along with parts of the Yorkshire–Lancashire industrial belt, the West Midlands, and South Wales in the UK; Lille, Valenciennes, or St Etienne in France; Dortmund, Essen, Bochum, Duisburg, and Saarbrücken in the Federal Republic of Germany; Charleroi and Liège in Belgium; Rotterdam in the Netherlands; Bilbao, Gijón, and Aviles in Spain; Genoa and, perhaps, Torino in Italy. Some of these cities do also have some of the traditional functions, but it is their fading or faded industrial function which is more significant.

In the UK the problems are of population and capital out-migration, and net job losses on a large scale. The multiplier effects are considerable. Not only has Liverpool lost its port function as the direction of trade has shifted, but the whole marine administration, insurance and financial function along with the food processing industries have all but disappeared as well. So, too, have the service industries which existed on the wealth generated by those former functions The West Midlands component industry has fared similarly whilst much of the economy of Torino is still tied to the fortunes of FIAT. In decline, the problems of decentralization are replicated on a greater scale: housing is abandoned and falls derelict while large holes appear in the city fabric – much of it former industrial land that is too polluted or unstable and therefore too expensive to bring back into productive use. Infrastructure breaks down and the further decline in public transport use brings ever increasing deficits.The effects upon the population are unemployment, deprivation, social malaise, and increased criminality, to name but a few. And, of course, there is much less money circulating in the local economy – again with significant knock-on effects for retailing. Perhaps the only gains for these areas have been a reduction in atmospheric and water pollution and the removal of congestion. In 1982 Bradbury *et al.* concluded, after an in-depth case study of the prospects for Cleveland:

> that it is highly unrealistic to expect any severely declining city to stop declining either descriptively or functionally in the near future. Not enough households or businesses would change locations in response to any feasible revitalization policies.[11]

Also in 1982, van den Berg *et al.*, having described the characteristics of FURs at each of the stages of urban growth along with the types of problem typically to be found at each stage, then list the types of policies and policy instruments that appear most relevant to reducing those problems.[12] Here, by definition, policies are generally those of adjustment in response to changing conditions in order to ease cities into the next stage with the minimum of disruption and hardship. To help achieve this, there may even be a case for retaining the status quo, at least temporarily; for example, by modernizing existing industry and updating the skills of the work-force so that comparative advantage is maintained over the competitors elsewhere. Or it may be appropriate to diversify the local economy to reduce dependency on one main type of industry. Planning controls or incentives or other policies may channel activity to those areas most needing it or alternatively prevent it: 'faced with it [the progression through the stages], the urban or regional policy maker may want to try to manipulate the process'.[13]

Apart from the United States, the UK, and perhaps The Netherlands, few countries have had any specific urban policy. There have in the past been policies which have been concerned with overall national industrial or welfare aspects, but there have been fewer which have been directly targeted at individual or selections of urban areas or at individual urban problems. This is hardly surprising given the relatively recent emergence of serious urban problems of decline; and so, to date, many urban-decline-specific policies have been *ad hoc* or experimental. Traditional regional policy has previously been concerned with guiding and equalizing rather more than preventing or solving. Sectoral policies have been geared towards the re-creation or the conservation of the old economic base; i.e. they are defensive (preserving the status quo) rather than offensive (promoting positive adjustment for restructuring in response to change).

However, the policy climate is changing. The rise of neo-conservative governments is resulting in a shift away from interventionist and welfare policy and towards the use of macro-economic policy, with a minimal social safety net, in the hope, or with the assumption that increased wealth generated by market forces will filter down to bring about a solution to local urban problems. But this 'assumes a perfect capital market and perfect labor mobility and ignores the spiral decline of local revenues that impinge on the range of potential responses of a particular urban area'.[14]

It has been argued that traditional regional policy promotes inefficiency by channelling activity to sub-optimum locations whilst sectoral policy promotes inefficiency by failing to restructure. On the other hand, the manipulation of money markets, interest rates, and taxation levels, or the right to exercise privatization, or to relax planning controls, are seen as creating the necessary economic climate for optimum economic development and the generation of mainly private capital to offset local adjustment problems.

Marxist theory of urban decline suggests, however, that it is the very flight of capital and the expropriation of profit which have significantly contributed to the problems in the first place. The more conservative counter argument to this is that government interventionism does not provide capital within a proper business climate – 'redistributive programs that were doomed to fail'.[15] Even spatially targeted urban policy comes under fire: 'It is our contention however that these well meaning assistance programs [in the US] have had the unintended consequence of anchoring disadvantaged persons in localities of continuing blue collar job loss'.[16] The Urban Programmes (UPs) in the UK were not given a chance to have that effect – Lever describes how five times the amount provided by UP grants in London between 1979 and 1984 was lost by reductions in the Rate Support Grant to local authorities.[17] It may, however, be useful for Europe to scrutinize the successes and failures of American urban policies, for North American cities have already undergone many of the industrial and urban experiences and problems, especially of decline, that Europe is only beginning to come to terms with.

Policy is used as an instrument to bridge the gap between actual and desired states. That there is a need for some policy is clear, but van den Berg *et al.*[18] caution that the process of policy making and implementation is cyclical or cumulative with the measures that are introduced causing changes which may solve some of the problems but in so doing create others for which further policy is then needed. In addition, policy has very different scales of operation along with many different implementing agencies, often competing against each other and sometimes nullifying the impacts. Thus there is a much greater need for policy integration – co-ordinated in the horizontal (policy sector) direction as well as in the vertical (policy level) direction.

But is there an optimum level for the implementation of any one policy or groups of policy? Again, in the countries under scrutiny, a multitude of politico-administrative systems exist, and the responsibilities for the performance of any one function or part of a function vary considerably from country to country, as do the means of raising the revenue for operation. In terms of the exercise of relevant functions, some countries are more centralized than others; but some are increasing that centralization whilst others are decreasing it. Some relatively decentralized countries are seeking greater central powers whereas again others are seeking less. Thus, in recent years, Greece, The Netherlands, Spain, and France have seen the devolution of significant responsibilities to the regions, and, in the case of France, to the smallest administrative level also – the commune – of which there are over 36,000. In The Netherlands it was clear that not all local authorities were equally equipped to cope with urban renewal powers, and there has been a return to intermediate administrative levels for these functions. On the other hand, the UK has witnessed an increasing assumption of formerly local powers by central government, and, at the same time, the transfer of other powers from intermediate metropolitan government to local authority government or to *ad hoc* agencies.

There is also the question of the efficiency, for some policy intervention, of the very small administrative units which are characteristic of certain countries (Spain, Italy, France). The lack or weakness of an intermediate level of government in these countries means that not only is there a problem of duplication of some functions, but also the risk, within one metropolitan area, of non-cooperation of neighbouring authorities with contradictory political or ideological complexions. Conversely, the greater the area and population that the administration covers, the more impersonal the function becomes, with the risk that certain groups will be missed.

The success of any policy, national or local, is difficult to judge, but there is some evidence of revival, at least in the traditional cities of the US, triggered by the injection of private capital into the growing service production economies within a context of national economic growth. The extent to which this is attributable to direct urban policy, or lack of it, or to indirect national economic policy creating the climate for business, is debatable. The growth of the service sector (transport, communications, finance, and personal services) in older cities has been seen as a reversal of decline and, indeed, suggests that a new role for cities is emerging. On the other hand, two features have not changed: fiscal stress persists, and concentrations of the poor and minorities have not diminished.[19] So it seems that macro-economic policy can address some of the problems, but there is no evidence yet that it is of any help to those who most need it.

Thus there seem to be four broad trends in the reorganization of the urban-regional space economy: the first is the decline of the obsolescent heavy manufacturing sector resulting in net job losses, out-migration and decay; the second is the suburbanization and ex-urbanization of the more mobile populations, effectively redistributing the nature and location of economic activity and service demand; the third is the emergence at a much smaller scale of new manufacturing and communications industries which have new locational requirements – here a new, very low density, axial metropolitan phenomenon is emerging; and the fourth, in the US at least, is a reverse trend – an increasingly important role for office, financial, and knowledge-based services for the older 'traditional' cities and for a very few adjusting 'advanced industrial' cities. Not only is a new generation of 'yuppies' returning to city environments, creating enormous economic potential for revitalization there, but this has also coincided with the introduction of new technologies that have contributed to new patterns of settlement elsewhere.

Notes and References

1. This chapter draws on the following papers presented to the Future Cities' Conference at Oxford Polytechnic on 23/24 April 1987: Hay, D.G. 'European cities: trends, problems and policies'; and Barras, R. 'Cities and new technology'.
2. Knight, R.V., (1986) 'The advanced industrial metropolis: a new type of world city', in H.-J. Ewers, J.B. Goddard, and H. Matzerath (eds) (1986) *The Future of the Metropolis: Economic Aspects*, Berlin and New York: De Gruyter.
3. See: Hall, P.G. and Hay D.G., (1980) *Growth Centres in the European Urban System*, London: Heinemann Educational; and van den Berg, L., Drewett, R., Klaassen, L.H., Rossi, A., and Vijverberg, C.H.T. (1982) *Urban Europe: A study of Growth and Decline*, Oxford: Pergamon.
4. Mathias, P. (1969) *The First Industrial Nation: An Economic History of Britain 1700–1914*,. 2, London: Methuen.
5. See: Klaassen L.H., and van den Berg, L. (1978) *The Process of Urban Decline*, Working paper 1978/6, Rotterdam: Netherlands Economic Institute; Hall and Hay, op. cit. n. 3; van den Berg *et al.*, op. cit., n. 3.
6. Berry, B.J.L., (1973) *Growth Centres in the American Urban System*, Cambridge, Mass: Ballinger.
7. Ganz, A. (1986) 'Where has the urban crisis gone? How Boston and other large cities have stemmed urban decline', in M. Gottdiener, (ed.) *Cities in Stress,* Beverley Hills, Calif.: Sage Books.
8. van den Berg *et al.* op. cit., n.3.
9. Cheshire, P.C., Hay, D.G., Carbonaro, G., and Bevan, N. (1987) *Urban*

Problems and Regional Policy in the European Community of 12: Analysis and Recommendations for Community Action, Final Report to the Commission of the European Communities, University of Reading.

10. Eurostat (Statistical Office of the European Communities) (1975–86) *Yearbook of Regional Statistics,* annual publication, Luxembourg: Eurostat.
11. Bradbury, K.L., Downs, A., and Small, K.A. (1982) *Urban Decline and the Future of American Cities,* Washington D.C.: 253, The Brookings Institution.
12. van den Berg, op. cit., n. 3.
13. Hall and Hay. 190, op. cit., n. 3.
14. Fox-Przeworski, J. (1986) 'Overview: national government responses to structural changes in urban economics'. 315 in Ewers H.-J. *et al.*, op. cit., n.2.
15. Gottdiener, M. (1986) 'Retrospect and prospect in urban crisis theory', in Gottdiener, M., op. cit., n. 7.
16. Friedrichs, J. and Kasarda, J.D. (1986) 'Economic transformation, minorities, and urban demographic-employment mismatch in the US and West Germany', in Ewers, H.-J. *et al.,* op. cit., n. 2.
17. Lever, W. (1986) 'Economic development policy in London', in Ewers, H.-J *et al.* op. cit., n. 2.
18. van den Berg *et al.,* op. cit., n. 3.
19. Ganz, op. cit., n. 7.

Chapter 2

The future economic role of urban systems[1]

Iain Begg and Barry Moore

In this Chapter, again from the perspective of the mainstream, academic urban and regional economist, Iain Begg and Barry Moore look forward to the future of the city. Relating their analysis to the cities of western Europe and North America, they start by identifying the determinants of economic function. According to this analysis, two types of activity underlie the economic rationale of the city – 'non-tradeables', which are produced and consumed within the city, and 'tradeables', which are produced within the city and then 'exported'. It is these 'tradeable' activities that are most important in securing the economic survival of the city, and three major processes of structural change are identified as influencing them – broad movements in the international division of labour, the substitution of capital for labour, and the growth of the service sector. Finally, having examined the demographic, technological, and economic factors affecting future cities, Begg and Moore make their predictions. Like Hay, in the preceding chapter, they do not believe that there will be any significant return of conventional manufacturing activity to the urban core. Nevertheless, they do see some evidence of urban renewal brought about by both a change in residential preferences favouring some inner-city locations and the emergence of new specializations for cities. However, it is clearly stated that this renewal will not be evenly distributed and, in a rather chilling analysis of what is termed 'balanced decline', a typology of future city development is presented in four categories – 'expansion or recovery', 'bottoming-out', 'further decline', and 'maturing'. This typology indicates, first, that no single formula can be predicted and, second, that 'casualities are to be expected'.

Iain Begg is a Senior Research Officer in the Department of Applied Economics at the University of Cambridge. He has carried out research on economic and social aspects of urban change in the UK and elsewhere in Europe and has published a number of articles based on his research. His other interests include high technology location, local economic development and the regional implications of completing the

54

EEC 'internal market'.

Barry Moore is Assistant Director of Research to the Department of Land Economy, Cambridge and a Fellow of Downing College. He was an advisor on the OECD's Urban Programme and a Special Advisor to the House of Commons Select Committee on Welsh Affairs. His main current interests are in the field of government policy evaluation, particularly of urban and regional policy.

Introduction

Ever since ancient times, cities have played a leading role in the functioning of economic systems. As commercial or administrative centres, cities are the focus of economic activity for their surrounding regions, and are typically the location for major economic decision-making. They act both as centres for production – by providing the mix of factors needed to create output – and for consumption – by bringing together the infrastructure required to distribute output. Different types of cities do, however, perform different functions. Moreover, the economic specializations of cities have evolved over time, as economies themselves become more complex and as the competitive advantages of cities for particular types of activity have changed.

In most advanced industrial economies, the future economic role of cities, especially large conurbations, has been called into question by recent developments.[2] Technological change has radically altered methods of production and, thus, the suitability of cities for different kinds of economic activity; improvements in communications and rising real incomes have contributed to marked shifts in the distribution and demographic composition of population between different parts of countries and different types of settlements; and national and international economic developments have brought about major changes in the structures of economies – most notably, the change in the pattern of economic activity away from manufactures and towards services.

Highly-urbanized countries like the UK, Germany, or the United States, are bound to be particularly affected by forces which modify the economic role of cities. The bulk of resources, both human and material, are located in urban areas and are orientated towards an economic system based on the urban economy. However, many of the historical reasons for this outcome have ceased to be valid; with the result that, in many countries, the existing urban system is, in several respects, ill-suited to the likely future demands it will face.

The aim of this chapter is to appraise the prospects for cities in the advanced industrial economies of western Europe and North America in the light of social, technical and economic trends in the next few decades. In the next section, determinants of the economic functions of cities are discussed. The following sections consider the main influences on change expected in the future, and assess their likely impact on cities. The fourth part of the chapter relates these prospective changes to the circumstances of cities in western Europe (with continuing contrasts between growing and declining cities) and the United States (where many of today's trends anticipate likely developments in other industrialized countries). This is followed by a section on the UK, which is, in many ways, representative of trends occurring elsewhere.

Determinants of the economic functions of cities

The economic rationale for cities is that, through agglomeration, certain activities can be carried out more effectively and efficiently. To understand how the effects of agglomeration shape the pattern of economic activity in cities, it is useful to draw a fundamental distinction between two basic types of activity. The first is non-tradeables, comprising all those economic activities for which demand and supply are physically contiguous. Most personal services fall into this category, as do the majority of minor construction works, retailing, repair services and a proportion of food manufactures. The essential characteristic of non-tradeables is that it is local economic conditions which determine the demand for them. In practice, there is a considerable overlap between non-tradeables and those economic activities which cater for consumption of output.

The second category is *tradeables,* where (potentially, if not actually) the sources of demand for the activities in question can be physically remote from the location in which they are produced. Clearly, goods and services which are traded internationally fall into this category. Other types of activity may be tradeable only within national boundaries (such as many central government services) or within parts of a country. The main features of tradeable goods and services is that their location is influenced primarily by the suitability of the area from the perspective of the producing unit, not the purchasers of the activity; for example, the location of a power station adjacent to sources of fuels like coalfields.

At the margin, the distinction between tradeables and non-tradeables becomes somewhat arbitrary, since it depends on how a local economy is defined. Conceptually, however, the difference is reasonably unambiguous, and the separation of economic activity into these two components provides an initial framework for analysing the development of the economic functions of cities. These are shown schematically in Figure 2.1, which itemizes the main elements of the two types of activity.

Traditionally, cities specialized in providing economic functions that served their catchment areas, and their economies were thus, in the terminology adopted here, dominated by non-tradeables: administration, commercial activities, retailing, wholesaling, transport

Figure 2.1 Types of economic activity

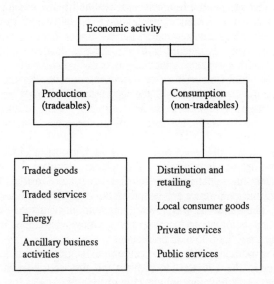

and so on. Since the Industrial Revolution, however, a second class of cities has sprung up with specializations that owe far more to their perceived competitiveness for tradeables activity. The urban system consequently comprises two quite distinct types of city functions, so that the prospective realignment of these functions can be expected to play an important part in shaping the future of the urban system.[3]

A major influence on this reshaping will be changing residential preferences. In most of the older industrialized countries, inequalities in the distribution of income per head between areas are not great. This is partly the result of social transfers and the integrated nature of their economies. One consequence of this is that there is a close relationship between the size of the resident population and the number of jobs in the local economy which directly service that population by providing largely non-tradeable services for immediate consumption. An approximate figure puts this job demand at between twenty and thirty jobs per 100 population – typically half or more of the working population. It follows that if there are population movements from one type of settlement to another – for example, from conurbations to smaller towns (as in northern Europe and the US), or from rural hinterlands to cities (as in southern Europe) – there will also be an induced shift of economic activity.[4]

Population movements occur for a variety of reasons, ranging from concern about the attractiveness of the local environment (crime, housing type, density and quality, or social mix), through economic necessity (access to employment), to availability of amenities. As a rule, relatively short-distance moves tend to be motivated by pursuit of an improved living environment, whereas longer-distance migration is more likely to be associated with job change. Shifts in the relative importance of these various factors (such as high income elasticity of demand for better housing), or developments which alter the extent to which they matter (for example, the separation of place of employment from the place of residence made possible by easy commuting) are bound to lead to shifts in residential preferences with far-reaching implications.

For instance, with much of the stock of housing in cities in social ownership or of increasingly dilapidated quality, the inner-city environment has deteriorated relative to other residential areas, reinforcing the preference for suburban and smaller town areas. In the UK this phenomenon has been apparent not just in the large conurbations but also in some smaller cities where the 'inner city' problem has not been so well publicized.[5]

Planning policies such as the retention of 'green belts' around the main cities in the UK tend to prevent the further suburbanization of larger cities, and thus contribute to the growth of smaller towns around large cities. The process has been encouraged by the growth of commuting to work, made possible by improvements in surface communications and vastly increased car ownership, and the willingness of higher paid staff to undertake long daily journeys to work. It is also a reflection of agglomeration diseconomies of very large cities which manifest themselves in higher costs of living, especially of housing. In some countries, central, regional, and local government policies have also played a part in shifting the balance of residence away from larger cities – not only through overt polices like inner-city slum clearance or the construction of new towns, satellite cities, and so on, but also by less direct means like fiscal policies which promote owner occupation.

In the mature industrial economies, the upshot is that, just on the basis of changed patterns of settlement, a growth in economic activity in the smaller towns and rural areas would be expected, as activity moves to follow population. Moreover, as disposable income grows, there is a greater likelihood that an increasing proportion of GDP will be devoted to the consumption of non-tradeables.

Turning next to the location of tradeables activity, the OECD[6] has identified three major processes of structural change in the international economy of importance to the evolution of the urban system. Broad movements in the international division of labour are a first factor. Much low-skilled assembly work in motor vehicles, textiles, and electronics (previously heavily concentrated in older industrialized cities) has relocated to countries offering low labour costs. There are, therefore, certain types of manufacturing (whether defined in terms of *products* or *processes*) in which the industrialized countries have lost their competitive edge, and are unlikely to recover it. Equally, there are other segments of the market for manufactures for which the economic characteristics of the older industrialized countries seem well-suited. Products requiring a technological input, or employing specialist skills – aerospace, pharmaceuticals, and engineering goods fall into this category – are the sort in which Britain, Germany or the United States must expect to retain a competitive advantage through possessing a qualified labour force and an appropriate industrial tradition. Few of these newer industries are attracted to old industrial cities.

In parallel with the internationalization of manufacturing, the OECD notes the substitution of capital for labour as a second fundamental structural change affecting city economies. Manufacturers require more floorspace per unit of output, and are characteristically less able to compete with many non-manufacturing activities for the available land.[7] As a result of this development, a significant proportion of manufacturing jobs which were once central to city economies have disappeared or have been dispersed to other, less urbanized locations.

The third factor cited by the OECD is the growth of the service sector, particularly of producer services and non-profit services which do not immediately serve local demand. Tourism has also emerged as a major growth sector. Much of the new service activity has been concentrated in urban areas, such as central business or tourist districts, and has been instrumental in transforming urban economies. There has, too, been a reorientation of trading relationships from a pattern dominated by North Atlantic exchanges to increased intra-European and cross-Pacific exchanges. Other structural changes include the expansion of oil and electricity as the main source of energy in place of coal, and the emergence of new manufacturing activities replacing old staple industries like textiles or steel-making. It has, indeed, been suggested by some commentators that the advanced industrial economies are living through another industrial revolution.[8]

Policy has also played its part in shaping the urban economy. One set of policies has been those with explicit spatial objectives, designed, for example, to disperse activities away from major urban concentrations such as Paris or London. More recently, urban policy has sought to regenerate and stem the decline of larger cities. Some of the consequences of these new policies are beginning to emerge. Previously run-down tracts of inner city areas – in cities as diverse as London, Copenhagen, or Baltimore – are being 'gentrified' with the result that their appeal as residential areas has begun to rise. Where, 10 or 20 years ago, the young and affluent were drawn to suburban housing, leaving the inner cities to deprived social groups, now there is some evidence of a reversal of that trend.

Recent policy initiatives are also playing a part in shaping the structures of city economies. Much more emphasis is being placed on promoting the development of cities' functions as satisfiers of consumer needs – retailing, tourism and other services – through land-use planning and economic development strategies, rather than on attempting to recoup for cities their previous relative specialization in industry. Policies without explicit spatial objectives have also had a significant impact on the urban system. Fiscal advantages for home owners, for instance, have encouraged a flight of population from inner cities to suburbia and smaller towns. Policy decisions on communications infrastructure have, similarly, facilitated the movement of population and economic activity.

Figure 2.2 Determinants of economic activity in cities

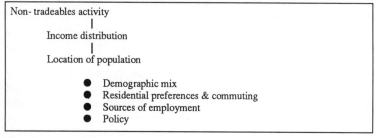

Non- tradeables activity
|
Income distribution
|
Location of population

- Demographic mix
- Residential preferences & commuting
- Sources of employment
- Policy

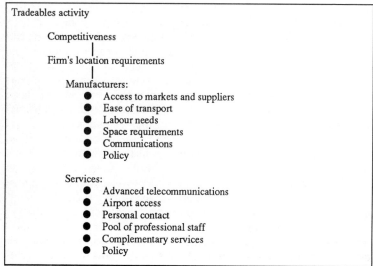

Tradeables activity

Competitiveness
|
Firm's location requirements
|
Manufacturers:
- Access to markets and suppliers
- Ease of transport
- Labour needs
- Space requirements
- Communications
- Policy

Services:
- Advanced telecommunications
- Airport access
- Personal contact
- Pool of professional staff
- Complementary services
- Policy

All of these changes have played a part in shaping the economic role of urban systems (summarized in Figure 2.2). Older, 'smokestack' cities with a long industrial tradition in declining industries like steel, coal, textiles, or shipbuilding, have signally failed to attract the newer industrial or commercial activities. New growth centres have emerged. Cities which previously acted as ports, or as regional centres in parts of countries which have gone into decline, have seen much of their *raison d'être* stripped away.

Future developments and their implications for cities

Given the complexity of the processes which influence the evolution of urban systems, there can be no all-encompassing vision of how cities will develop in the coming decades. Nevertheless, there are systematic structural changes already underway which will, inevitably, play a significant part in shaping the urban system. Demography, technology, and economic developments will all exert an influence, as will social and environmental factors.

Demographic factors

A key demographic influence in the coming decades will be the growth of the retired population. Medical breakthroughs, early retirement, and a natural bulge in the numbers reaching pensionable age by the first decade of the next century account for this projected rise.[9] Unlike previous generations of pensioners, a large proportion of these will be asset rich, having paid off mortgages on their own homes, and can anticipate a comfortable standard of living from their state and occupational pensions. Clearly, therefore, the residential choices of this group of people will have a major impact on the location of economic activity serving their demands. It will also contribute to a projected increase in numbers of households,[10] which could influence construction activity, possibly requiring new settlements. The pattern of expenditure of pensioners will, in addition, affect the structure of economic activity, possibly increasing the proportion of locally provided services.

In particular, the retired of the future will have the means to pay for greatly increased consumption of leisure activities, and to demand more and better medical and personal services. Much of this new demand must be expected to be concentrated in areas where the elderly choose to live, as their propensity to travel is lower than other social groups. Indeed, increased leisure time and spending is certain to be a general social phenomenon, implying that economic activities which cater to it can look forward to expansion. Since larger cities, generally, are able to offer and sustain a range of such activities, the implication is that they will specialize increasingly in these service sector activities. However, the outcome may be the emergence of a new generation of 'grey cities' – within easy reach of larger cities – specializing in retired population services.

Technological factors

The broad direction of technological change in the next few decades is already evident from advances such as those in the fields of biotechnology, electronics, and communications. Innovations and inventions resulting from the application of these new discoveries will lead to far-reaching changes in the organization and location of economic activity, and will alter the pattern of resource use. Where previous waves of technological development could be characterized as having a centralizing effect (the rapid urbanization which accompanied the developments, successively, of steam power and the rise of mass production), it is arguable that emerging technologies will be much more de-centralizing in their impact.[11] These economic transformations must, inevitably, affect the future economic role of cities, and can be expected to favour those parts of the urban system – be they smaller 'salubrious' towns, or established metropolitan areas – which offer the best combination of location factors.

Although the revolutionary technological developments of the next generation are bound to remain conjectural, other, more evolutionary changes can already be guessed at with a degree of precision. For instance, the effects of research into new methods of cultivation, together with genetic 'engineering' in livestock strains, can already be built into projections of the land required for agricultural use. For the UK, as an illustration, it is forecast that, in the next 30 years, the land needs of agriculture could fall by 40 per cent or even more if the most efficient techniques are adopted.[12] Compared with the relatively small fraction of the country devoted to urban settlements, this represents a huge increase in land potentially available for urban development. Assuming little or no overall population growth in the UK, these biotechnology developments, alone, could radically alter the pattern of settlement by greatly increasing the potential living space per inhabitant.

Electronics have already caused major changes in the working environment, not only by giving rise to the so-called information technology revolution, but also by stimulating an irreversible shift in methods of manufacturing production. Robotics have made it possible, for example, for a large integrated steelworks to be run by a handful of technicians at consoles. Similarly, modern mass-production lines are equipped with robots which replace manual labour in carrying out repetitive tasks. This vastly enhanced capital intensity of manufacturing, a trend which must be expected to continue, has two key implications. First, industry will demand more space for mass production so that greenfield sites will be needed. Second, the labour requirements of manufacturing will not just shrink, they will change in character: a growing proportion of manufacturing employees in the future will be not assembly-line workers or semi-skilled craftsmen, but highly trained technicians or electronic engineers. What this indicates, in turn, is that the link between the location of manufacturing and the location of major concentrations of population will be weakened still further, the more so as improvements in transport infrastructure permit increases in commuting.

Information technology and communications

The information technology revolution, too, is capable of causing a restructuring of employment patterns. Definitions vary, but it is beyond dispute that a significant proportion of economic activity is concerned with the acquisition, processing, and retrieval of information. As new methods of handling information emerge, the capacity to shift the place of work grows. Trading, for instance, could be carried out from home using computer links, rather than from offices. Equally, many business services which have traditionally been carried out at production locations can now, as easily, be produced from remote offices, possibly in service orientated cities.

Other forms of communication development can also be expected to affect the future economic role of cities.[13] On the one hand, centres of communications infrastructure will be needed: cities will be obvious candidates for providing these because they can offer the range of complementary activities needed to sustain a communications centre, particularly the range of occupational skills. On the other hand, the implementation of computerized networking of most aspects of information will greatly extend the choices open to firms when making location decisions internationally as well as within a country.

Economic development

Increasingly, in the future, competition in activities like financial services will be international rather than intra-national. This will come about both because of enabling technological change in the field of communications and because of deregulation in world markets. The post-war period saw unprecedented growth in the volume of world trade, bringing with it the rapid industrialization of many Third World countries. In the next generation, all the signs are that this opening-up of markets will be extended to traded services.

In financial services, this process is well advanced. Dealing in the principal financial centres (London, New York, Tokyo) has become much more closely integrated in the past few years, and the days of a global market are not far off. On the evidence of the pattern of trade liberalization, this must be expected to lead to an intensification of competition between the established financial centres, with new entrants seeking to break into these lucrative markets. In this context, it is not unreasonable to think in terms of a global urban system in which London, New York, Chicago, Paris, Frankfurt, and Tokyo contend with one another for supremacy.

International tourism, similarly, can only continue to represent a growing proportion of world GDP, while many other services are also likely to proliferate. Just as the growth of trade brought with it a New International Economic Order, the coming internationalization of services will lead to a further evolution in the economic specializations of countries. This is bound to influence the pattern of economic activity within countries, and thus to have an impact on activity in cities.

According to Ayres,[14] technological developments mean that manufacturing, certainly in the advanced countries, will change from mass production of standardized products to flexible batch production of advanced technological products. As Schmandt points out,[15] there is an increasing dependence on research to drive the search for product innovation, to the extent that the distinction between research and production activities becomes blurred. The location of activity is likely to be increasingly governed by the preferences of the articulate and highly educated professionals central to such activities.

The future of urban systems

What, then, can be inferred about the future economic role of urban systems? Are we about to witness a new twist in the cycle of major cities as they emerge from a phase of deindustrialization, poised to take on new economic functions, or are many condemned to irreversible decline? Are emerging trends like gentrification indicators of a recovered role for cities as desirable places to live? Will developments be similar in different countries, or, as the OECD note,[16] sharply differentiated between countries? The preceding sections have tried to establish a framework for appraising the future of cities in terms of the major influences on their economic roles.

Some general observations can be chanced. First, it must be considered unlikely that there will be any significant return of conventional manufacturing to urban cores. For cities which owed their prosperity largely to such activity, this poses a stark choice: either they adapt to new economic activities, or they are faced with decline and its attendant problems of adjustment. A second observation is that many cities in the industrialized world are witnessing a form of urban renewal, brought about both by a change in residential preferences which has seen upgrading of inner city areas[17] at the same time as dispersal of lower income groups to more suburban locations, and by the emergence of new specializations for cities. Pittsburgh, the East End of London, and parts of Paris are examples of areas which have gained from such processes.[18]

Yet, although there are encouraging signs that decline is not inevitable for cities, questions remain about the sheer scale on which such transformations can take place. In the US, cities like Cleveland, St Louis, or Baltimore – all of which had seemed condemned only a decade ago to progressive decline – have successfully adapted to a producer services future. Similar metamorphoses appear to be under way in many European cities – for instance, Dusseldorf, Lille or Milan – with a dynamic and innovative service sector leading the way. Doubts must remain, however, about how much scope there is for the urban system as a whole to pin its future on the new service activities, since there is only so much of this (tradeable) activity to go round. Thus, as Dusseldorf prospers, the adjacent cities of Duisburg and Dortmund have seen their decline accelerate; while the success of Lille is no consolation for nearby Roubaix, Tourcoing, and Valenciennes as they see their staple industries drift away. Buffalo or Newark show no real signs of emulating the apparent renaissance of New York and Boston.

Edward Mortimer, writing in the *Financial Times*, has noted that across northern Europe there is a swathe of declining industrial cities: 'The power house of the world has become the "rustbelt"'.[19] This could well extend in the next few decades to encompass some of the centres of heavy industry in southern Europe, like Bilbão or Genoa which lack appeal for the newer forms of tradeables activity, while problems of chaotic growth continue to plague other southern European cities with poor rural hinterlands, like Naples or Athens. Indeed, even though cities like Dortmund or Glasgow are making determined efforts to alter their images through cultural development and positive promotion of the cities' virtues, they are leaning against the wind. As Mortimer notes: 'The trouble is, of course, that Bavaria and Baden-Wurttemberg have symphony orchestras just as good, and they have ski slopes and mountain scenery as well.'[20]

In short, what works for one city cannot necessarily be used for another, let alone for the urban system as a whole. Science parks, high quality residential developments, retail complexes, and innovation centres are the fashionable responses of today to securing economic recovery, but it is inconceivable that the demand for these facilities can be spread so widely that it provides an answer for all. On the contrary, there is a remorseless logic of location which means that cities offering the most attractive characteristics will ultimately do better than those which are struggling. Whether this means that the less favoured must wither and die, may depend on their ability to exploit alternative niches in the spectrum of economic activity.

Policy is, as always, the joker in the pack. Given the influence of new location requirements of tradeable activity and population, the critical task for policy is to achieve a viable urban economy. This does not necessarily imply a return to an urban system similar to that of the past. Smaller, more specialized cores with closer links to satellite settlements could come to characterize the urban structure, calling into question the emphasis of policy on individual cities and urban problems. Urban renewal, which has become a major preoccupation in many countries, as social problems multiply and as the dangers of social divisions become more acute, needs to be governed by a strategic assessment of the evolution of the urban system, rather than individual cities.

In the coming decades, the main driving forces from policy may be much more population orientated: where are the new housing developments to be located; where will immigrants be steered to; or where will leisure activities be promoted? This will depend on a complex interaction of land-use planning policies, on fiscal incentives, and on major infrastructure programmes. It will also be driven by the complementary decisions of individuals and of productive units on choices of location.

The future of the urban system in the UK

The UK, at present, exemplifies many of the themes addressed in the previous sections. Its urban system contains the whole spectrum of city types, from the apparent despondency of cities such as Liverpool which look to be bereft of economic function, through resurgent areas like Bristol, to cities which seem, like Cambridge, to have found the key to a bright future.

Population trends will be dominated by the growth of the retired. This would indicate a growth of existing, mainly coastal retirement towns and of smaller residentially attractive market towns within easy reach of major cities. If past trends persist, the South of the country would be favoured over the North on account of its relative lack of industrial dereliction, but lower property prices outside the South and East might counter this. These trends are also likely to be reinforced by the progressive obsolescence of much of the country's existing urban housing stock.

At the same time, growth in leisure spending can be expected to promote economic activity in cities which offer a range of such activities. In terms of an urban hierarchy, this points to larger cities in a region providing leisure and other services which complement those provided in smaller, predominantly residential cities. To some extent, a hierarchy based on a 'central-place' model can be anticipated, although many of the activities in which larger cities were relatively specialized will be provided in future either remotely (e.g. video and televised entertainment or home banking) or by the development of new patterns of activity (such as the growth of retail chains offering the same goods everywhere). Ease of travel may also, in a country as small as the UK, limit the need for wide proliferation of urban centres supplying central place activities.

The country's international trading links will constitute a second major influence on the urban system. Financial services and other traded services will require a sound base, and it is difficult to envisage any city other than London, or some of its satellites close to Heathrow, securing the agglomeration economies that will be needed for Britain to compete successfully in the world market. Tourism, however, is another matter. For the country to prosper in this market the need will be for a diversified tourist infrastructure, which again indicates a role for regional centres in serving the wider regional market. What this points to is the development of key gateway cities like Southampton, Plymouth, Derby, Swansea, or Glasgow (none of which would spring to mind as tourist destinations today) much more as service centres than as the commercial and industrial centres they were previously.

For the UK, the challenge of the future will be to secure a niche in the market for manufactures to complement its presumed competitive advantage in traded services. Achieving an adequate market share will be an essential prerequisite to maintaining income growth. The national interest will dictate that this sort of industry be located so as to attain optimal cost competitiveness, and this consideration will be a potent factor in determining the role of cities in manufacturing activity. The likelihood that trade with Europe will continue to grow as a proportion of the country's exports, a process that will be given added impetus by the planned completion of the European Community's internal market by 1992, means that the drift of activity towards the South and East of the country must be expected to continue. The marked locational preference of high-technology activities (widely believed to be the sectors in which Britain can be internationally competitive) for new towns and for the more dynamic areas of the south of the country also provide pointers to future patterns of activity.

The prospective trends of the different types of manufacturing will help to shape the future economic role of the urban system. If large-scale manufacturing continues to demand increasing amounts of floorspace, the evolution towards industrial development outside large cities will continue. Together with the need to have access to markets and suppliers, this suggests a concentration of manufacturing on the periphery of cities and towns in the South and East. At the same time, it implies that the large conurbations in the West of the country (Liverpool, Glasgow, Manchester, possibly also Leeds and Birmingham) cannot look forward to a return of manufacturing. By the same token, many of the smaller towns which have, traditionally, acted as suppliers of components to the manufacturing centres will face a reorientation of their economic function. Specialized engineering and electronic skills will, of course, remain in demand, and the smaller cities with a tradition in these fields will probably continue to be active in supplying national and international markets. Many local services, however, are essentially dependent on the traded goods sector – transport being a case in point – so that the absence of manufacturing would also mean a loss of activity in these complementary activities, few of which have any stand-alone viability.

The conclusion that seems to emerge from this analysis of manufacturing's location needs is that the biggest impact is likely to occur in the West Midlands, the North West, Central Scotland, and South and West Yorkshire, all areas where the concentration of urban areas reflects past rather than future need of manufacturing. This prompts the question of whether these areas are likely to take on an alternative economic function in future. Part of the answer has already been indicated in relation to 'central place' functions of cities. There will always be a place in the urban hierarchy for cities large enough to provide economies of scale in meeting demand for consumption. Indeed, with the forecast increase in leisure spending, larger cities can cater to the demand for variety in a way that smaller towns cannot. Similarly, to the extent that moves in the location of manufacturing are short distance, for example from a conurbation like Liverpool to one of the necklace towns in the region, it is conceivable that the core city would retain many of the complementary activities which service manufacturing. Larger urban areas could well follow the pattern emerging in the US of becoming increasingly specialized in business services.[21]

Nevertheless, the direction of probable change is unambiguous: even those larger cities which do succeed in developing regional capital functions (and it is already evident in the economic strategies of cities as diverse as Glasgow, Sheffield, or Southampton that there is a growing emphasis on such service functions as the attraction of corporate headquarters, or of regional retailing functions, rather than promotion of new manufacturing) cannot hope to generate enough economic activity fully to compensate for the decline of manufacturing. In the absence of some other source of new activity, it follows that these types of city are confronted with economic decline.

This need not be a cause for concern. In fact, a balanced decline, in which the supply of labour contracts to match the falling off in demand, as job opportunities emerge elsewhere, is not intrinsically worrying. Past experience, however, is that the decline, especially of inner city areas, has been decidedly uneven, with the 'employable' leaving and those least competitive in the labour market remaining behind, so that unemployment rises, and the economy goes into a vicious cycle of cumulative decline. The answer is in the policy response. Policy is also capable of affecting the forces that initiate decline so that the influence of policy will, itself, be a determinant of the future of the urban system.

Many recent urban policy initiatives have been aimed at regenerating city economies by removing dereliction and by trying to foster indigenous activity. The reclamation of docklands for new activity, in London, Liverpool, or Southampton, using the catalyst of public money, or the designation of Enterprise Zones across the country, are examples of the types of schemes that have been undertaken. Such policy initiatives do not just provide relief for economically depressed areas, they also increase the scope for new types of economic activity. In London, for instance, the huge investment in Docklands has led to a resurgence of middle-class housing in what was previously a moribund area. This is bound to be accompanied by the growth of population-related personal services, a local construction boom, and demands for public services in education, health and community services.

Whether this phenomenon is peculiar to London, given the spur of the 'big bang' in the City of London and the consequent upsurge in demand for high-quality office and residential accommodation, is an open question. It is beyond doubt that cities which *do not* attempt to bring about a transformation of derelict environments have little chance of attracting office or residential growth. Cities do, in principle, have a competitive advantage in providing variety in leisure services, so that it is conceivable that wholesale refurbishment of city environments could attract residential interest, and thus population-related activity.

Whether or not this occurs depends, in part, on policy decisions. Strict adherence to existing 'green belt' planning policies could favour cities as residential areas. On the other hand, if the decisions on surplus agricultural land include the construction of a fresh wave of new towns, the economies of larger cities could be significantly undermined. Fiscal reliefs, energy choices, and a host of other policy decisions also have the potential to influence the future development of the economic role of the urban system.

Some cities will, no doubt, succeed in making the transition to the changed economic environment of the next century. Others will struggle because, with changing economic functions, the 'demand' for urban areas may fall short of the urban capacity available. Whether this is comprehensive, with a shift from intensive urbanization to an urban hierarchy more like that in France, or is confined to the less advantaged regions of the country, is a matter for conjecture.

Concluding remarks

The future of urban systems is necessarily uncertain. Many of the key influences remain in the realm of conjecture. Equally, there are other determinants which can be foreseen with reasonable certainty: the directions of demographic and technological change, and the changing economic structure these imply. Figure 2.3 summarizes the main factors that come into the reckoning in shaping the future of different urban areas, and indicates the principal developments that are implied. Thus, it can be anticipated that growth areas will be those where there is an influx of population: retirement centres, attractive residential towns, possibly the revived inner areas of larger cities, although there may still be compensating outflows from the remaining tracts of rundown and derelict areas.

Figure 2.3 Determinants of future activity in urban areas

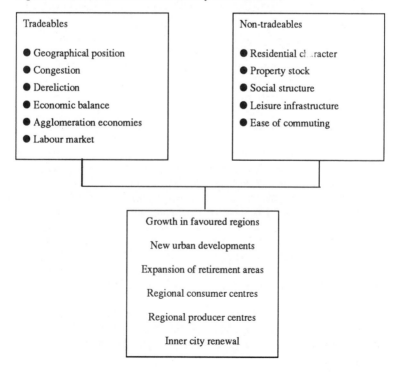

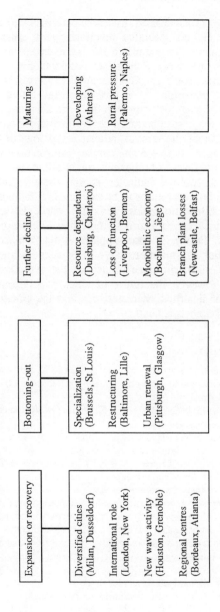

Figure 2. 4 Typology of future city developments

Expansion or recovery	Bottoming-out	Further decline	Maturing
Diversified cities (Milan, Dusseldorf)	Specialization (Brussels, St Louis)	Resource dependent (Duisburg, Charleroi)	Developing (Athens)
International role (London, New York)	Restructuring (Baltimore, Lille)	Loss of function (Liverpool, Bremen)	Rural pressure (Palermo, Naples)
New wave activity (Houston, Grenoble)	Urban renewal (Pittsburgh, Glasgow)	Monolithic economy (Bochum, Liège)	
Regional centres (Bordeaux, Atlanta)		Branch plant losses (Newcastle, Belfast)	

The role of urban areas in tradeable activities will concentrate more on services and on specialist functions, while many manufacturing activities gravitate to greenfield sites or even to countries outside the advanced country bloc. This poses problems for many of the older industrial cities, some of which may find it very difficult indeed to manage the transition to a post-industrial future. Casualties are, therefore, to be expected, although there are too many imponderables to allow a firm forecast to be made as to which cities they will be. Figure 2.4 attempts, none the less, to indicate a typology of city types within which examples (drawing on current information, and thus highly speculative) are shown of cities that might fall into the types.

What this typology indicates is that there is no single formula allowing the future of cities to be predicted. Although there are forces which will affect all cities, it is the particular characteristics of individual cities which will determine how successfully they adapt to these forces. Policy, no doubt, plays some role in this process of adaptation, but its limitations have to be acknowledged. Good or bad fortune may, similarly, have influenced the evolution of some cities. Ultimately, however, the future of cities will depend largely on the interaction of inherited characteristics and the emerging dynamics of international economic change.

Notes and references

1. This paper draws on the papers by R. Barras, D. Hay and I. Begg, and B. Moore presented to the 'Future Cities' conference at Oxford Polytechnic on 23/24 April 1987.
2. See Cameron, G.C. (ed.) (1980) *The Future of the British Conurbation*, London: Longman.
3. See Knight, R.V. (1982) 'City development in advanced industrial societies', in G. Gappert and R.V. Knight (eds) *Cities in the 21st Century*, Urban Affairs vol 23. See also J.F. Richardson (1982) 'The evolving dynamics of American urban development', in Gappert and Knight, op. cit. Knight, for instance, comments that:

   Cities appear to be returning to their more traditional roles, roles they played before they were overrun and overwhelmed by the forces that fuelled the Industrial Revolution ... It is clear that the eventual form of the industrial city will not only be different from that of early industrial centers but its function will also be different from that taken by traditional cities.

   Similarly, Richardson concludes that:

   Perhaps the most banal but still important conclusion is that the city of the future will not be like the industrial city of 1850 to 1950, and there is not much point in planners and policy makers trying to bring it back.
4. See Hall, P. and Hay, D. (1980) *Growth Centres in the European Urban System*, London: Heinemann Educational; OECD (1983) *Managing Urban*

Change: Policies and Finance, Paris: OECD; Cheshire, P.C. and Hay,
D.G. (forthcoming) *Urban Problems in Europe*, London: Allen & Unwin.

5. See Begg, I.G. and Eversley, D.C.E. (1986) 'Deprivation in the inner city',
   in V.A. Hausner (ed.) *Critical Issues in Urban Economic Development*,
   vol. I, Oxford: OUP.
   Cheshire and Hay (op. cit., n. 4 have, similarly, shown that there have
   been significant shifts in settlement patterns in most European countries.
6. OECD, op. cit. n.4.
7. See Ermisch, J.F. (1983a) *Locational Comparative Advantage and Land
   Use and Employment in London and the South East*, ESRC Inner Cities
   Working Paper, London: Policy Studies Institute.
8. See Ayres, R.U. (1984) *The Next Industrial Revolution: Reviving Industry
   through Innovation*, Cambridge, Mass.
9. See Ermisch, J.F. (1983b) *The Political Economy of Demographic
   Change*, London: Heinemann. Ermisch shows for the UK that there will
   be a large surge in numbers of pensioners from the turn of the millennium,
   and that, on one assumption about fertility, the ratio of workers to
   pensioners in the UK could fall to as low as 2 : 1 by the year 2030.
10. ibid.
11. Advances in communications, for instance, are cited as a reason.
    Telecommunications make it possible to separate the place of production
    of services such as accountancy, consultancy, or even head office
    functions, from their place of consumption.
12. See North, J. (1986) 'Use and management of the land: current and future
    trends', Bawden Lecture, Nov. 1986, Department of Land and Economy,
    University of Cambridge (mimeo).
13. A city like Atlanta in Georgia is a good example of the powerful effect of
    being such a centre – in this case through being a major hub point for
    airline networks. St Louis is another city where recent recovery has been
    much assisted by its pivotal air transportation role.
14. Ayres, op. cit. n. 8.
15. See Schmandt, J. (1987) 'Growth policy and the changing role of the
    states', paper presented to the IRER Conference on Regional Strategies
    and Innovation and Enterprise Competitiveness, September 1987, at the
    University of Neuchatel, Switzerland.
16. OECD, op. cit., n. 4, pp. 54 – 5.
17. Gentrification may, however, be somewhat illusory as a solution. See Ganz,
    A. (1986) 'Where has the urban crisis gone? How Boston and other large
    cities have gone into decline', in M. Gottdiener (ed.) *Cities in Stress: A New
    Look at the Urban Crisis*, Urban Affairs, vol.30. Ganz notes that even among
    ostensibly successful US cities, there is: 'new deprivation amidst booming
    growth', and quotes the *Washington Post* (1984) thus, on Baltimore:
    Few cities have tried so long, so hard, or so creatively to reverse their
    decline as Baltimore ... Yet even as more projects are announced and
    new buildings take their place on the skyline, nagging questions persist
    about Baltimore's future ... An increasing proportion of those who
    remain in the city are poor.
18. See Noyelle, T.J. and Stanback, T.M. (1984) *The Economic*

Transformation of American Cities, Totowa, New Jersey: Rowman & Allanheld. Noyelle and Stanback have shown that there is a sea-change occurring in the forms of economic activity which are growing in importance in some of the older cities in the US. Indeed, it is largely as a result of such cities acquiring new roles in providing producer services that the decline of the US 'snowbelt' in favour of the southern states has been arrested.

19. Mortimer, E. (1987) 'A flicker of the Northern Lights', *Financial Times*, London, August 1987.
20. ibid.
21. See Noyelle and Stanback, op. cit., n. 18.

Additional reading

Begg, I.G. and Moore, B.C. (1987) 'The Changing economic role of Britain's cities', in V.A. Hausner (ed.) (1986/7) *Critical Issues in Urban Development* (2 vols.), Oxford: OUP.

Coates, J.F. (1982) 'New technologies and their urban impact', in G. Gappert and R.V. Knight (eds) *Cities in the 21st Century*, Urban Affairs vol. 23.

Fothergill, S. and Gudgin, G. (1982) *Unequal Growth*, London: Heinemann.

Glickman, N.J. (1983) 'International trade, capital mobility and economic growth: some implications for American cities and regions in the 1980s', in D.A. Hicks and N.J. Glickman (eds) *Transition to the 21st Century: Prospects and Policies for Economic and Urban-Regional Transformation*, Greenwich, Conn.: Jai Press.

Hausner, V.A. (1986/7) *Critical Issues in Urban Economic Development*, vols I and II, Oxford: OUP.

Hicks, D.A. and Glickman, N.J. (eds) (1983) *Transition to the 21st Century: Prospects and Policies for Economic and Urban-Regional Transformation*, Greenwich, Conn.: Jai Press.

Leven, C.L. (1978) 'Growth and non-growth in metropolitan areas and the emergence of the polycentric metropolitan form', *RSA Papers* 41.

O'Connor, J. (1981) 'The fiscal crisis of the state revisited', *Kapitalstate* 9.

Shostak, A. (1982) 'Seven scenarios of urban change', in G. Gappert and R.V. Knight (eds) *Cities in the 21st Century*. Urban Affairs vol. 23.

Washington Post (1984) 'Is Baltimore truly back? New showcase city faces old problems', Nov. 24th.

Chapter 3

Urban change in the Third World: are recent trends a useful pointer to the urban future?[1]

Jorge E. Hardoy and David Satterthwaite

In this Chapter, Jorge Hardoy and David Satterthwaite provide a detailed analysis of the data concerning urbanization and urban growth in the Third World. They begin by discussing the accuracy of urban statistics and show that there is a lack of reliable, contemporary or comparable data on which to make accurate forecasts to the end of the century, let alone beyond. They then identify some general trends in Latin America, Asia, and Africa which suggest that the growth of metropolitan centres is actually decreasing in many cases relative to some secondary cities. On this basis, forecasts of mega-city populations appear highly questionable and indicate a need for studies which take into account the economic, social, physical, and political forces which condition it in each case, and limit projections to shorter time-frames where the degree of reliability – and hence the practical value – is greater. The central message of the chapter is that future cities in the Third World are unlikely to resemble those currently forecast and that new approaches will be needed to assess trends and develop more appropriate forms of urban management.

The authors have researched and published widely on urbanization and development. They are Director and Researcher respectively with the Human Settlement Programme of the International Institute for Environment and Development. Dr Hardy is also President of IIED-America Latina, based in Buenos Aires.

Introduction

For more than 15 years, it has been widely assumed that around half the world's population will be 'urban' by the year 2000. For instance, a book on Third World urbanization published in 1985 stated that 'Third World cities are growing at extremely rapid rates' and uncritically accepted projections that the world would be 50 per cent urban by the year 2000 and 90 per cent urban by 2050.[2] A book published in 1986 talked of Third World cities 'mushrooming', and stated that by 2000, not just half the world's population but almost half the Third World's population would be urban.[3] Many authors have translated this into half the world's population living in 'cities' by the year 2000, although, as will be described later, the terms 'urban centres' and 'cities' are not synonymous.

Given the volume and range of literature on 'exploding cities' and 'rapid urbanization', there is a hardly surprising tendency to assume, first, that all cities are growing rapidly and, second, that urban trends (evident in the last few decades) are likely to continue. This implies that trends in the past few decades provide a reliable guide for projections into the future. For many years, the United Nations Population Division has published projections for the year 2000 on national urbanization levels and on large cities' populations; in recent years, projections have been given up to the year 2025. These have suggested an ever increasing proportion of the world's population living in urban centres and large cities; United Nations projections made in 1982 (and published in 1985) forecast close to 500 'million cities' (i.e. cities with a million or more inhabitants) in the Third World in less than 40 years, compared to 119 in 1980.[4] The number of Third World cities with 4 million or more inhabitants is also projected to multiply several times from 22 in 1980 to 114 in 2025; by this date, more than 1.1 billion Third World people are projected to live in cities with 4 million or more inhabitants, more than six times the number in 1980.[5] According to such projections, by the year 2010, a higher proportion of Third World inhabitants will live in cities of this size than in the First and Second World. But an examination of recent census data and of the forces and factors which have underpinned urban change in different Third World nations raises serious doubts as to the validity of such projections and suggests that levels of urbanization and the dominance of very large cities may be far less than projected.

Before discussing the validity of projections on the Third World's urban future (and the assumption on which such projections are based) this chapter will review urban change in recent decades in Latin America, Asia, and Africa, and the forces and factors responsible for such change. This allows a discussion of whether the factors underlying rapid urbanization in recent decades are likely to continue in the future. The first section now points to the difficulties in arriving at an accurate understanding of the scale and nature of urban change.

The difficulties of describing urban change in the Third World

The best basis for making projections about city population sizes or about the proportion of people who will live in urban centres in the year 2000 or 2025 is a detailed understanding of urban change in the past few decades and its causes. But the statistical base to describe urban change accurately in the Third World does not exist. One problem is a lack of recent, reliable census data for many nations; for instance, Nigeria's last reliable census was in 1963.[6] No accurate figures can be given for urban trends in sub-Saharan Africa without accurate figures for Nigeria, since around a quarter of the region's population is in Nigeria.

Another problem arises from the lack of statistics which allow accurate international comparisons of the number (or proportion) of people in urban or rural areas. Despite the fact that so many publications have tables which list different nations' urbanization levels (i.e. the percentage of the population in urban areas), there are major differences in the criteria used by different governments to define which settlements are 'urban', which limits the validity of such comparisons.[7] To give just one example, if the Indian government decided to adopt the urban criteria used by the Peruvian government in recent censuses, India would change from being predominantly rural to one of Asia's most urbanized nations.[8] This in turn would radically alter aggregate urban statistics for South Asia which would become much more urban. Even the statistics for the proportion of the world's population living in urban centres would change significantly. If this change in criteria was applied to 1985, the world would move from being 41 per cent urban to around 47 per cent urban.

In fact, the usefulness of dividing any nation's population into 'rural' and 'urban' is diminishing. The assumption is that most of the agricultural population live and work in rural areas, while most of the non-agricultural population live and work in urban areas. But most national definitions of 'urban areas' mean that small market towns are included along with the largest cities when the two have very little in common. In many small urban centres, more than half the economically active population works in agriculture, with virtually all the rest making a living either working in agro-processing or selling goods and services to those deriving a living from agriculture. Meanwhile, many examples could be cited of high-technology industries and non-agricultural workers being in rural areas.

The fact that so many statistics are available to compare 'urban areas' with 'rural areas' has helped to sustain a belief that governments and aid agencies should give a high priority to addressing rural – urban disparities – in income and in access to basic services. But simply disaggregating national populations into 'urban' and 'rural' is a crude and often inaccurate way of identifying the people most in need. For instance, figures on infant mortality in 'urban areas' may be lower than those for rural areas, so the assumption is made that the urban population is better off than the rural population. But there are likely to be far more significant differences in infant mortality rates between richer and poorer urban districts within the same city or between richer and poorer rural districts. There are likely to be even more significant differences between richer and poorer income groups. Not surprisingly, a report by an Expert Group meeting to review United Nations Human Settlements statistics pointed out that, within most nations, there is such diversity between different rural areas and between different urban centres that aggregate statistics 'for all urban centres' or for 'all rural areas' are very misleading. More disegregation by income group, gender, and location is needed to help identify population groups most in need of government services and support.[9]

Comparisons of two urban centres' population growth rates can also be very misleading. Even within the same nation, if two urban centres with comparable population sizes had comparable population growth rates, this can hardly be stated as evidence that they are experiencing comparable economic changes. For instance, the relative contribution of natural increase and net in-migration to population growth may be very different. Or one of the centres may have a rapidly expanding population as a result of an inflow of refugees or of local rural inhabitants because of a drought, while the other centre's population growth is largely due to in-migration by people attracted by a growth in retail and service trade, which in turn was stimulated by rapid growth in production in surrounding farming areas. The contributions of wars and natural disasters to population movements (and urban growth) may be considered a special case; the movements might be assumed to be temporary. But it seems that the influence of such 'natural disasters' on population movements is growing and that their impact is often greatly exacerbated by human action (or inaction). In many instances, population movements produced by natural disasters are permanent moves.

An additional problem is the confusion between 'urban centre' and 'city'. In many nations, the term urban centre includes settlements with only a few hundred inhabitants. Although there is no agreement as to the definition of a city, no one would consider that small urban centres with a few hundred or a few thousand inhabitants, and with a high proportion of the labour force working in agriculture, can be counted as 'cities'. For many Third World nations, between a quarter and half of their urban population live in relatively small urban centres which would not be regarded as 'cities'.

There are also problems with international comparisons of city populations. To allow accurate international comparisons of cities' populations and growth rates, agreed criteria are needed as to how city boundaries are defined. But very different criteria are used to define city boundaries. In some instances, official figures for a city's population understate the real population since no change has been made in a city's boundary to include new developments which have grown beyond this boundary. In other instances, official figures overstate the city's population, since the boundary encompasses large areas of agricultural land and substantial numbers of rural inhabitants. One example of this is the figure of over 10 million inhabitants commonly cited for Shanghai urban agglomeration. This figure is actually the population in an area of over 6,000 square kilometres which includes large areas of highly productive agriculture and many villages and agricultural workers.[10]

One final problem in making international comparisons for cities' populations is the fact that there may be many different figures for the same year, based on different boundaries. For example, for metropolitan Manila, in the Philippines, in 1978, there were at least eight different definitions in use by different government agencies, all of which gave different figures for metro-Manila's population.[11] For Dhaka, Bangladesh, population statistics may refer to the historic city (5.6. square kilometres), the metropolitan area (414 square kilometres), the Statistical Metropolitan Area (1,121 square kilometres), Dhaka Sadar subdivision (1,601 square kilometres) or the District (7,459 square kilometres). A study of metropolitan Dhaka in 1981 chose yet another boundary which differed considerably from all those mentioned above.[12]

What generalizations are valid for urban change in the Third World?

Because it has proved possible to arrive at some generalizations about urban trends in the First World in recent decades, as nations there underwent comparable economic and demographic transformations (although during different decades), it has been assumed that comparable generalizations can be made about the Third World. In fact it is more difficult to point to 'Third World wide' trends than it is to 'First World' trends. There is more diversity between nations in their economic structures, population growth rates, levels of per capita income, and population sizes. The Third World includes many large, resource-rich, and small, resource-poor, nations. Differences between the rich, more industrialized nations such as Brazil and South Korea and the poorer nations such as Chad, Mali, or Nepal make it difficult to generalize about urban trends. It is even more difficult to generalize about future prospects for urban development 'for the Third World' when it contains dozens of nations which have little possibility of developing stable, viable economic bases, and several nations which have become major industrial powers within the world market.

An understanding of urban change in the Third World needs to be built up from detailed national, regional, and local studies. These point to the complicated mix of local, regional, national, and international factors which influence population movements within each nation or region, or in and out of urban centres. While many different urban centres may share a common factor which encourages or discourages in-migration, its importance relative to other factors and its interaction with other factors are unique to each urban centre. Of course, for each urban centre, both the range of factors and their relative importance change over time. A notable aspect of a review of empirical studies of small and intermediate urban centres in the Third World, is the enormous diversity discovered in the factors underlying economic and demographic changes in the different urban centres. A second notable aspect is the number of urban centres with very slow population growth rates or declining populations which calls into question the notion of universal, rapid urban growth.

Even with such diversity, it is useful to seek some generalizations which have validity beyond one particular urban centre, region, or nation. It seems that four generalizations about urban processes in the Third World have some validity in recent decades. The first is that most nations experienced a far more rapid growth in urban population than in rural population which means that an increasing proportion of their national populations now live in urban centres (however these urban centres are defined). The second is that in most nations, there has been an increasing concentration of population and economic activities in one or two cities, metropolitan areas, or 'core regions'; Table 3.1 gives some examples of cities which contain a high concentration of national production or trade. The third is that rapid growth has taken place simultaneously in both urban and rural populations; only relatively recently have rural populations declined in a few Third World nations and, in most, they seem likely to continue growing rapidly in the foreseeable future. The fourth is that, in aggregate, natural increase has contributed more to the growth in urban population that net rural-to-urban migration. But on this last point, as examples given later will show, for many cities and for some nations, net rural-to-urban migration has contributed more than natural increase in recent decades. And in many instances, a high proportion of migrants into cities are young people, soon to have children, while many migrants from urban to rural areas are relatively old and infertile. So a high rate of natural increase in a city's population may owe much to rapid in-migration of young, fertile people in previous years.[13]

Although serious doubts can be raised about the validity of international comparisons for levels of urbanization, one is faced with the problem that there are no alternative statistics which give Third

Table 3.1 Examples of cities with high concentrations of their national industrial production, commerce or government investment.

Nairobi (Kenya)	In 1975, Nairobi had 57 per cent of all Kenya's manufacturing employment and two-thirds of its industrial plants. In 1979, Nairobi contained around 5 per cent of the national population.
Manila (Philippines)	Metropolitan Manila produces one-third of the nation's GNP, handles 70 per cent of all imports, and contains 60 per cent of all manufacturing establishments. In 1981 it contained around 13 per cent of the national population.
Lima (Peru)	The metropolitan area of Lima accounts for 43 per cent of GDP, four-fifths of bank credit and consumer goods production, and for more than nine-tenths of capital goods production in Peru. In 1981, it contained around 27 per cent of the national population.
Managua (Nicaragua)	In 1983, Managua concentrated 25 per cent of the national population and 38 per cent of the GDP.
Lagos (Nigeria)	In 1978, the metropolitan area of Lagos handled over 40 per cent of the nation's external trade, accounted for over 57 per cent of total value-added in manufacturing, and contained over 40 per cent of Nigeria's highly skilled personnel. It contains only some 5 per cent of the national population.
Mexico City (Mexico)	In 1970, with some 24 per cent of the national population, it contained 30 per cent of total employment in manufacturing, 28 per cent of employment in commerce, 38 per cent of employment in services, 69 per cent of employment in national government, 62 per cent of national investment in higher education, and 80 per cent of research activities.
São Paulo (Brazil)	Greater São Paulo, with around one-tenth of Brazil's national population in 1980, contributed one-quarter of the net national product and over 40 per cent of Brazil's industrial value-added.
Rangoon (Burma) (Renamed Yangon in 1989)	Located at the centre of the national transport and communications network, Rangoon is the economic, political, and administrative heart of Burma. It is the dominant tertiary service centre and virtually all the import and export trade passes through its port. More than half of Burma's manufacturing industry is said to be located there. In 1981, it contained around 6 per cent of the national population.
Port au Prince (Haiti)	Approximately 40 per cent of the national income is produced within the capital, although only 14 per cent of the national population live there. It virtually monopolizes all urban economic activities. Its primacy is buttressed by both a highly centralized political and administrative system, as well as development policies geared towards the manufacturing sector, which have favoured a high level of expenditures within Port au Prince.
Bissau (Guinea Bissau)	With only 14 per cent of the national population, the capital city received 39.1 per cent of total state investments between 1978 and 1980. Davila notes that, ever since the last decades of Portuguese domination – which ended in 1974 after a 10-year war – most of the city's population has depended on external assistance for its survival, largely because it is cheaper to import foodstuffs from as far away as Pakistan than it is to transport the agricultural surplus from the south of this small West African nation.

81

Jorge E. Hardoy and David Satterthwaite

Dhaka (Bangladesh) (previously Dacca)	Apart from its role as national capital, some 60 per cent of all establishments surveyed by the census of manufacturing industries are located in Dhaka, while 47 per cent of all manufacturing employment is also concentrated here. Jute processing and textiles, the two principal industrial groups of Bangladesh, are centred here. Dhaka has also been the major beneficiary of public sector employment. The manufacturing sector and the public sector are the two major employment generating activities; they also comprise the formal sector of Dhaka's urban economy. In the 1981 census, the city contained less than 4 per cent of the national population.

Sources:

Nairobi – Richardson, Harry W. (1980) 'An urban development strategy for Kenya', *The Journal of Developing Areas* 15 (1), October.
Manila – Apacible, M.S. and Yaxley, and M. (1979) 'Manila through the eyes of the manilenos and the consultant' PTRC Summer Annual Meeting.
Lima – Richardson, H W. (1984) 'Planning strategies and policies in metropolitan Lima', *Third World Planning Review* 6 (2).
Managua – MINVAH (1983) 'Politica de ordenamiento y desarrollo de los asentamientos intermedios y rurales en Nicaragua', Managua, September.
Lagos – Aradeon, David, (1986) Aina, Tade, and Umo, Joe (1986) 'Southwest Nigeria', ch. 6 in J. Hardoy and D. Satterthwaite (eds) *Small and Intermediate Urban Centres; their role in Regional and National Development in the Third World*, London: Hodder & Stoughton.
Mexico City – Scott, Ian (1982) *Urban and Spatial Development in Mexico*, The World Bank, Baltimore and London: Johns Hopkins University Press.
São Paulo – Hamer, Andrew M. (1984) *Decentralized Urban development and Industrial Location Behaviour in São Paulo, Brazil: A Synthesis of Research Issues and Conclusions*, Discussion Paper, Water Supply and Urban Development Department, Washington DC, The World Bank.
Rangoon – Leonard, John B. (1985) 'Rangoon – city profile'; in *Cities* 2. (1) February.
Port au Prince – US AID (1980) *Haiti Shelter Sector Assessment*, Office of Housing and Urban Development, December.
Bissau – Davila, Julio D. (1987) *Shelter, Poverty and African Revolutionary Socialism: Human Settlements in Guinea Bissau*, London, Washington DC, and Buenos Aires: IIED.
Dhaka – World Bank Urban Sector Memorandum quoted in ESCAP (1985), *Study and Review of the Human Settlements in Asia and the Pacific*, vol. 11; Country Monographs, Bangkok: United Nations.

World coverage. Many recent censuses contain sufficient information as to the proportion of national populations in settlements within defined ranges of population size but, as yet, they have not been used to produce a reasonably comprehensive alternative to figures based on each nation's own criteria.

Separate sections for Latin America, Asia, and Africa review urban change between 1960 and the early 1980s but comparisons of different nations' level of urbanization are avoided. However, comments are made about the extent to which the proportion of different nations' populations living in 'urban centres' has changed since 1960, since this provides some measure of the extent to which national populations are concentrating in settlements which have some urban characteristics. These should be interpreted with caution for the reasons noted already. The sections also seek to link urban trends with forces and factors which underpin these trends.

Latin America

As Table 3.2 shows, in 1980 the various regions in Latin America had among the highest proportion of their populations living in cities, with more than 100,000 inhabitants and with more than 1 million inhabitants of all the Third World regions. Indeed, the southern cone of Latin America had a higher proportion of its inhabitants in such cities than both the Second World and most First World regions in 1960 and in1980. By 1985, four metropolitan centres (Mexico City, São Paulo, Rio de Janeiro, and Buenos Aires) had populations exceeding 10 million inhabitants and were among the world's fifteen largest urban agglomerations.

Nations with the most rapid growth in their economies and in manufacturing output during the 1960s and 1970s (such as Mexico, Colombia, and Brazil) tended to have the largest increase in the level of urbanization. Between 1960 and 1982, the level of urbanization grew from 51 per cent to 68 per cent in Mexico, from 45 per cent to 69 per cent in Brazil and from 48 per cent to 65 per cent in Colombia. However, urban growth rates in all sub-regions are declining and, apart from the Caribbean, they have been doing so since the late 1940s.[14]

The three nations in the southern cone – Chile, Uruguay, and Argentina – had much slower rates of urban population growth and less dramatic increases in the level of urbanization; the proportion of Argentina's population living in urban areas only grew from 74 per cent to 83 per cent in these 22 years, while that of Uruguay only grew from 80 per cent to 84 per cent. But these three nations are unusual not only in being the most urbanized nations in Latin America and among the most urbanized nations in the world, but, in addition, they had the slowest growing economies and slowest growth in manufacturing output in Latin America during the 1960s and 1970s. Argentina and Chile also had a decrease in the proportion of their labour forces working in industry. In 1980, some 36 per cent of their national populations were in 'million cities' which was a higher proportion than in Japan, North America, or West Europe. The reasons are rooted in their economic and demographic histories. In Argentina and Uruguay, rapid immigration from Europe in the late nineteenth and early twentieth centuries took place at a time when there was no change in rural land tenancy; the 'latifundia' and poor transportation networks generally prevented immigrants moving into farming. The only exceptions were a few areas being settled for the first time and where official colonization programmes were implemented, but these only covered a small percentage of good agricultural land. At that time, one should recall that it was easier, cheaper, and quicker for immigrants from Europe to travel to the east coast of South America rather than to

Table 3.2 Distribution of the world's population by urban areas and by cities with 100,000+ and 1 million+ inhabitants, 1960 and 1980 (in percentages)

	Population (millions)		Population in urban areas* (%)	
	1960	*1980*	*1960*	*1980*
Third World				
*Africa*ᵇ			18.4	28.7
Eastern Africa	76.0	136.7	7.4	15.7
Middle Africa	34.9	54.6	18.2	34.4
Northern Africa	65.1	108.2	30.0	44.1
Southern Africa	20.8	32.8	42.2	49.2
Western Africa	80.7	143.8	13.4	22.8
*Latin America*ᵇ			49.3	65.3
Caribbean	20.4	29.5	38.7	52.3
Central America and Mexico	49.5	92.3	46.7	60.7
Tropical South America	116.1	198.0	46.1	65.8
Southern Cone of South America	30.7	42.3	72.7	82.4
*Asia*ᵇ			20.6	26.6
China	667.3	1,002.8	16.8	20.3
Other East Asia (not including Japan)	39.7	63.0	36.3	60.4
South Asia	864.5	1,408.2	18.3	25.4
Second World				
USSR	214.3	265.5	48.8	63.2
Eastern Europe	116.7	134.9	44.5	56.3
First World				
Western Europe	308.4	349.1	66.6	76.8
North America	198.7	251.9	69.9	73.8
Japan	94.1	116.7	62.5	76.2
Australia and New Zealand	12.7	17.9	79.8	85.8
*World*ᶜ	3,013.8	4,453.2	33.6	39.9

Notes:
ᵃPercentages in this column are not comparable due to use of different definitions of an urban population in each country.
ᵇCountries included in list of nations within each of the African, American, and Asian categories are the same as those used by the United Nations. Europe is divided into two categories: Eastern Europe (Albania, Bulgaria, Czechoslovakia, German Democratic Republic, Hungary, Poland, Romania, and Yugoslavia) and Western Europe (all other countries).
ᶜ Columns do not add to world totals since figures have been rounded and Melanesia and Micronesia were not included.

Population in cities with 100,000 + residents (%)		Population in cities with 1 million + residents (%)	
1960	*1980*	*1960*	*1980*
2.7	8.4	0.0	3.1
7.1	18.7	0.0	9.7
19.9	25.0	9.7	14.6
22.8	23.0	6.3	13.0
5.6	15.8	0.0	5.5
19.1	28.8	7.1	15.6
23.1	37.2	10.5	22.6
24.7	41.5	14.3	26.2
46.7	54.2	32.7	35.9
11.4	11.0	6.6	7.0
26.1	49.1	15.9	32.1
9.7	15.9	4.0	8.2
25.6	36.2	6.0	14.0
19.5	26.4	8.0	10.4
42.9	48.2	22.6	25.7
49.5	56.3	28.7	34.7
30.5	45.6	21.7	27.0
54.8	69.1	31.7	47.0
19.9	24.7	9.9	13.6

Source: United Nations (UN) (1985) *Estimates and Projections of Urban, Rural and City Populations, 1950–2025: The 1982 Assessment*, New York: UN.
N.B.: Figures for Table 3.2 could have been presented for 1960 and 1990 rather than 1960 and 1980, which would have made them more up to date. But figures for 1990 would have been projections based on data from censuses taken in the late 1970s and early 1980s. Figures for 1980 were felt to be more appropriate and more accurate, given the authors' reservations about the assumptions which underly the techniques for making projections of urban populations.

the Andean nations. It was in the southern part of this coast that investments concentrated, most of them coming from overseas. Urban developments there were much stimulated by investments in industries and in infrastructure such as railways, urban services, and ports; most were to serve national or international economic interests located in the largest cities. Buenos Aires and Rosario in Argentina, Montevideo in Uruguay, and São Paulo and Rio de Janeiro in Brazil experienced more rapid population growth in the late nineteenth and early twentieth centuries than they have in recent decades.

In most Latin American nations, over the last four decades, available statistics suggest an increasing concentration of productive activities and of urban populations in only one or two cities, metropolitan areas, or 'core regions' – although, as earlier examples suggest, for many nations this process began many decades ago. A high proportion of Latin America's industry is concentrated in relatively few 'core-regions'. Three of the most prominent examples are: the La Plata – Buenos Aires – Campana – Zarate – San Nicolas – Rosario – San Lorenzo region in Argentina; the triangle of Rio de Janerio – São Paulo – Belo Horizonte in Brazil; and Mexico City – Toluca – Cuernavaca – Puebla – Queretaro in Mexico. While the trend in cities has been for much of the new (or expanding) industry to be within or close to city centres, in recent years in many large cities, industrial and commercial employment has grown more rapidly outside the inner cities. There are examples both of central cities growing much more slowly than suburban rings (or even losing population) and of cities beyond the commuting range of the largest centres sustaining population growth rates higher than the metropolitan areas, a process termed polarization reversal.[15] For instance, in Buenos Aires, the central city (the Federal District) lost population between 1970 and 1980, while the population in the counties within the Greater Buenos Aires Metropolitan Area but outside the Federal District had a total population increase of 30 per cent.[16] Perhaps more significantly in the long term, Greater Buenos Aires only increased its share of the national population by 0.1 per cent during the 1970s compared to an increase of 2.0 percent during the 1960s.[17]

Within Greater São Paulo, since 1940, the population *outside* São Paulo City has consistently grown more rapidly than that in the city; between 1940 and 1980, São Paulo City's population grew more than six fold, while the population *within* Greater São Paulo but outside the city grew more than sixteen-fold.[18] During the 1970s population growth rates in cities *close by but outside* Greater São Paulo have come to exceed that of Greater São Paulo itself.[19] Comparable trends have also been apparent for many years in Mexico City's metropolitan area, where population growth within the area but outside the central city (the Federal District) began to sustain higher rates of population growth than the central city during the 1950s. The proportion of metropolitan areas's population and industrial and commercial activity located within the Federal District is likely to continue to decline.[20] Furthermore, during the 1970s, various cities close by but not within the metropolitan area had more rapid population growth rates than that of the metropolitan area. It is also worth noting that between 1972 and 1981, the population growth rate of Lima–Callao in Peru (with 4.4 million inhabitants in 1981) was among the slowest of any urban centre in Peru, with 50,000 or more inhabitants,[21] although this may be partially explained by an undercount in the 1981 census.

In terms of changes in population distribution, an examination of migration flows within nations will reveal and clarify trends which city population growth rates alone obscure. Latin America's large metropolitan centres may have slower population growth rates than many other smaller cities, but some may still be the dominant centres for receiving net rural-to-urban migration flows. This was certainly the case for Mexico City during the 1940s and 1950s. Mexico City attracted 49 per cent of all migrants between 1940 and 1950, which was nine times the number received by the next largest migrant-receiving city (Guadalajara). But between 1950 and 1960, Mexico City's share in attracting migrants for the nation was down to 42 per cent and the number of migrants it attracted was only three times that of Guadalajara.[22]

Cuba's pattern of urban development does not bear much relation to that of other nations which experienced comparable rates of rapid economic growth during the 1960s and 1970s. Since the mid 1960s, a declining proportion of its urban population has lived in Havana, the capital and much the largest city. The agrarian reform implemented shortly after the revolution in 1959 removed one of the main causes of rural-to-urban migration. Since then, a combination of economic and social development outside Havana (in rural and selected urban areas), the rationing system, and a postponement of new housing and infrastructure investments in Havana reduced its dominance of the national urban system.[23]

Asia

South and East Asia[24] have a lower concentration of population in cities of 100,000 or more, or 1 million or more, inhabitants, than aggregate figures for Africa and Latin America. But such aggregated statistics are heavily influenced by circumstances in China and India, which together represent more than two-thirds of Third World Asia's population. In Table 3.2, the very large differences between China and the rest of

Third World East Asia (which includes Hong Kong and both North and South Korea) are notable in terms of the level of population concentration in cities with 100,000 or more, or 1 million or more, inhabitants. By 1985, Third World Asia had five of the world's largest urban agglomerations: two in China (Shanghai and Beijing), two in India (Calcutta and Bombay), and one in South Korea (Seoul). Each had more than 10 million inhabitants.[25]

Within Asia, during the 1960s and 1970s, it was richer nations with the highest economic growth rates which tended to have the largest increases in the level of urbanization. Between 1960 and 1982, the level of urbanization grew from 30 per cent to 69 per cent in Saudi Arabia, from 43 per cent to 70 per cent in Iraq, and from 28 per cent to 61 per cent in South Korea. In Saudi Arabia, immigration certainly contributed significantly and, perhaps, a significant proportion of the growth in urban population in this period was accounted for by temporary workers.

Meanwhile, in this same period, it was the far poorer Asian nations with relatively slow economic growth that generally experienced the smallest increase in their level of urbanization: Bangladesh, Nepal, Burma, India, and (although to a lesser extent), Pakistan and the Philippines. While growth in the output of manufacturing was often rapid during this period – as in the case of Bangladesh and Pakistan where the annual growth in output averaged more than 7 per cent – there was little change in the proportion of the labour force engaged in agriculture.

Urban trends in India between 1971 and 1981 illustrate how aggregate national statistics provide a poor idea of what is happening in large, populous nations. Among the 12 cities with 1 million or more inhabitants in 1981, Lucknow, Kanpur, and Calcutta were probably experiencing net out-migration but Bangalore was growing rapidly.[26] A study of population growth rates (and their causes) in urban centres with 20,000 or more inhabitants in a relatively rich, urbanized region and a poor, un-urbanized region, failed to show any clear correlation between the size of urban centres and their population growth rates over eight decades.[27] In India as a whole, most of the more rapidly growing cities during the 1970s had less than 500,000 inhabitants in 1971, and were either single industry cities, centres for raw material extraction, or state capitals. Many were a long way from the most densely populated areas. However, for large metropolitan centres such as Bombay, Calcutta, and Hyderabad, cities close by but outside the metropolitan area often grew more rapidly than the metropolitan centre. Examples include: the two major industrial centres of Asansol and Durgapur (among others) close to Calcutta; and, for Bombay – Nasik and Khopoli, or, further away, Aurangabad. These industrial centres are not so much residential or industrial suburbs, although many enterprises there have very strong economic links with the metropolitan centres. It may be that 'polarization reversal' is taking place in many of India's largest urban centres. Certainly, within several of India's metropolitan areas, population growth outside the central city exceeded that within the city during the 1960s and 1970s.[28] The population of Calcutta city hardly grew slowly in the period 1961–81 and its share of the metropolitan area's population has fallen rapidly since 1951.[29] In Bombay, population in the original city grew very slowly between 1971 and 1981; population in its inner suburbs has grown far more rapidly than in the city since at least 1941, while, since 1951, population growth rates in the outer suburbs have exceeded those of both the city and the inner suburbs.[30] Both Bombay and Calcutta provide examples of where the traditional concept of a city as a concentration on non-agricultural economic activities is no longer very useful. The original cities have grown into much larger urban agglomerations but, more significantly, they have become part of even larger 'core regions' which in some ways are comparable to those noted in Latin America. If population movements within core regions are analysed, they point to a decentralization of population and economic activities. But nationally, the trend still seems to be towards centralization within core regions.

Within Asia, China stands out in terms of urban trends, for it had very rapid economic growth and very rapid growth in industrial production during the 1960s and 1970s but relatively little change in the proportion of population living in urban areas. Richard Kirkby, in his study of urbanization in China, suggests that an understanding of such trends is best achieved by considering three periods in China's development since the revolution in 1949. The first is between 1949 and 1960 when there was very rapid growth in urban population, most of it from net rural-to-urban migration. These 11 years included both the First Five-year Plan and 'The Great Leap Forward'; while having very different approaches to the form that development should take, both shared a common purpose of accelerated industrial growth. The period 1961–76 can be characterized, in terms of urban trends, as a period of 'de-urbanization'. A combination of forced mass resettlement and strict state control of individuals' access to jobs, housing, and food provided the means. Urban population growth was also kept down by the practice of recruiting peasants to work in industry but not allowing their dependents to live with them in the city, a technique widely used by colonial governments in sub-Saharan Africa to limit urban growth in earlier decades. The third phase, between 1977 and 1982, saw a return to rapid growth in urban population, once again with net rural-to-urban migration playing a larger role than natural increase. Much of the increase in urban population has been the officially sanctioned return to urban areas of many of the millions of people removed during the previous period.[31]

Urban change in different South East Asian nations is too diverse to allow much generalization. The so called 'newly industrialized countries' in Asia – Singapore, Hong Kong, Taiwan, South Korea – would be expected to have urbanized rapidly in the period 1960–82 as their economies grew rapidly. This is certainly the case in South Korea where, as noted already, the level of urbanization grew from 28 to 61 per cent. Singapore and Hong Kong were so urbanized in 1960 that they could not 'urbanize rapidly' in this period; both have such small rural areas that they can be considered as 100 per cent urban. Taiwan did not urbanize as rapidly during this period but it was already much more urbanized than South Korea in 1960.[32]

Nations such as Indonesia, Thailand, and Malaysia are notable because they had much smaller increases in the level of urbanization, despite relatively rapid economic growth. Three possible explanations can be suggested. The first is that this is simply the result of statistical inaccuracies which hide the fact that these nations urbanized rapidly in this period. Urban populations in 1982 could be understated if the government made no adjustments to the boundaries around growing urban centres, so that much of the growth in population took place 'outside' their boundaries and did not register as growth in their population. Alternatively, new urban centres may have been left out of the figures for 1982. In recent decades, in many Third World nations, many 'new' urban centres grew up – for instance new mining towns, tourist centres, frontier towns or centres serving areas where new land was bought into cultivation. In addition, many 'villages' have grown to sufficient size or have been selected as a centre for local government to qualify as 'urban centres'; if no allowance was made to add the populations of these 'new' urban centres to those of more longstanding urban centres, this too would mean that urbanization levels were understated. One specialist suggests that close to 30 per cent of Indonesia's population lived in urban areas in 1980 rather than the official figure of 22.4 per cent, if a more realistic definition is used for Jakarta and Surabaja, the nation's largest and third largest cities.[33]

Two other possible explanations can be suggested for the relatively small change in these three nations' urbanization level. One is that booming agriculture helped to keep the work force in rural areas and this may have special relevance to Thailand where, between 1960 and 1982, the growth in agricultural output was very rapid and the fall in the proportion of the labour force working in agriculture was low. Another explanation is that there was a rapid growth in jobs and incomes in rural areas but not in agriculture. Many studies in Asia have shown this in particular regions.[34] For instance in Kelantan, the poorest state in Malaysia, a survey of rice/paddy farming families found that 50 per cent of their income came from 'off-farm' activities.[35] A study in Java, Indonesia's main island, points to highly diversified rural industries and services:

> From small textile and cigarette factories to batik-making and brick-making, repair of bicycles and agricultural implements, production of coconut oil or tempe (fermented soya bean cakes) to weaving of mats and hats. Trading ... provides supplementary incomes for large numbers of rural families and the main source of income for many others. Carpenters and builders are active throughout the rural areas as are barbers, dukuns, midwives and other service activities of various kinds ....The rural based transport network is also very labour intensive.[36]

It is interesting to note that a paper documenting recent trends in migration flows to core regions within forty-six Third World nations found that several centrally planned economies do not have the continued concentration of production and urban population that most nations with market or mixed economies experienced, at least up to 1980.[37] The case of China's de-urbanization between 1961 and 1976 and the case of Cuba in Latin America have already been noted. In North Korea, the population in P'Yongyang metropolitan area (the capital) has also been carefully controlled.[38]

Africa

Africa has long been the least urbanized of the world's continents, despite a rich and varied (if poorly documented and often ill-understood) urban history which stretches back centuries in many nations and millennia in some. As in other continents, there is great diversity in levels of urbanization and urban growth trends. By 1985, according to UN estimates, no urban agglomeration had reached 10 million inhabitants, although other sources suggest that, by then, Cairo had more than 10 million inhabitants.[39] The urban agglomeration in and around metropolitan Lagos is probably the second largest in Africa, and estimates suggest that there were more than 5 million inhabitants there by 1985.[40]

While most sub-Saharan African nations had three-quarters or more of their population still living in rural areas and most of their economically active population working in agriculture in 1980, it is in sub-Saharan Africa that some of the most spectacular examples of increases in the population of cities have been evident in the last four decades. For instance, the populations of cities such as Khartoum (Sudan), Nairobi (Kenya), Abidjan (Ivory Coast), and Dar es Salaam

(Tanzania) have increased more than six fold since 1950, while that of Lagos (Nigeria) increased more than sixteen-fold.[41] Estimates suggest that the population of Nouakchott (Mauritania) has increased more than forty-fold since 1965.[42] Examples of very rapid population growth in other sub-Saharan African nations' largest cities could be given. For most of these, net in-migration contributed more than natural increase to their population growth in the 1950s, 1960s, and 1970s – despite the fact that many sub-Saharan African nations have among the world's highest rates of natural increase.

At least for the 1960s and 1970s, it was not uncommon for sub-Saharan African nations to experience rapid growth in their level of urbanization and relatively slow growth in production. Indeed, for nations such as Chad, Zaire, the Central African Republic, or Ghana, economic indicators suggest little change during these two decades. But the proportion of their national populations living in urban centres changed relatively rapidly between 1960 and 1982: from 7 per cent to 19 per cent in Chad; from 16 per cent to 38 per cent in Zaire; from 23 per cent to 37 per cent in the Central African Republic; and from 23 per cent to 37 per cent in Ghana. If these estimates accurately reflect what was happening in these nations, they contrast with trends in Latin America and Asia where, in recent decades, a combination of slow economic change and rapid urbanization has been rare.

Certainly, part of the reason is the fact that, on gaining political independence, many sub-Saharan African nations had very small urban populations, due to restrictions on urban population growth imposed by the colonial powers which were removed after independence. These nations also lacked the institutional structures for independence. Building this institutional structure and attempting to lessen dependence on imported manufactured goods through government-funded industrial development, however unsuccessful, have been important factors underpinning urbanization.

The case of Tanzania can serve as an example. In 1952, 27 per cent of the inhabitants of the colonial capital, Dar es Salaam, were 'non-African' and among the 'African' population, there were 1.5 men to every woman. An important part of the migration from rural to urban areas during the 1950s and 1960s was the movement of women and children to join their spouses. Under colonial policies in previous decades, women and children had been strongly discouraged from living with their husbands in urban centres. Between 1951 and 1967, a period of rapid growth in urban population (with net rural-to-urban migration contributing more than natural increase), it was generally the urban centres with the highest proportion of men to women which grew most rapidly. Women made up a higher proportion of the migrants than men, as the much less imbalanced urban sex ratio in 1976 attests. By then, there were 1.2 men to every woman in Dar es Salaam. Other urban centres also experienced large reductions in the imbalance of their sex ratios.[43] We suspect that processes such as these, plus the consolidation of the institutional base of independent governments, the general enthusiasm among newly independent governments for promoting import substitution industry and the low priority given to agriculture have been the main factors behind the rapid urbanization that many sub-Saharan African nations have experienced over the last four decades.

South Africa stands out as an exception, in that relatively rapid growth in GDP between 1960 and 1982 was accompanied by very little change in the proportion of population living in urban centres. South Africa is the only Third World nation with a market or 'mixed' economy which has had relatively effective policies to control migration flows to large cities. There, the apartheid system, which denies to the majority of the country's population basic economic, political, and social rights on the basis of race, also denies them the right to free movement in response to, for example, the lack of employment and the poverty in predominantly rural 'homelands' to which many have been forcibly relocated.

In North Africa, the relationship between economic change and urbanization is more like that evident in Asia and Latin America. For instance, between 1970 and 1982, Algeria, Tunisia, Libya, and Morocco had among the highest growth in GDP and in industrial output in Africa; they also had among the highest increases in the proportion of their population living in urban centres.

In terms of population growth rates in different size cities, or population distribution within core regions, the data base is too poor to point to continent-wide trends. The largest cities within each nation may be attracting a lower proportion of new productive investment; it is perhaps surprising to find that the two largest cities in Kenya (Nairobi and Mombasa) had the slowest population growth rates of any of the sixteen urban centres, with more than 20,000 inhabitants in 1979 during the last inter-censal period, 1969–79.[44] Recent reports suggest that population growth in Cairo has slowed considerably in recent years.[45] The population growth rate of one city close to metropolitan Lagos was recently estimated to have been more rapid than that of metropolitan Lagos itself.[46] But it would be unwise to consider these to be pointers to trends towards decentralization of urban development from the largest cities in Africa.

The underpinnings of urban change

To understand urban change, one needs an understanding of the economic, social, physical, and political forces which underpin it.

Increases in any nation's or region's level of urbanization cannot merely be the result of population growth.[47] While certain regularities in urban changes for certain nations, or groups of nations, have long been recognized, perhaps insufficient attention has been given to the differences which are often more significant. Today, the most important influence on urban change is changes in the nature of nations' economic and employment base. In most nations – population movements are essentially responses to where employment (or, on occasion, education opportunities) are concentrated. In many nations, population movements are largely responses to where survival is more certain. This is in sharp contrast to the richer western nations where, for a substantial proportion of the population, individual and household choice as to where they want to live has become increasingly important.

Economic change has a major influence on income distribution and thus on the nature and level of demand for goods and services and its spatial distribution. This, too, is a powerful influence on urban change. The highly unequal distribution of income within many nations shows up within cities in the quality of housing: the minority living in high-standard, well-serviced residential areas, and the majority living in very poor conditions in different sub-markets (such as inner city tenements, cheap boarding housing, squatter settlements, and shelter built on illegal subdivisions). Unequal income or asset distribution also shows up in national or regional urban systems. For instance, many Third World regions which are predominantly rural have had little growth in the level of urbanization because poorly paid landless labourers or cultivators with small, largely subsistence oriented plots do not generate much demand for the kinds of goods and services commonly provided by urban based enterprises.[48] Equally, inequitable land-owning structures or crop pricing and marketing structures can keep down such demand and minimize local urban development even in areas with highly productive commercial farming.[49] Conversely, there are a few regions where rapid growth in agricultural production and relatively equal distribution of land ownership have been the main factors in supporting rapid urban development there.[50] The more even spread of urban centres of different sizes across the national territory of most First World nations reflects both higher average incomes and a more equal income distribution.

Changes in political structure – as in the case of nations gaining political independence or of nations where governments committed to central planning come to power – are also important influences on urban change; the examples of the influence of political changes on urban change in Tanzania and Cuba have been given already. But the extent of governments' influence on urban change varies enormously from nation to nation and from government to government within each nation. Perhaps surprisingly, the slower growth experienced by many of the world's largest cities in recent decades seems to owe relatively little to explicit government policies to slow their growth. In centrally planned economies, the role of government is usually more explicit. A desire to lessen regional differences in industrial development and strategic military thinking have often influenced the location of productive investment. For instance, in China, a dispersed pattern of industrial development and initiatives to develop the interior have been much influenced by the government's desire, until recent years, to reduce the concentration of industry on its vulnerable eastern seaboard.[51] The government of North Korea has also sought to reduce the concentration of productive activities close to its southern border for comparable reasons.[52] But even in market or mixed economies, public investments in infrastructure and services, public expenditures and incentives, or controls to encourage or discourage investments in certain regions or cities are an important influence on urban change. Just as the US government's expenditures in defence and the space programme helped underpin the redistribution of population and productive activities towards the south and west, so too have comparable expenditures by the Indian Federal Government (and by the former colonial government for defence) helped to underpin Bangalore metropolitan centre's rapid growth.[53] South Korea, like North Korea, has sought to reduce population and industrial concentration close to the border which divides them.

What may be more significant, although certainly less well understood, is the influence on urban change of government's macro-economic policies, tax systems, interventions in setting prices for certain goods or services and the distribution of power and resources between national, regional and local governments. Within many Third World nations, the spatial effects of these have helped to encourage a high concentration of productive activities in a few cities (or core regions).[54] This happens when such policies explicitly or implicitly favour the better off inhabitants of larger urban centres and the more powerful industrial, commercial, and financial interests which are also generally concentrated there. To characterize this as 'urban bias' is incorrect for two reasons. The first is the fact that the population living in small and intermediate size urban centres are frequently as starved of public investments and public supports as most of the rural population. They do not benefit from 'urban bias'; even though they may represent half or more of a nation's urban population. The second is that, within the few urban centres which do benefit from 'urban bias' (typically the national capital and cities which are the birthplace or political constituency of powerful politicians), low-income residents there do not necessarily benefit. Services and facilities may be better in such centres in per capita terms, but these are not necessarily accessible to lower income groups who may make up half the population. Programmes to provide urban groups with subsidized food or other services may not reach most of the poor. To obtain such food or services, people must obtain a special card, and certain case studies have shown how these are only granted to people with 'legal' addresses. The poor who live in illegal settlements cannot obtain these.[55]

There is also the influence of the world market on the economic structures (and thus the urban systems) of all nations. All nations have been affected by the unprecedented transformation of the world's economy and political structure over the last 150 years or so. The changing role of city-based enterprises within the world market are just as relevant to rapid population growth in and around São Paulo and Seoul in recent decades as they were to London's rapid population growth during much of the nineteenth century and its decline since the 1940s.

Take the example of the growing importance within the world economy of nations around the Pacific Rim; this can be viewed as a region (including California and Japan) which challenges the dominance of the North Atlantic as the core of the world's economy.[56] In many Pacific nations, the form and pace of urban change is intimately tied to developments in the integrated network of production, trade, communications, and producer services which has developed there.[57] Cities such as Bangkok, Hong Kong, and Singapore serve as major centres for banking and other financial services and as administrative headquarters for multinational corporations; many other cities also have significant concentrations of offices of foreign companies. Some of these and certain other cities have developed as major centres for foreign (principally US and Japanese) investment in manufacturing or as centres for international tourism (or both). These in turn support a whole range of new service enterprises such as 'financial services from banking to broking, insurance underwriting, advertising, management consultancy, real estate consultancy, legal services and executive search' as well as 'all kinds of consumer oriented forms such as business hotels and retailing chains'.[58]

It is hardly surprising that the cities and city-regions in Asia which have been most successful in becoming what are sometimes termed 'world cities' (i.e. cities which are major centres of organization and control for world production and markets) have experienced among the most rapid and sustained economic growth. This in turn supports rapid population growth, except in Singapore where immigration is strictly controlled and where there is virtually no rural population left to migrate to the booming city-region. The entire nation is in effect a small city-region since Singapore is only some 600 square kilometres in size. Given the significant proportion of world production, trade and services controlled by multinationals, the urban future of many cities will be much influenced by the extent to which they can attract multinational investments and offices. This in turn has implications for the form of the city since a rapid growth in multinational investment can greatly increase prices – perhaps most notably for land – which in turn greatly increases housing problems.[59]

Certain governments have insulated their economies from world market forces; examples include the Chinese government for much of the 1950s, 1960s, and the early part of the 1970s, or the Burmese government in recent decades. Groups or blocs of nations have also sought to do so – for instance (in the east) COMECON, especially during the 1950s, or (in the west), the EEC in the case of agriculture. But no economy is completely impervious. In the present debt crisis facing so many nations, the changes in government spending and social orientation which many are obliged or forced to make will have a critical impact on urban change. So, too, will a continuing trend towards protectionism in the First World; a Third World city whose economic growth has been dependent on exports will have its economic structure and population growth rate considerably influenced if the market for enterprises located there is suddenly restricted. The decline in the availability of concessional multilateral aid may inhibit the construction or improvement of infrastructure to support urban development in many Third World nations. These are given as examples to show the complexity of seeking to identify the mix of factors which underpin urban change within any nation or region and to discover their relative importance.

The urban future?

Perhaps the most obvious conclusion arising from an examination of urban change in recent decades is to avoid generalizations and predictions too far into the future. Urban change is too sensitive to economic, social, political, and physical change to predict more than one or two decade into the future. Certainly, many examples can be cited to caution against long-range projections based on extrapolating past trends into the future. Extrapolating trends in urban population growth in China from 1949 to 1960 to give a guide as to what would happen in the next 40 years would make China's population 100 per cent urban before the year 2000 and could hardly provide a useful indicator of future trends after 1960 since the proportion of China's population in urban areas declined between 1961 and 1976.[60] Extrapolating population growth in São Paulo, from its growth from

48,000 inhabitants in 1886 to 484,000 in 1916, would have given it a population of some 48 million in 1976.[61] Less than 14 years ago, specialists projected that Calcutta would have 40–50 million inhabitants by the year 2000.[62] The projection was based on extrapolating Calcutta's rapid population growth for the 1930s, 1940s, and 1950s far into the future. Such rapid rates of population growth were largely due to an influx of refugees from what was formerly East Pakistan (now Bangladesh) after the partition of India in 1947,[63] and to population figures for 1941 being exaggerated for political reasons.[64] The most recent projections made by Calcutta's Metropolitan Development Authority suggest a population of 14.7 million by 2001 in the metropolitan district; this district covers 1,450 square kilometres and includes not only Calcutta urban agglomeration but also outlying rural areas.[65]

These may seem extreme examples to use in questioning the value of future projections – but United Nations projections published in 1980 for cities such as Dar es Salaam (Tanzania), Nairobi (Kenya), and various Nigerian cities seem as unreal. Even someone with a relatively unsophisticated knowledge of Tanzania's economy and potential for urban development would find it hard to imagine sufficient economic change to sustain an agglomeration of 4.6 million people in Dar es Salaam by the year 2000.[66] The obvious questions are – on what will they live and how will they be fed? People will not move to Dar es Salaam if there is no chance of an income or of food. For comparable reasons, suggestions that Nairobi will grow from under 1 million inhabitants to 18.9 million inhabitants between 1980 and 2025, as projected by the United Nations in 1982 must be treated with a measure of disbelief. This would mean that in less than 40 years, Nairobi would have three times the population currently living in Greater London.

There is also a certain measure of unreality in the fact that projections for some 40 years in the future can be made for cities for which there has been no reliable population data for more than 20 years. Population projections for the year 2025 are confidently given for certain Nigerian cities like Lagos or Ado Ekiti when there has been no reliable census in Nigeria since 1963. Ado Ekiti, a relatively unknown (and unimportant) Nigerian city even appears as the worlds twenty-fifth largest urban agglomeration in projections for 2025, with 15.4 million inhabitants in UN estimates published in 1982. A few years earlier, another relatively unimportant Nigerian city (Jos) had been listed as the twenty-fifth largest city in the world by the year 2000.[67]

Towards new forecasting techniques?

A parallel can be drawn between current techniques for forecasting cities' future populations and techniques used for forecasting energy demand in the early 1970s. At that time, it was assumed that energy demand in the west would simply continue to rise in line with past trends, just as urban trends in the immediate past are still assumed to be a guide to urban change in the future. The 1973 oil price rise led to energy demand forecasts being revised downwards a bit but no fundamental change occurred in the forecasting methodology.

Perhaps forecasts for future urban and city growth in the Third World are at this stage now with projections made 5, 10, or 15 years ago generally being scaled down, because of the recession. Successive United Nations reports in the last 15 years have generally given lower figures for the projected population for the year 2000. Table 3.3 lists the eight largest Third World urban agglomerations in the year 2000 according to the 1973–5 assessment of the United Nations Population Division and how the projections for the year 2000 have changed in subsequent assessments.

Table 3.3 Examples of changing projections for city populations by the year 2000 (in millions of inhabitants)

| Urban agglomerations | UN projections for populations in the year 2000 | | | | |
	1973–5	1978	1980	1982	1984–5
Mexico City	31.6	31.0	27.6	26.3	25.8
São Paulo	26.0	25.8	21.5	24.0	24.0
Calcutta	19.7	16.4	15.9	16.6	16.5
Rio de Janeiro	19.4	19.0	14.2	13.3	13.3
Shanghai	19.2	23.7	25.9	13.5	14.3
Bombay	19.1	16.8	16.3	16.0	16.0
Peking/Beijing	19.1	20.9	22.8	10.8	11.2
Seoul	18.7	13.7	13.7	13.5	13.8

Source: United Nations Population Division, Department of International Economic and Social Affairs.[68]

Mexico City's projected population for 2000 was 31.6 million in the Population Division's 1973–5 assessment but down to 25.8 million in the 1984–5 assessment. Projections for the population of Rio de Janeiro by 2000 were 19.4 million in the 1973–5 assessment and only 13.3 million in the 1984–5 assessment. Perhaps more significantly, the 1984–5 assessment no longer talks of a world population being half urban by the year 2000 but of more than 50 per cent of the world's population 'projected to live in urban areas' before 2010. The date when more than half the Third World's population becomes 'urban' is put off until 2016.

Although the techniques used by the United Nations Population Division have changed – for instance, to reflect the fact that the rate at which a nation urbanizes is likely to slow as its population becomes increasingly urban – there is still an assumption that urbanization will continue and that large urban centres will continue to grow. Even some of the most recent UN projections seem questionable, especially for sub-Saharan Africa. For instance, Maputo in Mozambique is projected to have a population of 2.7 million by the year 2000; in the 1980 census it had some 740,000. Given long-standing problems of economic destabilization and disruption from the South Africa backed guerillas and the enormous economic hardships facing the nation, it is difficult to imagine how Maputo's economy could develop to the point of allowing its population to more than triple between 1980 and 2000. Only through massive camps for displaced persons developing in Maputo as a result of war and famine could such a prediction be realized. As noted earlier, certain factors acting in recent decades led to very rapid urbanization in many African nations but these factors are no longer present or are not acting so powerfully. Similarly, UN projections may understate the future growth of certain cities which substantially increase their role in the world economy within the next two or three decades. For instance, certain Southeast Asian cities may continue to grow very rapidly, if this region remains one of the most dynamic parts of the world economy. But even here, the rapid growth of cities is not certain, since many of the new or expanding enterprises may locate outside the main city or metropolitan area – so again, core regions consolidate while populations within them decentralize.

To return to the comparison with projecting energy demand into the future, it needed rigorous studies of the economic and social changes which would underpin changes in energy demand to show that past trends were not a reliable guide to future demand. Projecting past trends, even if adjusted a bit, does not take into account the economic and social changes which underpin changes in energy demand. In most western nations, there is a very slow growth in population, a slow growth in the number of households, a declining importance for energy intensive industries, and a growing importance for economic activities with very low energy inputs per unit of value added. Clearly such factors have a major influence of how energy demand changes. If realistic projections for Third World cities' populations are to be produced, then these too must be based on comparable understandings of social and economic change for each city and nation and not on a set of equations applied in the same way to all nations.

Specialists looking at urban change in the west may have stronger grounds for claiming that there are trends which are comparable between nations and comparable factors underpinning such trends. Recent censuses there suggest urban change is best characterized as 'counter-urbanization' in many nations or regions, and thus in the opposite direction to the steady progression to 'megalopolis' which little more than 10 years ago was widely projected as 'the urban future'. The fact that there are comparable trends in terms of population redistribution at regional level (within metropolitan centres: and between metropolitan centres, non-metropolitan centres, and rural areas) gives more scope for a study as to whether comparable factors underly such trends. There may also be the beginnings of some 'counter-urbanization' in certain poor Third World regions, but the First and Third Worlds will often not be comparable. In poor Third World regions, there are likely to be people moving from cities to rural areas to ensure they can obtain sufficient food to survive whereas, in the First World, 'counter-urbanization' reflects the ability of people to live or work in rural areas but maintain ways of life which are more urban than rural – due largely to enormous advances in transport, communications technology, and higher incomes.

The real danger of the United Nations making projections far into the future of urban and city populations is their widespread misuse and misinterpretation. When a UN Population Division publication published in 1980 talks of Mexico City with 31 million inhabitants by 2000, it makes explicit the assumptions on which this projection is made. When UN figures are quoted by other sources, these qualifications are rarely repeated, and what was a projection becomes a 'certainty'. This figure of 31 million inhabitants is still quoted in books published in 1986, despite three revisions by the United Nations in this projection since 1980.[69] United Nations projections have been widely used by other institutions to focus governments' attention on 'city population growth' as 'the problem'. But this is misleading. First, enormous numbers of urban centres have not grown rapidly and yet have major problems with regard to poverty and environmental degradation. Second, most of the really serious problems of poverty, very poor housing conditions, and environmental destruction which have arisen in and around major cities need not have arisen if per capita incomes were higher and more equally distributed and if city governments had the power, resources, and personnel to cope with rapid growth. The growth in population in the Tokyo–Yokohama metropolitan area in recent decades is on a scale comparable to that in Mexico City's metropolitan area. But there are enormous differences – in the health problems faced by lower income groups, in the quality of their housing, and in the extent to which they have access to basic services and facilities. Since 1900, the population of the Los Angeles – Long Beach urban agglomeration has grown more rapidly than that of metropolitan Calcutta. Today, both have close to 10 million inhabitants. But no one would suggest that the scale and nature of housing problems in the two centres is comparable. The evidence presented in this chapter suggests that the issue of how fast or slow a city is growing is of secondary importance. The real issue is whether economic change is increasing the proportion of people with adequate livelihoods. It is also whether government agencies at national, regional, and local level are increasing the proportion of people protected against preventable diseases who also have access to safe and sufficient supplies of water, secure housing, education, health care, and (where needed) provision for the hygienic disposal of household and human wastes. In cities, the evident failure, or limited achievement, of most governments on this second issue of social provision is far more to do with inappropriate institutional and legal structures at national, city, and local government level (for many a hangover from colonial rule), and the low priority these have received from both governments and aid agencies, than it is to do with the rate at which cities have grown.

Peter Hall has suggested an alternative to the vision of the urban future dominated by large cities. He suggests that there is a general model for urban growth and change which can be applied to nations, as their urban systems go from those dominated by a primate city, through decentralization of urban development away from city cores to suburban rings, and finally to urban growth concentrating in non-metropolitan areas.[70] Thus, in time, regions or nations in the Third World will also arrive at 'counter-urbanization'. This almost implies that Third World governments need not worry about the growth of their largest cities since, in time, urban developments will become decentralized. This model receives some support from recent changes which have become apparent in, or close to, some of the Third World's largest urban centres, as described earlier.

But this model assumes that economic change in all Third World nations will be comparable to that now apparent in much of the west. For it is economic change which is usually the most important influence on social change, which in turn also impinges on urban change. But there are two reasons which make this vision of the future as unlikely as that of the United Nations. The first is the enormous diversity within the Third World; a common model for urban change seems as unlikely as a common model for economic change. As more research on urban change and its causes is undertaken by groups within each Third World city, we suspect that this will show an ever greater diversity in the rate of urban growth and the form it takes. The second is the fact that there are so many Third World nations which, without a major modification to the world economic system, have no hope of developing prosperous and stable economic bases. As such, they can hardly be expected to develop along the lines of an urban model which depends on very large capital investments, major economic changes, and a very considerable level of prosperity. Most of their citizens are never likely to have the luxury of being able to choose where to live, based on anything but a search for an adequate economic base for their lives.

Thus, there is a need to go beyond broad and often inaccurate generalizations about 'urban change in the Third World'. New classifications other than 'rural' and 'urban' are needed in analyses of the form, content, and spatial distribution of non-agricultural population and production.[71] The concept that there is 'urban bias' in development expenditures must be tested on a nation-by-nation basis; certainly in many nations, it is not evident that poorer groups in large cities or smaller urban centres are benefiting more than the rural poor. In urban issues, studies of urban change must build 'from the bottom up' from detailed city and sub-city studies. Research undertaken by Third World based non-government research groups have long pointed to complex processes at work within any individual city. For instance, a recent study by a Kenyan NGO pointed to the importance for most households in Nairobi of food they grow or produce themselves; under such circumstances, access to land on which crops can be grown and some livestock raised becomes of great importance to most households.[72] This is hardly a conventional view of a nation's capital city. Discussions with researchers from other African and Asian cities suggest that we may be underestimating the proportion of people in other cities who depend on food they grow themselves, within or outside the city, or on complex reciprocal arrangements with extended families or friends who have access to cultivable land. If, for a substantial proportion of city dwellers in Africa (and perhaps elsewhere), an assured, adequate diet now demands access to cultivable land or some other non-monetary transaction, this has major implications for the urban future. It means that there will be urban forms very different to western concepts of urban development. It also implies constraints on the development of large urban agglomerations. At present, there are relatively few 'mega-cities' of 5 million or more inhabitants in the Third World. In 1990, they are likely to house less than 5 per cent of the Third World's population, with less than 2.5 per cent in agglomerations of 10 million or more inhabitants, although verification of this will have to await the results of the censuses taken in the late 1980s and early 1990s. But if our concern is to improve the performance of governments and aid agencies, in providing basic services, in reducing poverty, and in controlling environmental degradation, the priority is to know to whom special attention should be paid; the question of where people live is dependent on this. To do this, more attention should be paid to understanding the 'what', 'how' and 'why' of change within individual cities and nations, and perhaps rather less to overviews of 'change in the Third World', such as have been presented in this chapter.

Jorge E. Hardoy and David Satterthwaite

Notes and references

1. This paper is an updated, shortened, and slightly revised version of a paper with this same title published in *Habitat International* 10 (3) 1986. This paper in *Habitat International* in turn developed out of an unpublished background paper prepared for the *World Resources Report* 1986 published by the World Resources Institute and the International Institute for Environment and Development, Washington DC, in 1986. We are grateful to Liz Mills and Julio Davila for their comments on an early draft and to Kate Sebag and Diana Mitlin for their comments on the draft of this revised and updated version.
   Statistics for nations' economic performance, changes in the proportion of their economically active population in different sectors, and changes in their level of urbanization for the period 1960 to 1982 were drawn from the World Bank's World Development Report, 1984.
2. Potter, R.B. (1985) *Urbanization and Planning in the Third World: Spatial Perceptions and Public Participation*, London: Croom Helm.
3. Repetto, Robert (1986) *World Enough and Time*, New Haven, Conn.: Yale University Press.
4. United Nations (1985) *Estimates and Projections of Urban, Rural and City Populations, 1950–2025: the 1982 Assessment*, ST/ESA/SER.R/58. New York: United Nations.
5. ibid.
6. Aradeon, David, Aina, Tade and Umo, Joe (1986) 'South-West Nigeria' in J.E. Hardoy and D. Satterthwaite (eds), *Small and Intermediate Urban Centres: Their Role in National and Regional Development in the Third World*, London: Hodder and Stoughton, UK and Westview, USA, 1986.
7. In most major Third World nations, the definition as to what constitutes an urban centre is based on a stated threshold for the number of inhabitants above which a settlement is 'an urban centre'. But this threshold may be a few hundred (or less) or up to 50,000 inhabitants. Most fall within the range of 1,500 to 5,000 inhabitants. Two other sets of urban criteria, not based on population thresholds, are widely used to arrive at 'national urban population'. The first is simply by stating that certain specified settlements are to be regarded as 'urban centres'; this is widely used in small-population and in relatively un-urbanized nations, with just a few named settlements being the only ones regarded as urban. In some of the smallest nations, just one settlement is regarded as urban. The second is based on the population in settlements which perform government functions; a settlement is 'urban' if it is the seat of a certain level of local government. In some nations, local-government status and population size are combined – so a settlement is urban if its population exceeds a defined threshold and it is the administrative headquarters of a certain level of local government. More sophisticated criteria may be added to population thresholds or local-government status, such as the proportion of the labour force working in non-agricultural activities, or population density, or other characteristics thought to be typical of an 'urban centre'. In a few nations, the 'urban population' are those people living in 'townships' or 'municipalities' or other forms of administrative area, within which most of

the population lives in one or more nucleated settlement said to have 'urban' characteristics. Research into how different Third World nations obtained the urban criteria they use today might prove interesting; for instance, several former French colonies' urban criteria are similar to that of their former ruler. But this is a question beyond the scope of this chapter.

The great diversity in the way that national governments arrive at the figures for their nation's level of urbanization greatly limits the validity of international comparisons. This is made most clear with some examples. In 1976, Bolivia's population was 32.2 per cent urban if a population threshold of 20,000 inhabitants was used to define whether a settlement was 'urban', or 42.6 per cent urban if the threshold was 2,000 inhabitants. Mexico's population would have been 43.3 per cent urban in 1970 if urban centres are settlements with 20,000 or more inhabitants, instead of 59 per cent urban, a figure based on an urban criterion of localities with 2,500 or more inhabitants.

Since the United Nations produces statistics for all nations as to the number of inhabitants in cities of 100,000 or more inhabitants, this should provide a more valid base for international comparisons, since the same criterion is used for each nation. But even here, the statistics for certain nations are known to be inaccurate. Many nations have not had a census in recent years. For such nations, United Nations figures for the population in cities of 100,000 + inhabitants are based on extrapolations of older data. These extrapolations do not seem to make allowances for cities which are likely to have grown into the 100,000 + inhabitant category between the last census and recent years. Thus, according to a recently published United Nations compendium of urban statistics, China had only one city with between 100,000 and 249,999 inhabitants in 1980. This is hardly believable in a nation with more than 1 billion inhabitants and (whichever way the urban population is calculated) one of the world's largest urban populations.

There also seems to be a considerable time-lag between the point when new national censuses become available and their use in United Nations statistics. For instance, the figures for the percentages of the urban population in cities of 500,000 + inhabitants in 1980 for nations such as Kenya (57 per cent) and Tanzania (50 per cent) are far higher than those suggested by the censuses in Kenya in 1979 and in Tanzania for 1978. Such United Nations figures were still being quoted in material published in 1987 – for instance, in the data tables of the *World Development Report, 1987*. Using statistics from theses nations' censuses would mean a much lower proportion of the urban population in cities of 500,000 or more inhabitants in 1980; in both nations, it would be of the order of 35 per cent. The extent to which national urban populations are concentrated in cities of 500,000 or more inhabitants may well be overstated for many other nations. But to list the proportion of nations' urban populations in cities of 500,000 or more inhabitants is in itself misleading, again because of the major differences in the criteria by which national urban populations are calculated.

Jorge E. Hardoy and David Satterthwaite

One final example of United Nations urban statistics which seem open to question are the estimates for the proportion of many small nations' or territories' populations living in cities of 100,000 or more inhabitants. Between 95 per cent and 100 per cent of the urban populations of many Third World nations with small populations are said to be living in cities of 100,000 + inhabitants in 1950, 1955, and 1960. But these nations or territories had no cities at all which had reached 100,000 inhabitants. Examples include Burundi, Djibouti, São Tome and Principe, the Gambia, Antigua, the Seychelles, Gibraltar, New Caledonia, Cook Islands, Niue, and the Faeore Islands. Indeed, for some of these, their national populations had not reached 100,000 inhabitants by these dates and some still have no urban centre with 100,000 inhabitants.

8. In recent censuses in Peru, 'urban centres' are defined as populated centres with 100 or more occupied dwellings. In India, the criteria are more complicated, but, with relatively few exceptions, urban centres have 5,000 or more inhabitants, a relatively high density, and more than three-quarters of the adult male population employed in non-agricultural activities. Most of India's rural population live in villages which have more than 100 occupied dwellings.

9. UNCHS (Habitat) (forthcoming) 'Expert group on human settlements statistics: report of the meeting held in Nairobi, Kenya, 12–16 October, 1987', Nairobi, Kenya.

10. Hawkins, J.N. (1982) 'Shanghi: an exploratory report on food for a city', *GeoJournal*, supplementary issue, 1982.

11. PADCO (1978) *Philippines Shelter Sector Assessment* vol. 1, Prepared for US AID Office of Housing, Washington DC.

12. Statistics for Dhaka drawn from United Nations (1986) *Dhaka*, in the series of monographs on 'Population growth and policies in mega-cities, population policy', Paper no. 5, ST/ESA/SER.R/65, New York: (1985) United Nations.

13. For further details, see United Nations (1985) 'Migration, population growth and employment in metropolitan areas of selected developing countries', Dept. of International Economic and Social Affairs, ST/ESA/SER.R/57, New York: United Nations.

14. UNCHS (Habitat) (1987) *Global Report on Human Settlements 1986*, Oxford University Press.

15. See Townroe, Peter M. and Keen, David (1984) 'Polarization reversal in the state of São Paulo, Brazil', *Regional Studies* 18 (1): 45–54, for a discussion as to how this is best measured.

16. Derived from census statistics quoted in Rofman, Alexandro B. (1985) 'Argentina: a mature urbanization pattern', *Cities* 2 (1), February.

17. Part of the reason for the decline in population of the federal district was the former military government's destruction of shanty towns ('villas miserias'), forcing their population to live outside the federal district.

18. Derived from census statistics presented in fact sheet on São Paulo City, 1985, prepared by the Municipal Planning Bureau, City Hall.

19. Townroe and Keen (1984), op. cit. n. 15.

20. Derived from figures in Unikel, Luis (1970) 'The dynamics of the growth

of Mexico City', mimeo, later published in Spanish by the Fundacion para Estudios de la Poblacion, A.C., Mexico, in 1972.

21. Derived from figures from the 1981 census quoted in Richardson, Harry W. (1984) 'Planning strategies and policies for metropolitan Lima' in *Third World Planning Review* 6 (2) May.

22. Scott, Ian (1982) *Urban and Spatial Development in Mexico*, Baltimore and London: Johns Hopkins University Press.

23. Gugler, J. 'A minimum of urbanism and a maximum of ruralism: the Cuban Experience', in: *International Journal of Urban and Regional Research* 4: 516–35; and Jorge E. Hardoy (ed.) (1979) *Urban and Agrarian Reform in Cuba*, SIAP/IDRC, Ediciones SIAP, 1979, Buenos Aires.

24. Note that Japan is not included in the discussion and aggregate statistics of East Asia.

25. Note reservations expressed earlier in the chapter about the validity of the population figure for Shanghai.

26. Harris, Nigel (1984), 'Some Trends in the Evolution of Big Cities' *Habitat International*, Vol 8, No 1.

27. Bhooshan, B.S., 'Mysore, Mandya and Bangalore Districts' and Misra, H.N., 'Rae Bareli, Sultanpur and Pratapgarh Districts', Chapters 4 and 5 in J.E. Hardoy and D. Satterthwaite (eds) (1986), op. cit. n. 6.

28. Buch, M.N., *Urbanization Trends in India: the emerging Regional Patterns*, mimeo; and Harris, Nigel, op. cit. n. 26.

29. Statistics drawn from United Nations (1986) *Calcutta*, in the series of monographs on 'Population growth and policies in mega-cities, Population Policy Paper no. 1, ST/ESA/SER.R/61, New York: United Nations.

30. United Nations (1986) *Bombay*, in the series of monographs on 'Population growth and policies in mega-cities', Population Policy Paper no. 6, ST/ESA/SER.R/67, New York: United Nations.

31. Kirkby, R.J.R. (1985) *Urbanization in China: Town and Country in a Developing Economy, 1949 – 2000 AD*, London: Croom Helm.

32. Jones, Gavin W. (1983) 'Structural change and prospects for urbanization in Asian countries'. Papers of the East–West Population Institute No. 88, August,Honolulu: East West Centre.

33. Jones, Gavin W., 'Structural Change and Prospects for Urbanization: South-East and East Asia with special reference to Indonesia', paper prepared for the Conference on Urban Growth and Economic Development in the Pacific Region, Tapei, quoted in Forbes, Dean and Thrift, Nigel, (1987) 'International impacts on the urbanization process in the Asian region: a review' in Fuchs, Roland J., Jones, Gavin W., and Pernia, Ernesto M. (eds) *Urbanization and Urban Policies in Pacific Asia*, Boulder and London: Westview Special Studies on East Asia.

34. Jones, Gavin W., op. cit., n. 32.

35. Shand, R.T. and Mohd, Ariff Hussein, (1983) 'Data requirements for a large-scale irrigation project: a case study of the Kemubu irrigation project, Kelantan, Malaysia', Development Studies Centre, Australian National University, Canberra, (forthcoming) quoted in Jones, op. cit., n. 32

36. Jones, Gavin W. (1980) 'Population growth in Java' in R.G. Garnaut and P.T. McCawley, *Indonesia: Dualism, Growth and Poverty*, Research School of Pacific Studies, Australian National University, quoted in Jones, Gavin W., op. cit., 32.
37. Vining, Daniel R. Jr. (1985) 'The growth of core regions in the Third World', *Scientific American* 252 (4) April.
38. ibid.
39. ibid.
40. Aradeon, David *et al*. op. cit., n. 6.
41. Derived from census data or estimates quoted in Hardoy, Jorge E. and Satterthwaite, David (1981) *Shelter: Need and Response; Housing, Land and Settlement Policies in 17 Third World Nations*, Chichester: John Wiley & Sons.
42. Theunynck, Serge and Dia, Mamadou (1981) 'Young (and less young) in infra-urban areas in Mauritania', *African Environment*, 14–15–16: Dakar: ENDA. 206–33.
43. Bryceson, Deborah (1983) *Urbanization and Agrarian Development in Tanzania with Special Reference to Secondary Cities*, IIED internal paper.
44. Derived from census data quoted in Kiamba, C.M., Maingi K., Ng'ethe N., and Senga, W.M. (1983) 'The role of small and intermediate cities in national development: the case study of Thika, Kenys', paper presented at an International Seminar on Small Cities and National Development, New Delhi, January, 1983.
45. Vining, Daniel R., op. cit., n. 37.
46. Aradeon, David *et al*., op. cit., n. 6.
47. Many authors still confuse 'growth in urban population' and 'growth in a nation's or region's level of urbanization'. Virtually all changes in the level of urbanization (i.e. in the proportion of population living in urban centres) are a result of population movements in or out of urban centres. Natural increase in population (i.e. the excess of births over deaths) does not contribute to increases in urbanization levels except where the rate of natural increase in urban centres is higher than that in rural areas. But, as was noted earlier, if this is the case, this may be the result of high proportions of migrants from rural to urban areas being of child-bearing age and their movement to urban centres changing urban centres' rate of natural increase. A small part of a change in a nation's level of urbanization is often due to rural settlements growing to the point where they become urban (and thus are added to the urban population) and rapid rates of natural increase can increase this contribution. But, in general, a nation's level of urbanization is not influenced much by population increases for it is essentially the result of changes in economic structure; increased proportions of national populations in urban centres reflect an increase in the proportion of employment opportunities (or possibilities for survival) concentrated in urban centres.
48. For examples, see: Misra, H.N. (1986) 'Rae Bareli, Sultanpur and Pratapgarh Districts'; and Hardoy, Jorge E. and Satterthwaite, David (1986) 'A survey of empirical material on the factors affecting the development of small and intermediate urban centres', Chapters 5 and 7 in

J.E. Hardoy and D. Satterthwaite (eds) (1986), op. cit., n. 6.
49. For examples, see: El Agraa, Omer M.A. *et al.* (1986) 'The Gezira Region, The Sudan'; and Bhooshan, B.S. (1986) 'Mysore, Mandya and Bangalore Districts', Chapters 3 and 4 in J.E. Hardoy and D. Satterthwaite (eds) op. cit., n. 6.
50. For a case study of this, see Manzanal, Mabel and Vapnarsky, Cesar (1986) 'The development of the Upper Valley of Rio Negro and Neuquen within the Comahue region, Argentina' in J.E. Hardoy and D. Satterthwaite (eds) op. cit. n. 6.
51. Kirkby, R.J.R. (1985), op. cit., n. 31.
52. Vining, Daniel R. Jr (1985), op. cit., n. 37.
53. Bhooshan, B.S. (1986), op. cit., n. 44.
54. Hardoy, Jorge E. and Satterthwaite, David (1986) 'Government policies and small and intermediate urban centres' in J.E. Hardoy and D. Satterthwaite (eds), op. cit., n. 6.
55. This discussion of the validity of 'urban bias' is developed in more detail in Hardoy, Jorge E. and Satterthwaite, David (1989) *Squatter Citizen: Life in the Urban Third World*, London: Earthscan.
56. Douglass, Mike, (1987) *The Future of Cities on the Pacific Rim*, Discussion paper No 3, Department of Urban and Regional Planning, University of Hawaii, July.
57. ibid. and Forbes, and Thrift, op. cit., n. 33.
58. Forbes and Thrift, op. cit., n. 33. See also Friedmann, John and Goetz, Wolff, (1982) world city formation: an agenda for research and action', *International Journal of Urban and Regional Research* Vol 6, No 3.
59. Friedmann and Goetz, op. cit., n. 58.
60. Kirkby, F.J.R. (1985) op. cit. n. 31.
61. Statistics drawn from Di Loreto, Maria and Hardoy, Jorge E. (1984) 'Procesos de urbanizacion en America Latina', *Boletin de Medio Ambiente y Urbanizacion*, Year 3, no. 9, Buenos Aires: IIED America Latina.
62. Brown, Lester (1974) *In the Human Interest*, New York: W.W. Norton & Co.
63. Roy, Dilip K. (1983) 'The supply of land for the slums of Calcutta', in Angel, Archer, Tanphiphat and Wegelin, *Land for Housing the Poor*, Singapore: Select Books.
64. United Nations, op. cit., n. 29.
65. ibid.
66. United Nations (1980) 'Urban, rural and city population, 1950–2000 as assessed in 1978', June New York: United Nations.
67. ibid.
68. All documents from the United Nations Population Division, Department of International Economic and Social Affairs, New York.
    For 1973–5: 'Trends and prospects in the populations of urban agglomerations, 1950–2000, as assessed in 1973–5', ESA/P/WP.58, 1975.
    For 1978: 'Urban, rural and city population, 1950–2000, as assessed in 1978', 1980.
    For 1980: 'Estimates and projections of urban, rural and city populations, 1950–2025: the 1980 assessment', ST/ESA/SER.R/45, 1982.

For 1982: 'Estimates and projections of urban, rural and city populations, 1950–2025: the 1982 assessment', ST/ESA/SER.R/58, 1985.
For 1984–5: 'The prospects of world urbanization – revised as of 1984–5', ST/ESA/SER.A/101, 1987.
69. For instance, see Repetto, Robert, op. cit., n. 3.
70. Hall, Peter (1983) 'Cities as dinosaurs: the end of the urban age?', keynote paper presented at the Royal Town Planning Institute Annual Conference, 1983.
71. See, for instance, the suggestions for new classifications in T.G. McGee, 'The urban transition in Asia: the emergence of new regions of economic interaction in Asia', paper prepared for Only One Earth Forum, New York, May 1987, available from Professor McGee, Asian Centre, 1871 West Mall, UBC, Vancouver,Canada V6T 1W5.
72. Mazingira Institute, *Urban Food and Fuel Study,* Nairobi, Kenya, 1987. Available from Mazingira Institute, PO Box 14550, Nairobi, Kenya.

Chapter 4

Can Third World cities be managed?

Carole Rakodi

The management issue is addressed in Chapter 4 by Carole Rakodi, who poses the fundamental question of whether Third World cities can, in fact, be managed. Just as Hardoy and Satterthwaite question whether cities will continue to grow at the rate and to the scale currently projected, so Rakodi questions popular images of the breakdown of city management. She identifies three main management options to cope with increasing pressures, namely: the strengthening of existing urban administrative systems; increasing opportunities for community organizations to help themselves in local developments; and, finally, increasing the role of the private sector. The characteristics, advantages, and disadvantages of each are compared in terms of how they have been interpreted and implemented so far. The chapter concludes by putting each option into a broad perspective which anyone advocating a particular option would need to address.

The author is an urban planner in the Department of Town Planning at the University of Wales College of Cardiff where she co-ordinates courses for students from developing countries.

The failure?

Popular images of Third World cities stress the breakdown of city management in the face of rapid urban growth at relatively low levels of national and individual wealth. Large proportions of city populations are unable to obtain access to wage employment, land for housing, piped water supply, an adequate sanitation system, and social facilities such as educational or health services. While the rich live in high-standard, often subsidized, housing, provided with adequate if unreliable utilities and services, the poor are driven to squat on land which does not belong to them, to erect unauthorized, poor quality housing, or to live in overcrowded and insanitary inner-city slums and tenements, and to rely on low-income, untidy, and sometimes illegal, economic activities to support themselves. The Third World city is thus one of contrasts –

between modern, high-rise city centres and roadside stalls and markets, and between formal, official housing schemes built by the public or private sectors and the informal, unofficial housing areas of the poor.

Cities, it is said, are growing too fast or too large. A popular solution is to attempt, with little success, to slow down large-city growth, by diverting migrants to smaller cities, or by rural development policies and programmes designed to improve conditions in the rural areas, so removing a major reason for migration. But in many cities, as Hardoy and Satterthwaite have shown in Chapter 3, half or more of the growth is due to natural increase of the urban population itself and the city provides an attractive location for the manufacturing and service activities on which most countries rely to foster economic growth and development. The adverse economic circumstances of the 1980s may be slowing down the growth rate of African cities to near the rate of natural increase. However, large population increments must be accommodated each year. Can city administrative systems be envisaged which can cope with the problems of rapid urban growth and enable cities to absorb their growing populations at standards of living which enable basic needs to be satisfied? What form might such urban management systems take?

The initial responses of many governments to the inability of existing city organizations to provide and maintain the infrastructure in conditions of rapid urban growth was to adopt a project-oriented sectoral approach to urban development. Special public works authorities were often established, to finance and install water supplies or sewage disposal systems, or to build public housing. While these proliferated, leading to problems of co-ordination, there was little attempt to ensure that the traditional local governments responsible for operation and maintenance could cope with the additional tasks. Urban service provision continued to deteriorate and the sectoral approach gave way in many of the largest cities to a multi-sectoral approach – by way of the establishment, by central government, of development authorities or special metropolitan governments with provincial powers and status. Thus, development authorities were established in cities such as Karachi, Manila, Bombay, Colombo, and Calcutta, and metropolitan governments in, for example, Jakarta and Bangkok. However, most have failed to adopt a truly multi-sectoral, metropolis-wide approach or to solve the problem of the gap between installation and operation of urban services, while the centralization of power and undermining of local government has further reduced any possibility for participation in city-level decision making.

In face of the failure of local councils, development authorities, and public utilities to cope with the problems of rapid urban growth, many have advocated instead decentralized, local community organization,

Can Third World cities be managed?

participation and self-help? But is this the answer? Are city-wide administrative systems inherently inefficient, unresponsive and inappropriate? Can an urban management system for a city of half-a-million or more people be based on local community organization and self-help.

In order to begin to answer these questions, we will first discuss briefly the basic alternatives which have been advocated to deal with urban management problems. The strengths and weaknesses of these alternatives will be then examined, with examples, in order to assess what evidence is available on feasible systems for urban management in future cities.

City administration or community participation?

The deficiencies of earlier attempts to manage cities are now clearly recognized and, in recent years, three alternative solutions have been advanced to solve the most common problems of urban management. First, institutional development may be recommended: the strengthening of existing administrative systems and management processes – by improving revenue generation, and planning and implementation capacity; by improving the mechanisms for co-ordination; by training; and, perhaps, by strengthening local government and giving it greater autonomy.

The second alternative is premissed on the inability of either multi-sectoral development authorities or sectoral agencies (which may both be arms of central government), or weak local government institutions, to respond to the needs of local people, and particularly to those of the poor. Such institutions, it is argued, are remote, inflexible, and controlled by bureaucrats and other powerful interests. Even if their efficiency is increased and they adopt policies and programmes more appropriate to the needs of those previously excluded from service provision, these will be merely palliatives, designed to appease the most immediate demands of the urban elite or the national government. The only solution, it is suggested, is to empower the poor: to foster local community organizations capable of understanding the needs of local residents; to provide opportunities for people to participate in decision-making on local planning, infrastructure provision, and housing issues; and to help themselves in the face of apparent official unwillingness or impotence to meet their basic needs.

A third alternative has become increasingly popular in the 1980s. In the face of inefficient government agencies and bureaucracies and the unending rise in the cost of providing services, the market is seen as a more effective mechanism for matching supply to demand. Privatization of urban service provision (refuse disposal, transport, education, health, water supply, electricity, telephones) and housing may be recommended, and is already extensive in many cities. It may take a variety of forms, including monopoly control over provision of a

113

particular service, limited competition between two or three private companies, tendering for contracts awarded by the local authority, or household responsibility for satisfying needs by some form of self-help.

All there is space for here is a preliminary consideration of these three alternatives, the potential and limitations of which will be assessed in the next section. However, it is important to note that urban management can only be considered within the context of the nature and functions of both the national and local state. Here, the state is taken to mean not just the administrative apparatus of government, but the constellation of interests whose relative power and concerns are reflected in the role and functions performed by the national and local states. These functions include providing a suitable environment in which capital accumulation can proceed, ensuring the reproduction of the labour force, particularly those aspects for which private capital is itself unwilling to adopt responsibility, and maintaining social control and its own legitimacy. The actions required – while fulfilling these roles and responding to the interests of landed and other capital, the bureaucracy, the armed forces and the police, the bourgeoisie, wage labour, the peasantry, and the urban poor – may be contradictory, resulting in apparent vacillation, confusion, and changes in policy. National governments are concerned above all to achieve economic growth, maintain their own legitimacy, and weld a sense of national identity and unity from an often very disparate set of ethnic and religious groups.

Industrialization has been widely adopted as the key strategy for achieving development, inevitably resulting in a concentration of capital, public enterprise, and infrastructure investment in the cities: so-called urban bias. However, an urban bias in investment does not imply local control of that investment. Instead, local autonomy is often seen as a threat, both politically and in terms of the control seen to be necessary over national resource allocation and policy priorities. Typically, the power of local government to generate resources of its own, make decisions on priorities for investment, and control its own affairs has been weakened in the last 20 years, leaving city governments deficient in resources and administrative capacity. At the same time, failure to achieve economic development, increasing inequalities, and the inability of food supply in many countries to keep pace with population growth has led to a recognition that some local knowledge and control is essential to effective development practice. Decentralization is, therefore, recommended, although implementation of decentralized structures and programmes is generally half-hearted and ineffective.

In considering alternative forms of urban management, therefore, we must relate these: to the interests represented in the local urban state (urban landowners, large firms, the bourgeoisie, the bureaucracy, wage employees and the urban poor); to the struggle for autonomy at the local (city and neighbourhood) level; and to the resources actually and potentially available for managing the urban system and providing services.

Potentials and limitations

In this section, an attempt will be made to review the actual and potential achievements of the three alternative forms of urban management introduced above and to assess their limitations. The evaluation will concentrate on what are arguably the five most important aspects of managing cities. A capacity to plan and manage growth at the city-wide level is required, including the ability to release land for development in appropriate locations and quantities and to prepare policies, plans, programmes, and projects within an overall strategy. Within such a strategy, long-and medium-term programmes for physical infrastructure installation must not only be drawn up and implemented, but also operated and maintained in such a way that the needs of all income groups are met. To carry out such programmes – which do not, of course, exhaust the range of potential interventions designed to foster urban economic and social development – a city must be capable of matching revenue sources against demands, both for capital and recurrent expenditure, and of using its budgeting procedures as a means of programming work. In addition to planning and budgeting strategically, a management system should be capable of planning for the needs of local residential areas and of balancing competing needs across the city. Finally, a prerequisite for effective administration is support, both national and local, to ensure a flow of resources, backing for policy, and continued legitimacy.

City-wide administrative systems

Administrative organization under this heading may take a variety of forms, including traditional local authorities (city or municipal councils), local divisions of central government departments, parastatals, and urban development authorities or corporations. What has been the experience of Third World cities with these forms of administration and why? Have they a role to play in the management of future cities?

Local authorities have traditionally been responsible for organizing services such as water supply, disposal of solid and human wastes, provision and maintenance of open space and community facilities, land use control, and building regulation. They have been organized on departmental, bureaucratic lines, under an elected, or partly elected and partly appointed, council, depending, for example, on the political composition of urban areas compared to the country as a whole. The extent of central control over revenue generation, budgeting, and standards for service provision varies according to the national state's views on the risks and benefits of local autonomy, but is generally considerable. Despite their land-use planning responsibilities, the ability of local authorities to develop a corporate strategy for urban development has been constrained by staff and resource shortages, deficient programming and budgeting procedures, and, in the case of some larger cities such as Calcutta, the fragmentation of the metropolitan area into a number of municipal councils. While their performance in general has been poor, over-generalization should be avoided and the strengths of this mode of local administration recognized.

Richard Stren, for example, contrasts the performance of the Francophone and Anglophone African countries, and of Abidjan and Nairobi in particular.[1] While Nairobi city council provides a wider range of services, including primary education, spends more per head, and has more employees than the local administration in Abidjan, the level of services provided in the latter city is superior. This can be explained partly by the higher per capita income of the Ivory Coast, partly because many services are provided by outside agencies and companies and billed directly to consumers, and partly because of closer central government financial control, which restricts the opportunities for mismanagement and corruption which have exacerbated Nairobi's problems.

In Calcutta during the 1960s not only were municipal councils poorly organized and financed, but also there was no metropolitan planning development process to deal with the conurbation's problems. Metropolitan planning, implementation, and infrastructure operation was seen as the answer, and was instituted during the 1970s. But the capacity of these large-scale agencies to implement small-scale projects and operate urban services has proved to be limited and now, in the 1980s, while retaining the Calcutta Metropolitan Development Authority, there are moves to strengthen municipal councils both by increasing their powers, responsibilities, and resource base, and by restoring local elections.[2]

The bureaucratic organization of local authorities and their political dimension have both advantages and disadvantages. Their sectoral, formal, permanent, hierarchical organization is, it is argued by Sivaramakrishnan and Green in a review of the Asian experience,[3] suitable for certain tasks of urban management; in particular, efficient service delivery, maintenance of infrastructure, and regulatory activities. However, this does not mean that these roles are fulfilled adequately at present, as is only too obvious, for example, from the failure of Tanzanian and most Nigerian cities to operate adequate systems of solid waste disposal. This administrative structure, on the other hand, is unsuitable to cope with the active management of development:

innovatory programmes, area-based development or improvement projects, capital works projects; all of these need informal, non-legalistic, unhierarchical, multi-sectoral approaches. It is in response to the latter needs that local divisions of central government, parastatals, and urban development corporations, or special project implementation agencies, have been established.

In Nigeria, for example, urban water supply is the responsibility of state parastatals, which, however, despite financial backing from state governments, are characterized by poor operational and cost recovery performances, and lack of co-ordination with other service providers, such as the national parastatals responsible for providing electricity. Problems of remoteness from local problems and of lack of co-ordination between bodies controlled by independent boards or central government ministries inevitably arise, even in relatively wealthy countries such as Saudi Arabia. Even where metropolitan development authorities or government have been established, there may be little metropolitan planning, little co-ordination of spatial and socio-economic planning, and projects implemented without regard to a metropolitan framework for development (for example, in Karachi or Bangkok). Elsewhere, metropolitan authorities have more teeth, especially when they have the backing of central government (as in Kuala Lumpur).

Finally, special project agencies have played an important role in implementing the upgrading and serviced-plot projects of the 1970s and 1980s, especially those financed by outside agencies: for example, the Kampung Improvement Programme of Jakarta or the squatter-upgrading and sites and services projects of Lusaka. However, such special units, while enabling resources to be assembled, implementation co-ordinated, and red tape cut, have led to problems of the handover to ongoing administrations and maintenance of the infrastructure installed. In addition, the lack of political accountability of many of these agencies may be seen as a danger.

While the proliferation of such administrative structures in response to new or intractable problems is undesirable, abandoning the various institutional arrangements is also impracticable. Instead, Sivaramakrishnan and Green recommend that: these structures should be used as appropriate for particular tasks; less attention should be given to changing existing and devising new institutional structures, and more to improving the operations of, and co-ordination between, existing institutions; it should be recognized that different types of institutions are suitable for the management of development activities and ongoing administration; it is necessary to clarify relationships between them, especially the 'handover' stage mentioned above and flows of monitoring and evaluation information. Such reforms depend on support both from political and bureaucratic interests within countries and, probably, on international development assistance.

Carole Rakodi

Community organization and self-help

In many cities, community organization and self-help has been advocated as a way of restoring to people both opportunities for consultation and a say in decision making, and enabling the basic housing and service needs of the poor to be met. Given the unresponsive nature of many city development authorities and governments, it has been argued that bottom-up participation (via neighbourhood-level, often traditional, organizations) may be the answer. The Kampung committees of Indonesian cities and the barangays of Manila are typical examples cited, although there is some doubt that the latter are either traditional or representative, as they have replaced (by government dictat) earlier indigenous barrio organizations. Given the limited resources available to both poor households and city administrations – and the failure of earlier policies to solve housing problems by the provision of complete houses or flats – neighbourhood organization and self-help, it is argued, can produce more appropriate and widespread improvements to residential conditions. Have community organizations and self-help processes in practice enabled the residents of local areas to control the planning and servicing of their neighbourhoods, solve their housing problems, and obtain a fair share of urban resources?

State-sponsored, self-help housing has generally taken one of two forms. It may occur in serviced-plot, or sites and services, schemes – in which serviced land is made available for purchase or rent, with or without a tap, toilet, and shower, or core house. The role of local government, public utilities or project implementation units is, thus: to provide land; install infrastructure; allocate plots; make available loans for house construction (and, perhaps, also house plans, technical assistance, and building materials); regulate standards of house construction (perhaps place restrictions on building additional rooms for rent or disposal of houses and plots); and recover the capital and recurrent costs of land, infrastructure, and building construction, as appropriate.

Even in these 'self-help' schemes, therefore, the role of the state is considerable and self-help is very often restricted to the contribution of household labour and finances in the process of house construction. Although this undoubtedly has the effect of mobilizing household resources, which otherwise might not have been transformed into an improved living environment and capital asset, the contribution of self-help in these circumstances is limited. From the list of functions typically adopted by public authorities in such schemes, it is clear that the process is carefully controlled, and that self-help means contributions over and above what government is prepared to allocate rather than self-determination. Community organization evolves slowly, if at all, and is felt by many to be inhibited by the individualistic nature of the land tenure.

The beneficiaries of serviced-plot programmes are rarely the poorest households; only exceptionally, therefore, do these schemes represent a redistribution of resources, although this is related to local circumstances rather than being an inherent characteristic of the strategy. Thus, the extent to which redistribution occurs reflects the balance of interests within the city, such as the ability of private property interests to either push up the price of land beyond that which the poor can afford, for example in El Salvador, or force implementation agencies to rely on publicly owned land, which is often in peripheral locations. In addition, it may depend on the access of lower-middle income groups to channels of political influence, or the concerns of professionals and politicians alike with 'proper' standards. In a socialist society with strongly redistributivist economic and employment policies, the most appropriate strategy for accommodating rapid urban growth would probably still be to lay out settlement areas with basic infrastructure, and to make it possible for residents to build, or arrange for the construction of, houses appropriate to their needs, as was done to some extent in the early years after independence in Mozambique.

The other main set of circumstances in which community organization and self-help is practised is when public authorities abandon the idea of demolishing unauthorized housing areas and resettling their residents in public housing or serviced plot schemes. In such unauthorized areas, house construction has already taken place, supposedly by 'self-help'; this can be capitalized on, to continue the process of improvement started by residents. In practice, the housing market in such areas is more complex and highly developed than implied by the term 'self-help'. While some residents build their houses with household labour and financial resources, many use hired labour, many have bought houses from previous owners, and a varying proportion rent their accommodation – either from local small-scale landlords renting out spare rooms (as, for example, in Lusaka or Calcutta) or from larger-scale landlords who may not even live within the area (as, for example, in Nairobi). In addition to the existing houses, the presence of existing residents, generally with some form of leadership or community organization, makes it essential to obtain support in advance of upgrading. The residents may be able to contribute labour and other resources to installation and maintenance of infrastructure and other community improvements, and may even be given the opportunity to participate in decision making.

Participation is a somewhat vague term, which may imply the opportunity for people to have control over decision making with respect to their living conditions, or may merely describe opportunities for consultation, obtaining support for actions proposed by outside bodies, or mobilization of labour and other resources to supplement those made available by public authorities. Upgrading programmes may be initiated from outside or may originate in the demands made by residents. In either case, residents may or may not be given the opportunity to decide, or even to have a more limited say in, what that upgrading includes. In order to deal with the large numbers involved, channels for participation are generally necessary and these may take a variety of forms, including the following: locally elected leaders (as in the slums of Indian cities); a hierarchy of appointed and elected officials (as in the kampungs of Indonesian cities); or a party organization (as in the squatter areas of Luska). The extent to which local leaders are linked to wider political or patron – client networks may be crucial in bargaining for recognition and resources.

Less important than the precise form of the community organization is the extent to which it is responsive to, and legitimate in the eyes of, residents, and the scope which is given for any real say in decision making. If community organizations are not themselves allocated resources in relation to which they can make expenditure decisions, then, even in programmes such as that in Hyderabad (which attempt to operate in a demand-responsive manner), leaders and community workers have an important gate-keeping role – interpreting residents' needs, and mediating between them and public agencies. Where public or donor agencies have predetermined modes of operation, criteria, or standards, the scope for participation in decision making may be very limited – even if project planners and implementors are, in principle, willing for this to occur. This is the case, for example, in World Bank-funded upgrading projects – such as that in Lusaka, where project preparation and appraisal, funding, disbursement, and supervision arrangements inhibited what is inevitably a relatively slow and unpredictable process of community involvement in decision making. Where the views of residents are not taken into account, the nature of project organization and infrastructure standards may be inappropriate.

Community participation may be advocated not just to obtain residents' views on proposals for upgrading and their support for implementation, but also to mobilize individual and household inputs to supplement the efforts of public agencies in infrastructure installed. As in the case of serviced-plot schemes, while mobilizing self-help inputs may release resources not otherwise available for improvements, this may also be used to divert attention from the meagre extent of the commitment of public funds in relation to other priorities (within the city and nationally), and may impose an additional strain on household budgets already insufficient to meet basic expenditure. Although, in principle, upgrading may be seen as a particular stage in a process of improvement initiated and continued by residents, in practice it generally takes the form of a short-term capital programme; maintenance of infrastructure is, therefore, a recurring problem. It is sometimes suggested that the community organization also takes responsibility for maintenance. Experiments along these lines (for example, in Bombay and Hyderabad), are in their early stages, and in any case may represent an unfair burden on the poor which the rich are not expected to adopt, exacerbated by the tendency for utilities provided to the rich to be subsidized. Raising resources for maintenance by appropriate pricing policies, probably involving cross subsidies, would seem a more appropriate strategy.

Upgrading proposals are area-based policies which assume that residential areas are homogeneous and harmonious communities, and, because infrastructure is uniformly deficient within an area, that residents are uniformly poor. This is, of course, often not the case. Residential areas may be made up of groups with conflicting traditions or interests. Some residents may have locational advantages either between or within areas. Those who are living in unauthorized areas suitable for long-term residential development may well be in a higher income group than those living in the most marginal areas, unsuitable for upgrading even in the long term. Within areas, those with plots fronting tracks adopted as permanent roads and public transport routes benefit more than those without road access or, where compensation and alternative plots are not made available, than those whose houses have to be demolished. Some residents may also be more able than others to take advantage of what is on offer (e.g. house construction loans), while upgrading may produce adverse effects for other residents (e.g. increases in rents which penalize tenant households).

Self-help, community organization, and participation should not, therefore, be romanticized. While these may provide the basis for planning local residential areas and organizing appropriate improvement programmes, they are often problematic. In many cases, they are a means of incorporating, controlling, and pacifying disadvantaged people without major concessions, a point strongly made by Alan Gilbert and Peter Ward in their studies of Latin American cities.[4] Local organizations are easily co-opted, and rarely provide the impetus for structural changes to the existing economic and political power structure where this is biased against poor people. Nor do neighbourhood based organizations provide a decision making structure in which the competing priorities of city-wide and local infrastructure and service needs, or the requirements of different residential areas within the city, can be balanced and resource allocations made.

Does privatization equal efficiency?

Allocating responsibility for utility provision to the private sector is not new: in colonial times, electricity, telephones, and public transport were often handled by private companies, and in some countries this persisted after independence, although in many others the companies were nationalized. However, in the light of the more general climate of conventional opinion, which currently favours market forces over bureaucratic administration as a means of achieving development objectives, there has been increased advocacy of privatization of certain urban services. Privatization and self-financing independent companies, contracting out by the local authority for a fee, and/or advocacy of individual or community self-help may be recommended, to improve efficiency and reduce the burden placed on public administrative systems. Thus self-help is recommended here for different reasons from those discussed in the previous section – here individual enterprise and initiative is regarded as a more dynamic force than bureaucratic provision, especially if it is directly rewarded by profits or benefits to the initiator.

What sorts of city services are handled by private companies, and what has the experience been, in terms of efficiency and equity? While in many cities, as noted above, public authorities took over responsibility for service provision at independence, in others services continued to be handled by the private sector – for example, in Manila (electricity, gas, telephones), Calcutta (electricity, buses, ferry), Bangkok (minibuses), Karachi (gas, electricity), Ivory Coast (water supply) or Kinshasa (public transport). In the Ivory Coast, Richard Stren describes the private company which has supplied water to the urban areas on contract since 1959 as giving a good quality, efficient service, subsidized to low income earners by the state.[5] However, funds for the latter have become less easily available in the 1980s and residents of unauthorized housing areas depend on vendors, from whom the water purchased is costly. Solid waste disposal is another service which is sometimes contracted out. For example, in face of the decreasing ability of Nigerian local governments to provide an adequate service, contracts for removal from areas or individual households have been agreed in cities such as Kaduna, Enugu, and Ibadan, as has been the case for some years in Abidjan. However, if government expenditure is cut and payments for services reduced, the low-income areas tend to suffer disproportionately, while Stren concludes that such contracting out is not feasible if shortages of foreign exchange prevent contractors from buying and maintaining sufficient equipment to provide an adequate service.[6]

Public transport has commonly been divided between the public and private sectors, with the balance varying from city to city. In Calcutta, for example, nearly two-thirds of all trips use privately operated bus services, controlled by voluntary route associations, while in other cities the private sector is dominated by various forms of para-transit and the stage buses are publicly operated. Public bus operations suffer from inefficiency, shortages of buses, and difficulties of maintenance, and while these problems may also affect private operators, the latter seem to be more resourceful in keeping vehicles on the road. Such a division between public and private appears to work reasonably well as long as the public sector is able to exercise a reasonable regulatory function and private bus operators are able to maintain their fleets, while it has the added advantage, where basic forms of para-transit such as cycle and auto rickshaws are permitted, of providing cheap services to urban dwellers and considerable numbers of jobs. In housing, likewise, the capacity of the indigenous construction sector to provide housing in sufficient quantities and at appropriate costs seems superior to that of bureaucratic agencies.

While there does seem to be scope therefore, for private provision and operation of some urban services and facilities, unless this is done on a contracting-out basis (when it is directly affected by government expenditure controls, given the limited local revenue base of most city administrations), it must not be forgotten that the motive of capitalist enterprises is to make profits, and so services will be provided only to those who can afford to pay for them. Government intervention will still be necessary to ensure (directly or indirectly) that the needs of the poor are met, while in the poorest countries the private sector may itself be insufficiently developed to take on such responsibilities. Support for further privatization may be expected from the commercial bourgeoisie, as well as from better-off residents who are willing and able to pay for privately provided services; whether the results strengthen large scale capital, the petty bourgeoisie, or the own-account workers of the informal sector depends on how these services are organized.

It is not possible to reach firm conclusions on the administrative structures which are most appropriate for the management of urban growth from this short review – and, indeed it is inappropriate to try and identify a single optimum administrative structure or financial framework, as this will depend not only on technocratic decision making but on the political process, in which various interests bargain over control of, and the incidence of benefits from, market forces and public actions.

From the limited evidence available, it is clear that – while large-scale bureaucracies are typically inflexible and unresponsive, local governments generally lack power and resources to deal with the problems, sectoral agencies give rise to difficulties of co-ordination, multi-sectoral development authorities are cumbersome and often ineffective, and special project implementation units give rise to problems related to the handover to normal administrations – all of these have a role to play in urban management in particular circumstances. It is important, therefore, not to reject the administrative structures outright, but to realistically appraise their strengths and weaknesses, define the tasks which they can most effectively carry out, and assess the degree of political, economic, and technocratic support for the reforms needed.

We have seen that the alternative solution often advocated, that of community organization, has a positive role to play in local planning and service provision for residential areas, but that such an administrative structure is less appropriate for planning and managing city-wide growth and land allocation, planning and operating many components of physical infrastructure and utilities, revenue generation, and resource allocation between services and areas within the city. In addition, the potential for community participation in decision making, and self-help as a means of meeting the needs of the poor, must not be exaggerated. Both are essential, but neither are unproblematic, raising questions of the relationship of community leaders, area organizations, and local demand-making to the wider political process. Resistance to local autonomy at the neighbourhood level, as at the local government level, may preclude full use of this management component.

The third alternative form of adminstration considered, that of entrusting the provision and operation of certain services and housing to the medium and large-scale private sector may be easier to implement, given the support likely to be forthcoming from local capital, but gives rise to questions of equity. The most typical framework for future urban management, therefore, seems likely to be a composite of city-wide administrative systems, special agencies, and private-sector service provision, with some scope for local-area planning and organization in favourable political circumstances.

Notes and references

1. Stren, R.E. 'Local government and the administration of urban centres in Africa' in R.E. Stren and R. White (eds) (1988) *African Cities in Crisis: Managing Rapid Urban Growth,* Boulder: Westview.
2. Lea, J.P. and Courtney, J.M. (eds) (1985) *Cities in Conflict: Planning and Management of Asian Cities,* Washington DC: World Bank.
3. Sivaramakrishnan, K.C. and Green, L. (1986) *Metropolitan Management: the Asian Experience,* Oxford: Oxford University Press.
4. Gilbert, A. and Ward, P. (1985) *Housing, the State and the Poor: Policy and Practice in Three Latin American Cities,* Cambridge: Cambridge University Press. See also Cornelius, W.A. and Kemper, R.V. (eds) (1978) *Metropolitan Latin America: the Challenge and the Response,* Beverly Hills: Sage Books.
5. Stren, op. cit., n. 1.
6. ibid.

About Part II

Having examined some common assumptions regarding the future of cities in both First and Third Worlds in Part I we are now in a position to address a range of issues related to the concerns of the 'new economics', or the future of cities 'as if people matter'. Some of these issues were discussed in our Introduction. Part II takes this exploration further by looking more particularly at a number of social, political, technological, and ecological perspectives. As in Part I, the essays cover both First and Third worlds, revealing in the process differences and similarities. Our purpose here is not to be prescriptive, nor to present a single alternative view. Indeed, to try to do so at this stage would be both presumptuous and counter-productive. Rather, the essays present a variety of views, each one focusing upon a particular aspect of the city.

To begin with, after an introduction which sets a context for considering the future of the city, three very different views are presented. The first, written by two British town planners, takes up the question of the relationship between town and country, identifying new social, economic, demographic, and environmental trends. The second, with the eye of the sociologist, brings us down to the level of the citizen and examines the way in which relationships of power are resolved, with winners and losers. The third examines the demands that cities in both First and Third Worlds place upon soil fertility and other natural resources, stressing the need for a metabolism of cities that recycles resources to maintain a ecological balance.

Looking more particularly at the Third World, but with implications for cities everywhere, the issue of community control or planning 'from the bottom up' is discussed in the light of experience gained from very different contexts. This demonstrates that we have not yet even begun to tap the enormous potential of ordinary people to organize, plan, build, and maintain their own environments. This concern with the local decision-making process is followed by a discussion of the macro-political issues which need to be addressed if more socially, economically and ecologically sustainable forms of city management are to be achieved. The technological means to implement such sustainable alternatives are discussed in Chapter 11. This demonstrates that the major task is to increase the range of technologies available to people and shows that although many options have already been developed and proven in practice, they are not yet as easily accessible as they need to be.

Chapter 5

Alternative futures for cities

James Robertson

*James Robertson provides an introduction to the essays of Part II.
Drawing upon his earlier work in* The Sane Alternative, *he sets a
context by offering four alternative futures. The first, 'Decline and
Disaster', envisages a future in which severe urban breakdown follows
from the failure of cities to adapt either to changes in economic
function or, in the case of the Third World, to uncontrolled expansion of
the urban population. The second, 'Business as Usual', offers a 'top-
down' approach in which cities rely upon the benefits of conventional
economic development to trickle down to their less advantaged citizens.
The third alternative, 'Hyper-Expansion', is the scenario that favours
the technical fix. New technology replaces conventional employment
'releasing' an increasing proportion of the workforce to extended
periods of leisure. The question raised, which echoes the analysis of
Begg and Moore in Chapter 2, is whether such a future would support
present levels of urbanization. Finally, in the fourth scenario, the 'Sane,
Humane and Ecological' alternative, changes in work and a continued
trend towards decentralization, lead to the development of greater self-
reliance at both a personal and urban level. In developing these
alternatives in terms of the future of the city, Robertson pays particular
attention to this last scenario, linking trends in technology to changes
in personal attitudes to work and life-style, and to the possibility of a
new economics, matched by a shift from urban to rural values.*

*James Robertson is internationally known as an independent
lecturer, writer and consultant on economic and social change. His
books include* The Sane Alternative: A Choice of Futures *and* Future
Work: Jobs, Self Employment and Leisure after the Industrial Age. *His
recent assignments include work for the EEC and OECD on local
employment initiatives and the World Health Organisation on healthy
public policies, including healthy cities.*

It is useful to imagine a number of alternative futures for cities. To a
greater or lesser extent, each would be part of a larger alternative

future, embracing changes in global, national, and local economic activity, in patterns of work and living, in culture, in education, in health and in other aspects of life and thought. Awareness of such alternative futures (or scenarios) can remind us of factors bearing on the actual future to come.

In this chapter I shall outline four alternative futures: Decline and Disaster; Business As Usual; Hyper-Expansion (HE); and Sane, Humane, Ecological (SHE).[1] I shall suggest some of their implications for the future of cities, and relate them briefly to the concerns of the new economics.

Four scenarios

Decline and Disaster

Decline and Disaster must be recognized as possibilities – the consequences of failing to pursue other more positive approaches successfully, so let us start with the pessimistic scenario, and get it out of the way – if we can.

In the global context, a Disaster scenario might include nuclear war and mounting ecological destruction, famine and drought, especially in the Third World. Rising levels of unemployment worldwide could lead, in the absence of any successful response, to economic and social disaster for millions of people. Epidemics like AIDS might sweep the world. And so on. Such developments would clearly contribute to decline and disaster for cities. Even without these wider changes for the worse, a Decline and Disaster scenario for many cities can be imagined. In the industrialized countries, severe urban breakdown might follow from failure to adapt to the decline of cities' industrial-age functions in mass-production, mass-employment, mass-consumption societies. In Third World countries complete urban breakdown might follow from the uncontrolled expansion of cities as millions of impoverished people continue to be driven off the land by the economic and social forces of conventional westernized development.

Business As Usual

The Business-As-Usual view of the future assumes that most things will remain broadly as they are, and we should aim to get back to normality. In terms of the world economy, the rich countries will be expected to resume a pattern of economic growth that keeps the path of progress open for the Third World, by providing expanding markets for Third World products. In national economies, restored economic growth will be expected to enable industry and commerce to create wealth out of which publicly financed social services can be supported. Urban industrialized patterns of life-style and employment will be expected to remain the norm. Residential and work locations will remain in separate zones. People will continue to use their homes for leisure and consumption activities only. The land, premises and equipment, and financial capital that people need to support their work will continue to be provided by employers. The top-down, trickle-down approach to social and economic progress – recently highlighted as yuppie-led and golf-course-led growth[2] – will remain the order of the day.

So far as cities in the industrialized countries are concerned, this top-down approach will continue to be relied on to bring employment back to the cities, and to create the conditions there which will attract employers. The natural instrument for fostering urban revival on these lines will be the business-led development corporation. This contrasts with the key part to be played by bottom-up, locally initiated, grass-roots development, if the aim is to enable local people to create a more self-reliant, resourceful city for themselves – as in the SHE scenario (see below).

Americans have described as 'smokestack chasing' and 'chip chasing' the Business-As-Usual efforts made by city and national authorities to attract new employers into cities. It is difficult not to be sceptical about the long-term effectiveness of this approach. Some years ago, when travelling from one city to another in the United States, I remember being told by each in turn that it was aiming to become the new continental centre for micro-chip manufacture. Today, when city after city is enthusiastically discovering the potential of its tourist attractions as a source of employment, one wonders where all the tourists are going to come from and whether there will be enough to go round.

So far as Third World cities are concerned, their explosive, uncontrolled growth makes it hard to define a Business-As-Usual scenario for their future. They are an even more obvious case where, on closer inspection, Business As Usual seems to lead directly to Disaster.

Hyper-Expansion (HE)

The HE scenario foresees that further economic progress in the industrialized countries will only be achieved by concentrating on high technology production and by marketing highly professionalized services. Economic activity will become more global in character, and multinational business will play an even more dominating part than today. Conventional full employment will not come back. Most of the necessary work will be done by a skilled elite of professionals and experts, backed by automation, other capital-intensive technology, and specialist know-how. The majority of people will not need to work. They will consume the goods and services provided by the working elite – including leisure, information, and education services. They will have more leisure time to spend at home, at local leisure facilities (theme parks, shopping centres, swimming pools, sports centres, etc.), and on trips away from home. The coming of the leisure society and the information age will help to reshape the built environment accordingly.

The HE scenario has two main implications for the future of cities in industrialized countries. First, there will continue to be great growth in the information and communications facilities located in cities, and in the demand for space (including office space) for people working in that sector. This will apply particularly to cities like London which are established centres for the financial, commercial, and technical services of the global economy, as well as for communications and information services more conventionally defined. Second, there will continue to significant growth in the role of cities as centres of leisure activity, including tourism, discretionary shopping (shopping for fun!), sightseeing and museums, culture and the arts. More old inner city areas – like Covent Garden in London, the Cannery in San Francisco, Faneuil Hall in Boston, and so on – will be converted to these new uses.

Among many questions left unanswered by the HE scenario is whether the role of cities in that kind of society will support urban populations on today's scale. So far as Third World countries and cities are concerned, the HE scenario largely ignores their situation and prospects. It simply assumes that they will follow the industrialized world along a superindustrial path of technical and economic progress.

Sane, Humane, Ecological (SHE)

If the HE scenario represents a super-industrial vision of the future and an acceleration of the trends and drives that have been dominant during the industrial age, the SHE scenario represents a change of direction. For example, where work is concerned, the keyword will no longer be 'employment' (as under Business As Usual) or 'leisure' (as under HE), but *'ownwork'*. In general, people will become less, rather than more, dependent on the large institutions of government, business, finance, trade unions, and the professions to give them work and provide them with goods and services. Most aspects of the economy and society will tend to become more *de-centralized*, rather than more centralized. A key aim of policy at every level will be to enable people *to organize themselves* for co-operative self-reliance and to develop the capacities, habits, and skills needed for that. More self-reliant cities and more self-reliant Third World national economies will be part of the overall picture.

This scenario envisages a change of direction not only from greater dependency to greater self-reliance, but also to more *conserving*, as opposed to more wasteful and ecologically damaging, patterns of production and consumption. In fact, the two go together. Conservation involves more efficient use of resources all round, including actual and potential human resources. And moves in that direction are one way in which people at every level – city as well as household and nation – can reduce the extent of their dependence for work, for goods and services, and for welfare, on external employers and suppliers who are outside their own control.

The SHE scenario has two immediate implications for the future of cities. First, it places emphasis on enabling the people who live in cities to take control of their own future development – on encouraging bottom-up urban revival based on local community initiatives. Second, it places emphasis on the resourceful, self-reliant city, minimizing waste of resources by energy conservation and recycling, and minimizing dependence on imports from outside its boundaries – even of such basics as food and energy – by establishing new forms of urban production such as city farms and combined heat and power (CHP).

But the SHE scenario raises more fundamental questions, too, about the future relationship between city and country. In this it differs from the other scenarios. They do not question that cities will retain the predominant position in the twenty-first-century world which they have always enjoyed in the past. So, while recognizing that the actual future of cities will contain elements of all the scenarios, we shall need to pay particular attention to the implications of SHE.

City and country

Most people, if they think about the future of the city and the future of the countryside at all, think about them as if the two are quite separate. Rural and urban matters are the specialisms of different professions, different government departments, and different academic disciplines. Moreover, since cities first came into existence some thousands of years ago, they have dominated the countryside. City-based priests, kings, soldiers, courtiers, merchants, industrialists, financiers, politicians, civil servants, professional people, and media bosses have each, in their own times, attracted into cities the surpluses generated in the countryside, thus reinforcing the position of cities as the centres of power and attention for society as a whole. In the hierarchical centre/periphery model on which all 'civilized' societies have so far been based, the city has been the centre and the countryside the periphery.

During the industrial age, the preponderance of urban over rural interests has grown – in ways clearly showing that developments in the countryside affect what happens to cities. In the industrial countries, the eighteenth-century modernization of agriculture contributed directly to the urban industrialization that followed, and to the movement of population from country to city (as described in other chapters). In Third World countries, following the pattern of development in the industrial world, economic progress has been sought primarily in the development of the westernized, urban, industrial sector, as opposed to the rural village-based sector. The resulting discrimination against the rural economy, and the displacement of population caused by it, has helped to create the urban crisis in the Third World today.[3]

The SHE scenario suggests that we may now be coming to a historical turning point in this respect, as in others. The traditional imbalance between city and countryside may be about to be redressed. The pendulum may be beginning to swing the other way.

In the industrialized countries the heyday of industrialized fossil-fuel-based agriculture seems to be over. Land hitherto reserved for agriculture is already becoming available for other purposes. Just as developments in robotics and information technology suggest that much of today's conventional large-scale industry may be replaced in the twenty-first-century economy by dispersed, flexible, small-scale, hi-tech manufacturing units, so developments in biotechnology and information technology offer the comparable prospect of an agricultural sector in which small-scale, sophisticated food-producing units will have replaced many of today's large monocrop agribusiness farms. It seems probable that the future will continue to bring more small-scale manufacturing to the countryside, and more small-scale food growing to the cities; and in city and country alike those activities will continue to become more closely linked with others, such as conservation, leisure and tourism. In those ways, certainly, the prospect is of the conventional distinctions between city and country being blurred. The greening and villaging of the city will parallel the civilizing and urbanizing of the countryside.

Already, modern telecommunications, including telephones, television and radio, have reduced many of the economic, social, and cultural disadvantages associated with Marx's nineteenth-century rural idiocy. As information technology reduces those disadvantages further, as ecological consciousness spreads, and as various aspects of contemporary urban idiocy become less and less tolerable, increasing numbers of people will choose to live in the country rather than the city. The decentralizing capability of information technology may even call into question the need for a centralized urban base for many of the financial, commercial, communications, and governmental services for which new city-centre office blocks are still being built today.

So far as Third World countries are concerned, scepticism is already growing about the Business-As-Usual approach to development, under which economic and social progress was supposed to trickle down from the cities to the countryside. Even established institutions like the World Bank are now giving increasing emphasis to self-reliant development from the rural grass roots upwards.

Creating tomorrow out of today

An important possibility for the future, then, is that in the industrialized countries the process of urbanization, which has been so marked a feature of the industrial age, has reached a limit. The coming urban-to-rural shift in outlook and values which that would imply would parallel other deep-seated shifts (e.g. from masculine to feminine and from anthropocentric to ecological) which many people are coming to see as aspects of an all-pervasive paradigm shift now occurring.[4]

Such a shift from urban to rural values, leading to a fresh movement of people out of cities and to more dispersed patterns of economic and social life, would cut across existing structures of power. Today's elites – politicians, financiers, businesspeople, trade union leaders, policy-making civil servants, academics, professional and media people, all kinds of opinion-formers – are predominantly urban elites; and today's masses are predominantly urban masses. Both assume that urban solutions must be found for urban problems. It does not readily occur to them that solutions may be in more fundamental changes – that is, changes in the wider context in which today's urban problems arise. Nor will they find it easy to accept such changes. Meanwhile, the forecast is that, up to and beyond the end of the century, Third World urbanization will continue to grow dramatically, even if the rate of growth is now slowing down – suggesting the possibility of an eventual turnaround, as in industrialized countries.[5]

This brings us to the crux of the matter. The actual future of cities will evolve from a criss-cross of conflicting trends. It will not be any one of the alternatives, but will contain elements of them all. The coming of a globalized, information-based economy; robots and biotechnology; increasing leisure; the shift from centralized, hierarchical patterns of organization to lateral networks and greater participation; new concepts of efficiency, based on less wasteful use of resources and more conserving treatment of the environment; new patterns of agriculture: all these and may other disparate and conflicting trends will help to shape the future development of cities. There will be no universally shared vision of future cities – no agreed ideas or plans on which their future evolution can be based. They will evolve from conflict between alternative visions of the future and between the competing interest groups who support those alternative visions.

James Robertson

The new economics

The future of cities will be closely bound up with future developments in economic life and thought. Of the four alternative futures I have outlined, the new economics (as recently developed in the work of the Other Economic Summit and the New Economics Foundation) is closest to SHE. But, while paying special attention to changes implied by the SHE scenario, the new economics will need to clarify the strengths and weaknesses of them all. Much of the work already in hand or proposed by the New Economics Foundation – on local economic and social initiatives, on the information economy, on socially directed investment, on alternative economic indicators, on the economic potential of the 4 Rs sector (re-use, repair, reconditioning, recycling), and on other aspects of 'A New Economics By The Year 2000' – will be relevant to the future of cities.

Within cities, the emphasis must be on homegrown approaches to urban development and revival, with the aim of creating more self-reliant, more ecological cities, whose inhabitants will have more control over their own economic destinies than most urban dwellers today. But the search for solutions to today's urban problems must also include a new emphasis on economic and social development outside today's urban areas. This accords with the new economics' emphasis on lateral thinking. Just as the new economists recognize that from now on a revived informal economy will be one of the conditions of a well-functioning formal economy, so it must see that – in industrialized and Third World countries alike – the evolution of sustainable twenty-first-century cities will depend on the revival and regeneration of more self-reliant rural and small-town economies.

Notes and references

1. These alternative futures are discussed more fully in '*The Sane Alternative*'. In '*Future Work*' they are applied in detail to a discussion of jobs, self-employment and leisure after the industrial age. See Robertson, J. (1983) *The Sane Alternative*, rev. edn, Cholsey: Robertson and Robertson, J. (1985) *Future Work*, London: Gower/Temple Smith.
2. The summer of 1987 saw much public comment on the invasion of the Isle of Dogs in London's redeveloped docklands by young upwardly mobile professionals (yuppies) from the City, followed by astronomical rises in property values, the pricing of local people out of the local housing market, and a failure to create significant numbers of local jobs for local people. About the same time Nicholas Ridley, the Secretary of State for the Environment, was widely reported as saying that more international-class golf courses would be needed in the North of England to attract Japanese businessmen to set up factories there to employ local people.
3. A clear account of this is given in World Commission on Environment and

Development (the Brundtland Commission) (1987) *Our Common Future*, ch. 9, Oxford: OUP.

4. Maurice Ash suggests that urban values 'are concerned with the possession of things', whereas rural values 'are to do with ways of life, with wholes and what is qualitative, and hence with where we belong'. See Ash, M. (1987) *New Renaissance*, Bideford: Green Books.

5. See *Our Common Future*. See also Brown, Lester, Wolf, Edward, and Starke, Linda (1987) *State of the World*, p. 38 ff., New York and London: Norton.

Chapter 6

Town and country

John Holmes and Geoffrey Steeley

In this Chapter, John Holmes and Geoffrey Steeley take up the question of the relationship between town and country in Britain. From their base as town planners living and working in rural Hertfordshire but making regular journeys to London, they identify what they see as emerging social, economic, demographic and environmental trends. These include an ageing population, with a higher rate of divorce and, as in Robertson's earlier analysis, changes in work and lifestyle and the possibility of an increase in time for leisure. Holmes and Steeley then introduce the concept of the 'Spread City'. This phenomenon is not to be confused with urban sprawl or megalopolis but is akin to Ebenezer Howard's vision of the 'Social City', a network of well managed and planned, but self-contained, cities offering the greatest opportunities for the enjoyment of both urban and rural life.

John Holmes is currently working on environmental management issues for the Wellington Regional Council in New Zealand. A teacher and a planner by professional training, he has spent fifteen years working in the British planning system and was recently a member of the editorial board of 'Town and Country Planning', the magazine of the Town and Country Planning Association.

Geoffrey Steeley is the County Planning and Estates Officer for Hertfordshire. He has an extensive knowledge and experience of the British planning system and in recent years has been responsible for the development of Hertfordshire's County Structure plan and development associated with Stansted Airport. He chaired the Green Belt Working Group and the Regional Monitoring Group of the Standing Conference on London and South East Regional Planning Officers and has been President of the County Planning Officers' society.

Introduction

We live and work in Hertfordshire, but the nature of our work – in town and country planning – frequently requires us to travel into Central

London. It's not always a pleasant experience! But a rush-hour journey to the capital, from commuter countryside to commercial city centre, does encapsulate the scale and nature of late twentieth-century problems that we must address if we are to seek a move to more sustainable, humanly satisfying, and self reliant ways of living.

As we gaze at the scenery out of the carriage window, one of the first difficulties we need to face is that many of our fellow passengers may not perceive any problems at all; or at least, they may interpret what they see quite differently from us. What we may see as the largely treeless, hedgeless, natureless, open landscape of industrial farming, someone else may think of as positive testimony to man's control of nature in the pursuit of human food production. Where we see the scarred scenery of sand and gravel extraction, a companion might claim that this is an acceptable price to pay for the pluses of economic development. We see dormitory settlements, may of whose inhabitants work elsewhere, unconnected with their home community; and we see cramped, old housing in the city, many of whose inhabitants have no job to go to anywhere, whilst their community cries out for useful work. Others may smugly think 'I'm alright, Jack', and reckon the unemployed are their own worst enemies. We see small historic market towns and motorways and out-of-town shopping complexes that threaten the vitality and the viability of those older towns. Others may see a hypermarket as a car-owning consumers' dream. We see the edges of towns and of London itself; a wasted no man's land between conflicting land uses and conflicting attitudes. Others may see the urban fringe simply in terms of development potential. And we see connections between all this happening outside of our carriage and wider problems we read about in our morning newspaper – Third World debt, ozone depletion leading to global and more local climatic change, poverty, pollution, and the social and psychological desperation of people almost everywhere. Our fellow travellers may prefer to simply bury their heads in their papers, their metaphorical sand, and not recognize the complex web of their own involvement and hence their response in these wider issues.

Our underlying belief, however, is that we do have to acknowledge these connections, these changes around us with their life forms, and indeed for places, people and life in other, future times. This chapter is about some of the changes taking place around us, the problems they pose and the opportunities they present. Our area of reference is the south-east of England, an area with which we are very familiar. But our feeling is that what we discern happening here may have wider utility for other regions around capital and large cities in the developed world. We see an emerging relationship between city and countryside that perhaps makes the conventional understanding of the words 'city' and 'countryside' inappropriate. We see expanding variety in personal life-styles, economic expectations, family structures, and human aspirations. And we see a need for governments – local and national – to play a role that balances regulation with enablement, individual freedom with social and environmental equity.

So, we'll be looking at some emerging trends and making predictions. But the only safe prediction we can make about predicting the future, is that the prediction will almost certainly be wrong! Therefore, in thinking about what the future might hold for what people do, where they might do it, how they do it, where they live, how much spare time they have, how they spend that time, and so on, we don't want to use the idea of a target date or a blueprint for our crystal ball gazing. Instead, we'd prefer to consider future change more like a journey – a journey where there is no set time-table or destination, but where a broad direction is apparent. Different people will chose their own routes, and indeed their own mode of transport. Some will go faster, taking life in the fast lane; some will find dead ends; and some will take more meandering byways and observe what's happening around them. Whatever routes these journeys, our lives, take, there needs to be some broad rules as we see it. First, however we improve the comfort and quality of our journey (be it materially and/or non-materially) we should recognize as far as possible the consequences of our actions, and try not to degrade the quality and comfort of our fellow passengers' ride. Second, the quality of potential future passengers' journeys must be equally respected. Third, we have to ensure that there's a vehicle – in this case the planet – for future passengers to actually ride on!

The idea of a journey is also a useful analogy for what we want to say, because travelling implies a number of different features. It implies a transition rather than a transformation and we expect an accumulation of transitional changes in the way people live and work, rather than overnight transformations of individual lifestyles and organizational practices. Also, a journey often needs major signposts, opportunities to review where we are going; our argument suggests the application of wisdom to technology in a directed way, so, in this sense, explicit choices will sometimes have to be made. Journeys may require us to build bridges and enter uncharted territory. We believe that improved knowledge of the consequences of our actions – in social and environmental terms – demands something more than mere neutrality, more than simply cataloguing trends; we will therefore also need to use advocacy and envangelism to build new bridges to new ground.

Conventionally, when we try predicting where trends are taking us, our first instinct is to look to the past, and then project patterns forward to the future. Sometimes, we try and discern longer-term patterns, or 'waves' of behaviour, of technological advancement, and of economic activity.[1] Then we produce quite complex theories about how and when the next wave will wash over us! Others say that this is too scientific, that it's impossible to predict for more than a year or two ahead, and so they look at short term 'ripples', confining their speculation to the next few months or years. In a new context of global connectedness, of finite boundaries to resources, of five billion inhabitants, and of the need for long-term planning for sustainability, we feel that it's goodbye to waves and raspberries to ripples! Put bluntly, the old rules are no longer relevant, or at least, of only limited utility. Rear-view-mirror forecasting, or as Charles Handy has put it, 'stumbling backwards into the future',[2] cannot possibly create for us new visions; all we do by this method is rework tired old images. New pictures need imagination, so we cannot paint by numbers – the economic quantities in life – alone. We can add imagination and breathe life into our pictures only when we add people, of all colours, to the flat and sterile canvas of conventional economics.

Some emerging trends

In what direction are social, economic, demographic and environmental trends taking us? Are there identifiable 'ends', or are we too wrapped up in the 'means' to worry about why we do what we do, and what the longer and wider consequences might be? Are there real individual choices about the future, or a deep-seated inevitability about the patterns of behaviour that will emerge? Whether there is choice or inevitability, how might they be reflected in how and where we live?

Over the next few paragraphs we shall try and address some of these issues in a broad sense, simply touching upon some major features of current trends.[3] The first point concerns the population structure in Britain, and the in-built inertia that demography imposes when considering future trends. The total number of people in Britain is largely static, at around 56 million, but within that steady total, all sorts of significant changes have been occurring. The birth rate has, for some time, been below 'replacement levels', and, at the other end of the scale, there are many more older people in the population. Broadly speaking, then, the significant feature is the ageing of the population, with widespread implications for health, social service provision, housing, pensions, employment, and standards of living.

The needs of the elderly, be they the 'long-term retired' or 'frail households' will increasingly impose constraints, obligations, and responsibilities on a whole range of families, volunteers, and professional carers; this will leave little scope for freedom of choice in their own lifestyles and behaviour. The correct climate of thinking on elderly care places a greater burden on the family to care for elderly relations at home, but with smaller families, more divorce, and more one-parent households, there are fewer carers about. Add to this the fact that economic pressures increasingly demand two-earner families, or at least a higher number of women at work, and the pool of traditional caring is thus further reduced. In brief, the demographic phenomenon of an ageing population is likely to impose considerable extra demands on many people in all sorts of ways, thus potentially restricting personal choice.

A further feature already alluded to has been the rise in divorce. A largely unresearched area, divorce is having considerable impact in developing a wide diversity of family structures, social needs, the housing market, and on employment patterns. The financial and human costs of family fission do not often create situations in which people's thoughts turn easily to higher altruistic motivation. Single parenthood, for example, now amounting to 12 per cent of all families and likely to increase further, puts tremendous logistical and economic pressures on people, often at a time of great emotional stress. So, again, personal choice about patterns of behaviour and aspirations are likely to be limited as a result of this significant social trend.

A further relevant trend to this discussion has been a perceptible increase in non-work time that people now have available to them. Gershuny is optimistic that new jobs will be created out of increased 'leisure' time.[4] He argues that new technologies enable new styles of living – new ways of doing domestic work, new patterns of leisure – which in turn mean new sorts of consumption and hence new sorts of employment. Gershuny's argument is set within the conventional paradigm of formal employment, a growing economy, a consumer society, and the attitude that if technology makes it possible then we should do it anyway. Others are more sanguine about job creation in the post-industrial 'leisure' world, raising questions about the types of jobs created, who may get them, the potential for social schism between the 'haves' and the 'have-nots', and what relevance this type of picture has for other less-developed parts of the world.[5] Perhaps the crucial point for us is the context for increased leisure time – has it been enforced by early retirement, redundancy, or youth unemployment, or has it been positively chosen by someone to reflect their value system and personal interests? Choice is not a luxury for all, and in thinking about emerging patterns of work and life-styles and their physical manifestation, we should not underplay personal choice or the lack of it. Both exist and both will have an influence on the shape of urban development.

The point about job choice is well understood by Charles Handy,[6] who clearly feels that as important as the total number of jobs, is the type of job that may be created in the future. Apart from fears that the workforce will not be sufficiently educated and trained for jobs that may materialize, Handy is also unhappy about present priorities, about what he refers to as the 'value for money aroma and pursuit of self interest which seems to be the byproduct of the market economy'. For Handy, continuation of this approach can create an 'alpha–gamma' society, whereas he would prefer to see a situation in which 'everyone had more free time with more money to spend in it – thereby creating more jobs – but also more time to do other types of work, whether for fun, for love, for charity, or perchance, for extra personal gain'. Handy argues for the 'convivial economy' of Ivan Illich,[7] but his analysis is rooted in realism rather than romanticism – our current ways of working cannot be disinvented, and will inevitably help shape future patterns. Handy identifies three current types of work organization:

a) *The Shamrock Organization* – this comprises three types of worker, each having different terms of employment and conditions. The *committed core* in well paid, lifetime careers, from whom the employer demands high commitments, flexibility and mobility. These people are expensive to pay, and as Handy says have made 'burn-out' a fashionable disease! Along with the core is the *contractual fringe*, a growing segment, or petal, of the Shamrock Organization, for whom life is freer but less secure. The third petal is the *flexible labour force*, usually in the service sector and brought in as needed.

b)*The Federal Organization* – this is a loose grouping of relatively autonomous activities, an organizational response to the twin pressures for large-scale operations and connectivity, and smaller, human-scale work units. This type of organization relies on well-trained, trustworthy, competent, and motivated people.

c)*The Professional Organization* – mix of the Federal Organization (in terms of autonomy) and jobs which demand knowledge. An organization of professionals, with flat management structures, huge spans of control, and individual responsibility.

Choice in the future may be limited to a career in the trained professions and the core – a full life, perhaps merry and rich, but increasingly a short one – or self-employment as part of an expanding part time work-force. From choice, or as we have seen for some people, perhaps personal necessity as a result of other demands on their time, more and more people will follow this latter route. In terms of the implications for physical form, there will still clearly need to be a city centre – a focus for meeting, exchange, and the 'hardware' of the future business world; this will include the office, associated high-tech equipment and the basis for some production processes. Equally, the part-time society will have physical ramifications – the time that people work, where they work, and the effects of this on transportation systems in perhaps smoothing out or lessening movement flows. The home might also become a centre of formal and informal work, which has implications for the provision of services and other associated jobs at a more local, community scale.

To achieve the necessary sea-change in the way we organize work, the type of work, where we do it, and the place it holds in our lives, Handy emphasises the responsibility for action and vision that lies with us all, but particularly 'the more competent of us'. These themes of choice and responsibility – individual and organizational – are ones to which we shall return.

Within the south-east of the UK, choice may seem to be a commodity in rather greater supply than in other parts of the country. A more plentiful supply of jobs and the resultant cash has enabled people to have a freedom of movement not enjoyed elsewhere. Business is booming, with smaller towns and villages becoming the preferred free market focus for new jobs and housing. All this activity is widely heralded as an indicator of the success of the economic growth model to which nearly all governments are wedded, of whatever persuasion and in whatever location. Leaving aside questions about the equity of that growth, and wealth distribution intra-nationally and internationally, not to mention fundamental doubts about the sustainability of growth, the ironic fact is that the 'success' of the south-east creates its own problems for those 'fortunate' enough to be living there! Not the least of these have been rocketing house prices, traffic congestion, and constant pressure on the physical environment. For those without that choice, one wonders whether the quality of life is perhaps being eroded rather than enhanced by economic 'success'.

Doubts about the value of 'progress', even to those directly enjoying the material benefits, are not confined to the UK. In analysing the urbanization of Japan over the last 70 years, Yoshihiko Oyama suggests that the adaptation of western values and ideas has had an impact of the whole spectrum of Japanese society.[8] On the one hand, this has enabled Japan to enjoy economic and material wealth, but the other side of the coin is the loss of many non-material qualities that provided meaning and importance for Japanese culture and for individual mental comfort. Thirty million people live within a 30-mile radius of Tokyo, and it is within the cities that Oyama senses that people are most losing identity and contact with living processes. Rapid development means a constantly changing scene and the depletion of 'green coverage'; such rapid change leaves little room for memory and attachment to the local environment.

In the rural areas of Japan, too, the relationship between people and land has changed. Historically, farmers' identification with their land and surrounding environment was not just emotional, but 'sensuous' (taste, smell, touching the soil), 'physical' (bodily involvement in cultivation, irrigation, weeding, and fertilizing) and 'physiological' (attachment through a cyclical process of planting, growth, harvest, and the need for sustainable methods of fertilizing). The industrialization and mechanization of farming in Japan has broken these ties.

Oyama describes the man-land relationship in terms of 'proto-scenes' (literally, root-values). An individual will have his or her own 'proto-scene' ingrained in their sub-conscious, gained through sensual, physical and physiological contacts with the climate, land, landscape, and customs of the area where they were raised. Thus, people living in different environments may be expected to have different 'proto-scenes'. The value of their own type of 'proto-scene' may be more important than universally applied standards of beauty, health, or cleanliness – the replacement of old shanty houses by concrete blocks is the example that Oyama uses and one that will strike a universal chord in eastern and western worlds. Oyama concludes that as we move forward, we must somehow enable people to redevelop a sense of place.

In Britain, it is not hard to see similar trends – town centres losing their individual identity as multiple shops take over the high streets; post-war development and redevelopment making inroads into building heritage and established communities; and the discontinuity between people and land. This last point is worth exploring more fully. For many of our predominantly urban population, food comes from supermarkets – convenient, sanitized, with shape and size conforming to smooth marketing images. The direct contact with the land's productive capacities and the processes of growth have been largely lost, and, not surprisingly, are little understood or respected. People see themselves dependent on the supermarket, the shop, rather than dependent on the soil, so their concern for soil health is negligible.

For farmers, too, some would say that the link with cycles of growth and decay and long-term fertility of the land has been lost, as 'science' and 'experts' provide all the answers and the ingredients for modern farming. The economic, social and environmental costs of 40 years of chemical, industrialized farming, and the unsustainable nature of its methods, are becoming increasingly apparent; to put it more agriculturally, chickens are coming home to roost! Currently, we have surplus mountains of food in Europe. We could do with lower levels of food production and we could do with more diverse and nutritious food. We could also do without the dependence on finite oil- and chemical-based fertilizers, pesticides, and herbicides, and the resultant pollution and wildlife damage. And perhaps we should also think about re-investing the soil with long term fertility to repair its damaged structure and hence its propensity to erosion.[9]

Just as consumers have choices and responsibilities in what they buy, equally farmers have a choice about their methods. A shift forwards, marrying the strengths of traditional husbandry with modern technology is quite possible and timely, given growing consumer interest in health and 'whole food', and the current need to debate 'common agricultural policy' and the land-use implications of reduced levels of production. Yet the colossus of the agrochemical industry, combined with the 'us' and 'them' attitudes of farmers and environmental interest groups alike, polarize the positions rather than providing an opportunity for creating objectives that satisfy agricultural employment, food production, and environmental protection. The Countryside Policy Review Panel[10] has calculated that some 4 million hectares of land could be available for purposes other than food production by the year 2000, and that much of this land could be on the urban fringe and between settlements in the more densely populated areas of the country. So, the debate about the future of the countryside provides an opportunity to re-think the whole relationship between town and country, and in terms of our journey analogy, here again is another important signpost.

Where might these issues and trends be taking us? There are clearly some underlying demographic trends that we can do little to influence, but there are emerging patterns of work that may provide greater individual freedom, if enough employers are enlightened to the mutual benefits that can accrue to the organization and the employee. There are also changing priorities for the countryside and agriculture. But are these separate, unrelated trends, or can we discern any structure or pattern that explains the changing relationships between work, home, life-styles, and the environment?

South-east spread city

In answering the question we have posed, it may be helpful if we think briefly about what cities, towns, or villages are. Essentially, they are the physical structures and spaces which enable increasingly complex human interactions to take place. In fact, the interaction could equally well take place at the level of the micro-chip or of the planet; there are interactions – direct and indirect consequences and relationships – between us all. So, we are really asking a question about future interaction, and those artefacts or structures where interaction might take place.

Historically, interaction, production, and accommodation have generally been in close proximity, but, increasingly, all three no longer have to be coincident in location or form. Interactions are able to take place over wide geographic areas, and, in different places, different physical forms are occurring. Without planning, this form could become urban sprawl, but it can also be seen in a more organized way in post-war new towns, or in the sort of landscape and activity we see in our own county, Hertfordshire. What we may be seeing in the south-east of England is one large unit of interactions, a city that has physical form and environmental character which is simply more spread. Indeed, the name 'spread city' has already be used to describe the phenomenon, and it may be one method of coping with millions of people and their interactions in such a way that the physical environment and infrastructure are more able to deal with the demands being placed upon them. The physical form of 'spread city' is thus a product of the interplay of population density, communication and production technology, and environmental capacity. Put simply, 'spread city' may be the next evolutionary form of human settlement, reflecting human aspirations as well as ecological constraints.

What exactly do we mean by 'spread city' and does it serve as a useful signpost for the future? Is it a signpost we should follow? It's perhaps easier to say what 'spread city' is not, at least to begin with. It's not urban sprawl, and nor is it the super-urbanization of megalopolis. sprawl suggests a lack of direction, little sense of purpose, and an absence of a sense of place. Megalopolis is vast, centralized and orientated to efficient systems rather than human foibles. 'Spread city' should offer opportunities and variety for people – in housing, work, lifestyles, environment, leisure and recreation, performing and visual arts, business, voluntary activity; indeed, the whole range of human interactions. It should offer identity, community, economic viability and human vitality. South-east 'spread city' is beginning to offer some of these opportunities, albeit for a minority of its populus at the moment, and this is the crunch: how might we enable and encourage further initiatives that help create a sense of place, a spirit of place, and a sense of purpose for those without the power of choice?

Responsibility for new directions

A distinction can usefully be made here between individual responsibility and organizational responsibilities. Some people are already taking steps to shape their own destinies in a more directed way, towards lifestyles that are environmentally benign and sustainable, personally enriching, and more self-reliant. With growing awareness of the local and global consequences of their daily activities, they have asked the responsible question, 'What can I do?', and they have taken decisions to decrease dependency on the resources of other people and other places.[11] Greater self-sufficiency for those with the financial means and the personal commitment is one way to 'uncouple' from the express train of undirected economic development, but there can be little doubt that, whilst small communities are individually and collectively developing lifestyles that respect principles of sustainability and greater self-reliance, it is hard work. Hard work physically, and hard work more generally, because the conventions and values of contemporary society (and the bureaucratic machinery that supports it) do not encourage such independence.

This is where organizational responsibility comes in. From his perspective as Director of Recreation and Community Services in Birmingham, J. Munn offers the view that the progressive local authorities in the 1990s will be those which not only operate efficiently, but can also harness the vast resources and skills of the community sector at the local level.[12] Munn believes that positively promoting non-bureaucratic, enabling structures in the leisure field will be a strategy which is more about the needs of people, their identifiable communities, and less about public sector bureaucracies. Drawing upon unemployment trends and demographic factors that we have noted earlier, Munn points to the need for inter-departmental, corporate working rather than defensive attitudes about professional specialisms and departmental independence; he is also scathing of those authorities which have failed to create planning and management structures which would allow the community to be involved in the process of identifying leisure facility and service needs.

For Munn, to achieve stable community structures at local level, councils have a straight choice. Either they can treat community development services as a low priority frill on the budget, with an environment where boredom dominates the scene beyond the home, surrounded by a crumbling social structure; or they can develop a positive commitment to co-ordinating resources as all levels of government, aimed at achieving effective community development through the provision of services and facilities identified by the community itself.

Within another part of the bureaucracy, the planning profession should perhaps also be reviewing how it uses its skills in co-ordinating, negotiating, and enabling, with a view to supporting and encouraging local initiatives, in the way that Munn has suggested. Individuals, interest groups, and communities are all working to take back some measure of control in shaping their environments and their lives, and the sort of activities and principles we would want to support and extend in the environmental field, for example, might include:

1. Expanding countryside management services, which draw together landowners, farmers, conservation interests and voluntary labour, co-ordinated by local authority or special project staff. There are now many success stories and the educational as well as the practical value of such work is apparent to all sides.[13]

2. Developing approaches to mediating conflicts on the urban fringe,

along the lines of the Groundwork model.[14] By combining local and central government resources, community enthusiasm and effort, and business skills and materials all together in partnership, Groundwork demonstrates an increasing recognition of joint responsibility for environmental management.

3. Small scale, less formal arrangements within public agencies for enabling amenity groups to carry out environmental improvement and maintenance. More and more local authorities of all political persuasions are seeing the value of making better use of land that lies derelict and buildings that stand empty.

4. Food production in urban areas. This might be through city farms,[15] or it could be achieved by allowing and encouraging the short- or medium-term use of vacant land through leasing arrangements or management agreements. Besides providing worthwhile work, personal financial savings can be made and contact with fundamental living systems can be re-established.

5. New urban strategies adopted by local authorities, reflecting a strong advocacy role in heightening public awareness and support for environmentally sensitive goods and services. In organizational terms, this might include: 'service delivery' at an appropriate scale; improved living, working and, leisure environments; locally generated employment; and the re-creation of community identity – 'villages in the city'.

6. Experimental forms of community development and decision making, both in urban and rural areas. The Town and Country Planning Association's support for the Divis Flats residents, and the Lightmoor Project[16] in self-build housing are but two examples of organization and support to enable greater participation and self-reliance.

These people-based initiatives are an essential component for the creation of identity – the sense and spirit of place; they are a reaction to conventional methods, a frustration that 'big brother' can't or won't help, and that 'do-it-yourself' or 'self-help' is the way forward. All these initiatives, individual or community, represent a transition rather than a transformation of society's values and *modus operandi*, and their net effect is currently small. However, as idiosyncrasy becomes a trend and a trend becomes fashionable, a more coherent pattern of behaviour may well emerge, and, indeed, be facilitated and strengthened by the availability of new 'solar-age' products, services, and attitudes. Until that time, however, 'spread city' and wider society may well see heightened tensions as the issues under debate – of sustainable development against undirected growth, of greater local and regional self-reliance compared with global exploitation, of participation and enablement rather than paternalistic and centralized control – become the subject of increasingly polarized views.

In the meantime, however, can we do more than simply support isolated initiatives? As planners from Hertfordshire, we can perhaps draw on our county's experience as the birthplace of garden cities, and identify the need for a balanced relationship between 'town' and 'country'. In developing his ideas for garden cities 100 years ago, Ebenezer Howard[17] clearly recognized the importance to the human psyche of a balance of town and country living. He recognized the pluses and minuses of both situations – that cities offered concentrations of poverty as well as wealth, crime as well as justice, disease as well as medicine, and so on; and the country offered a lack of society and a few amenities, as well as natural beauty. Writing in an essay in 1945 to introduce a later edition of Howard's 1898 book *Garden Cities of Tomorrow*, Lewis Mumford came to a conclusion that still has considerable relevance today for the issues we have discussed:

> Howard's ideas have laid the foundation for a new cycle in urban civilisation: one in which the means of life will be subservient to the purposes of living, and in which the pattern needed for biological survival and economic efficiency will likewise lead to social and personal fulfilment.[18]

The notion of 'spread city' may therefore be a modern form of Ebenezer Howard's 'social city' – the idea of a regional network of free-standing settlements, the garden cities, recognizing the intimate inter-relationships between them all. The context may have changed in the century since Howard's first exposition of the ideas, but the lineage is still apparent. Town and country, although aesthetically distinguishable, are operationally united. Small towns are set in well husbanded countryside, with an extraordinarily high variety of activities and social forms throughout. In terms of appearance and land-use distribution, urban and urban-related land uses (including villages) may cover perhaps 20 per cent of the area; agriculture for food and other types of countryside product (e.g. forestry, biomass for fuel) covering perhaps a further 50 per cent; and countryside for leisure, wildlife, wilderness, and access filling covering the remainder. Everywhere, principles of greater local reliance and genuine community participation will be crucial catalytic forces within the chemistry of change. This is the future for which we will plan.

Conclusions

Change is ever present. From a multitude of transitions, we have selected and merely touched upon a few, without doing justice to the complexity and inter-connectedness of all the changes that are taking place around us, locally, nationally, and globally. But dealing with complexity and burgeoning knowledge will continue to be part of the human condition as we move into the future. One of the problems, we would argue, has been the belief that specialization and expertise is the only way to handle ever increasing levels of knowledge. This lack of an overview, the failure to make connections across subjects and between places, has led us to our present, perhaps perilous state. So, our selectivity and superficiality are perhaps defensible if we can justifiably claim that we have applied wisdom and vision to our understanding; and we hope we can!

What then have we learnt from our travels in this chapter that may be useful preparation for the longer metaphorical journey we anticipated earlier – the future for human habitation on Planet Earth. First, we clearly recognize that in much of the developed world, the relationship between city and countryside is shifting such that the distinction between town and country, city, and village, may be irrelevant: they may look different and are physically separate, but with modern communication and telecommunications they are intimately and operationally linked.

This leads us on to a second conclusion – that in recognizing our interconnectedness (internationally as much as locally), we have to realize that we are all in this together. Ultimately, it is in our own interests to look after the interests of other peoples and other places. We have to seek out 'win – win' situations, which means recognizing that costs to others may well cost us too, unless we take responsibility – individually and organizationally – for the wider, not always obvious consequences of our actions. *Our* objectives and hence our actions may then change, which leads us to the third point.

We cannot passively 'stumble backwards into the future', dragged by market forces, by an economic system that can rarely see further than the next election, no wider than the formal economy, and no deeper than money as a measure of value. We must do more than merely accommodate trends, we have to recognize resource limits and human needs – for participation as well as for pounds, for choice as well as chops! We need to establish principles by which the wider interrelationships mentioned above can be acknowledged, and then we can advocate directions of change that enable sustainable development, increased self-reliance, and personal development in material and non-material ways.

Our fourth conclusion is some scepticism, but also some optimism, that what is happening in the south-east of England is the physical manifestation of a mix of old and new values, patterns of work, styles of living, and people-based community development. James

Robertson[19] has suggested that as we move to a post-industrial age, we will see evidence of three styles of working – basically, 'business-as-usual', a high-tech employment and leisure society, and 'Ownwork', akin to Charles Handy's more hopeful view of future work. In the south-east of England in 1987, these sorts of transitional characteristics are apparent, although not in equal proportions. 'spread city' may be a fact, or it may be an academic fiction, but whatever is happening, our earlier conclusions point to the need for positive advocacy if 'spread city' is not to become 'middle-age-spread city' or 'senile city'!

Our fifth conclusion, therefore, is the need to re-affirm governmental support in enabling and enhancing community initiatives. This may mean highly localized service delivery; it may mean helping initiate, fund, and manage good ideas; and it may mean the development and application of locally derived regulatory controls on a whole range of ecological criteria – on pollution, energy efficiency, habitat improvement, and so on.

The last conclusion is that we should not be either bold enough to suggest that what is happening in the south-east of England will happen elsewhere, or arrogant enough to imply that our answers are universally applicable. All we would say is that 'spread city' is a child of its time – that the raw material is a city which has evolved from a nineteenth-century economy and has the physical artefacts of that period to go with it, which together dictate the need for a 'next-generation' settlement response. The form and shape of 'spread city' can vary; design, by professionals working with the community, can make it something positive. But design is culture-specific, and so the south-east of England will clearly not be a universal model. As Oyama points out, different societies are at different stages of cultural and economic development, and have different values, and different political systems. 'Spread city' will not happen everywhere, and these societal differences will also mean that, intrinsically, and quite rightly, local responses rather than universal solutions are called for in managing future city form.

Notes and references

1. Barras, R. (1987) 'Technical changes and the urban development cycle', *Urban Studies* 24 (1) February: 5–30
2. Handy, C. (1987) 'The future of work – the new Agenda', *Journal of the Royal Society of Arts*, June: 515–25.
3. Champion, A.G., Green, A.E., Owen, D.W., Ellin, D.J., and Coombes, M.G. (1987) *Changing Places: Britain's Demographic, Economic and Social Complexion*, London: Edward Arnold.
4. Gershuny, J.I. (1987) 'Lifestyle, innovation and the future of work', *Journal of The Royal Society of Arts*, June: 492–502.
5. Roberston, J. (1985) *Future Work*, London: Temple Smith/Gower.

6. Handy, C., op. cit., n. 2.
7. Illich, I. (1973) *Tools for Conviviality*, London: Calder & Boyars.
8. Oyama, Y. (1987). Many of the points we have summarized were presented by Yoshihiko Oyoma to the conference on 'Future Cities' at Oxford in April 1987. The paper was entitled 'The urbanization of Japan – construction or destruction?'
9. Hodges, D. and Arden-Clarke, C. (1986) *Soil Erosion in Britain: Levels of Soil Damage and their Relationship to Farming Practices*, published by the Soil Association, 86–88 Colston Street, Bristol, Avon BS1 5BB.
10. Countryside Policy Review Panel (1987) *New Opportunities for the Countryside*, Countryside Commission.
11. Seymour, J. and Girardet, H. (1987) *Blueprint for a Green Planet*, Dorling Kindersley.
12. Munn, J.M. (1987). The ideas we have discussed were contained in a paper made available for the 'Future Cities' conference at Oxford. The paper was entitled 'Leisure services in post industrial society'.
13. Hertfordshire County Council. The County Planning and Estates Department has operated a Countryside Management Service for over a decade and considerable experience has now been developed on community partnership, practical action, staff training, equipment, and funding. Full training, equipment, and funding. Full details can be obtained by writing to the Countryside Management Service at County Hall, Hertford, Hertfordshire SG13 8DN. For other areas, information is available through the countryside Commission.
14. The Groundwork Foundation can be contacted at: Bennett's Court, 6 Bennett's Hill, Birmingham B2 5ST.
15. *City Farmer* is a quarterly magazine for community gardeners and city farmers and is available from: National Federation of City Farms Limited, The Old Vicarage, 66 Fraser Street, Windmill Hill, Bedminster, Bristol BS3 4LY. There are currently some eighty city farms in Britain.
16. Full details about how the Lightmoor Project was set up and is currently operating can be obtained from: The Town and Country Planning Association, 17 Carlton House Terrace, London SW1Y 5AS.
17. Howard, E. (1946) *Garden Cities of Tomorrow* (ed. by F.J. Osborn), London: Faber & Faber. (originally published in 1898.) The Faber edition has a very useful introductory essay by Lewis Mumford
18. Mumford, L., in Howard, E., op. cit., n. 17.
19. Robertson, J., op. cit., n. 5.

Chapter 7

Mad Maurice III: Metropolitans in the making[1]

Joe Cullen

Joe Cullen brings us down to the level of the citizen. With the eye of the sociologist, and in a style full of colour and literary reference, Cullen begins to throw some light upon the meaning of the city and citizenship. Linking the tragedy of Faust to the tragedy of urban development, he questions the primacy of conventional rationalism in general and economic determinism in particular. For Cullen, the 'base line' of urbanization is discovered in an examination of the nature of power. Drawing upon the theories of Foucault and the writings of Koestler, he posits a clash between city structures and existential action, between 'fixed rules and flexible strategies'. For him, the future of the city must be about the ways in which relationships of power are resolved. For the citizen there will be winners and losers.

Joe Cullen has researched, taught and written on a wide range of subjects, including environmental psychology, work and labour organization, artificial intelligence and urban sociology. He has worked at the University of Cambridge, the Open University, the Polytechnic of North London and, latterly, Loughborough University, where he was a Research Fellow in the Department of Social Sciences. He is currently working as a Senior Analyst for Property Market Analysis in London.

Introduction

Before large cities were invented, people, we are led to believe, enjoyed a symbiotic relationship with their environment. True, this relationship largely consisted of a wary accommodation to the forces of nature, but its hallmark was penetrability. Through the long and painstaking ecological process of creating *genre de vie*, rules governing man–environment relationships became enshrined within a historical continuity. The mechanisms and media through which this became possible have been analysed in a wide range of perspectives, among them Jungian psychology and linguistic structuralism.[2] Their currency – the totems containing coded blueprints to explain the world; vocabularies rich in the symbolism of the seasons; architecture depicting the lexicon of cosmic forces – suggests a deep understanding of sense of place. At the same time, it suggests that the narrative of the land and that of the human was seamless: the human existent was embedded in nature.

Urbanization appears as a cold shower on this sunny tranquillity, yet at the same time, like all sudden dousings, it stimulates. As the mass production machine lumbers across the land, drawing in people here and spewing them out there to create vast concentrations of humanity in burgeoning cities, it brought with it a quickening of the collective pulse. The sense of excitement, of standing on the edge of limitless possibilities that industrialization ushered in, is inscribed in the concrete artefacts of the period when capitalism was at its most vociferous: the proliferation of inventions, the shrinking of spatial and temporal boundaries, the dissemination of the products of mass consumption. Its cultural corollary – the imagery of urbanization – has been expressed in the idea of modernism, the shock of the new, and it, too, embraced a clear conviction: that the emerging modern city was an essentially liberating form. It provided a mechanism to escape being shackled to the land.

Right at the outset, then, the modern city posed a contradiction. On the one hand, it offered the allure of liberating practices. On the other, it cleaved a shocking disconnection between an age-old order and a brave new world. Already the distinction was being drawn between the idea of community, focused on intimate relationships with 'natural' environments, and society, focused on the amorphous social relations of the industrial city. Such a duality was there at the birth of sociology, in Durkheim's dichotomy of organic and mechanical solidarity; in Tonnies' distinction between *gemeinschaft* and *gesellschaft,* and in Weber's concept of traditional and rational forms of domination. Their message, that the unholy alliance between urbanization and capitalism contrives a separation of the intimate relationship between labour and community, has remained an enduring legacy. In literature, as Raymond Williams points out, this sense of atomism became a powerful metaphor, exemplified in Dickens' portrayal of individuals swallowed up in vast industrial maws like Coketown, ingrained in the hankering for a lost rural innocence imagined in the work of the Lakeland poets.[3]

The duality of citizenship

The transition between rural and urban life provoked a sort of collective schizophrenia, and has been marked ever since by a prolonged search to find the nature of citizenship. The concept of 'duality' became an alluring frame of reference within which to consider it, and citizenship is frequently expressed in an almost stylized compartmentalization of 'capitalism' and 'culture'. Thomas, in his work on the nature of 'life spaces' and their potential for supplying a soothing palliative to the atomism of urban life, draws a distinction between people's social and economic spaces.[4] Friedmann, as Thomas points out, portrays a tale of two cities, focused on the dual modes of 'economic space' and 'life space':

> Together the two constitute a unity of opposites, and although both are necessary for the sustenance of modern societies, they are inherently in conflict with each other.

For Friedmann, life space is the theatre of life (the convivial life of families and communities), whereas economic life embraces the narrow channels of securing basic essentials. He suggests that economic space imposes itself on life spaces in a way which is all too often capable of dominating the life space.[5]

This perception of the city as some giant carnivore, gobbling up communities at an accelerating rate and belching out the bones in the form of shrivelled ghettos, has prompted some serious soul searching. In a review of the city which unceremoniously equated urban economic and spiritual decay with monetarist policies, the Archbishop of Canterbury's Study Group, 'Faith in the City', has once again underscored the colonization of community by capitalism.[6]

Other writers, borrowing lavishly from the existential tradition in philosophy, have identified a tendency for people to become immersed in development and construction in order to stave off the terror of contemplating their own mortality. Naturally, existential preoccupations have been aired most frequently in America, that most anxious and insecure of cultures. Relph, in his description of the 'placelessness' of contemporary American urban society, seems to suggest a nation of refugees, desperate for a history, lacking in cultural substance and clinging on to Disney for comfort.[7] Ann Buttimer, in her discussion of the concept of 'inauthenticity', paints a similarly tacky vision of the American Way, with its celebration of ephemerality and disposability.[8] There is the clear influence of Heidegger in this polemic, with its emphasis on the 'lack of concern' implicit in the construction of modern urban habitats. There is also the suggestion that the contemporary urban dweller responds in a similarly empty fashion. In Tuan's analysis of the behaviour of contemporary home-owners,[9] human behaviour is presented as a frenetic, fearful deployment of 'objects' in order to build cocoons to shield people from existential storms, an analysis which is rooted in Sartrian concepts of 'reification'.[10] Marcel's portrayal of the 'acquisitiveness' of western culture, with its overtones of Marx's 'fetishism with commodities', interprets the conspicuous consumption inherent in urban life as a desire to fill existential void with 'thing-like traits'.[11]

One thing is clear. The great liberating force of urbanization, bringing with it the capacity to change nature through the forces of production, has eroded the nature of citizenship. Urbanization plucked people from place and deposited them in placelessness. The essential angst of modernism, this sense of displacement, is part of the tragedy of development. In his influential book on the experience of modernity, Marshall Berman tries to analyse the nature of a great twentieth-century obsession: the pre-occupation with development.[12] He does so by dissecting one of the most powerful literary symbols in modernist thought: Goethe's Faustian myth. In Faust's third and final metamorphosis, he

connects his personal drives with the economic, political and social forces which drive the world: he learns to build and to destroy. He expands the horizon of his being from private to public life, from intimacy to activism, from communion to organisation.

He achieves this by developing things; by harnessing the forces of nature through machines; by mobilizing the species through the division of labour to create vast earth-shaking projects; by building awesome cities. By so doing, Faust precipitates crucial changes in forms of economic, social, and ideological production.

As Berman points out, the tragedy of Faust is the tragedy of development. In order to achieve his vision, Faust throws himself and his subjects into a ruthless programme of construction. The comparisons with Stalin's mobilization of the masses to build the post-revolutionary Soviets are uncomfortably apposite:

Daily they would vainly storm,
Pick and shovel, stroke for stroke;
Where the flames would nightly swarm
Was a dam when we awoke.
Human sacrifices bled,
Tortured screams would pierce the night,
And where blazes seaward spread
A canal would greet the light.[13]

Yet the legacy of this process of development is dialectical. Out of the suffering comes progress; the construction of the dam breeds a new community in which men and women can feel proud. The modernization of the material world, as Berman points out, is a sublime spiritual achievement. The denouement of the tragedy, where, in order to remove the last obstacle to progress, Faust engineers the death of Philemon and Baucis and the obliteration of their archaic small-holding, has been interpreted in endless permutations by Goethe's successors. Anti-Marxists refer to Faust's own death in the face of the guilt personified by Philemon and Baucis as a sort of biblical casting-out of the godless totalitarian. Marxist interpretations allude to the tragedy of the capitalist process, Lukacs, for example, arguing that the last act of Faust is a tragedy of capitalist development in its early industrial phase.[14] Perhaps more topical, as Berman argues, is the interpretation attached to the myth by the contemporary ecological movement, where Schumacher's exhortation to 'think small' re-states the Faustian tragedy in terms of the destructive, de-humanized nature of modern corporate enterprise.

Rational Man

One of the supreme ironies in the tragedy of development has been the imposition of a rigidity and uniformity of life style based on a misplaced notion of 'Rational man'. The realization that Modernity could for the first time radically transform the environment through the practical application of scientific laws was accompanied by a similarly unquenchable belief in the capacity of Scientism to transform human behaviour. Urban Utopianism was the concrete outcome of this strand of thought, and it reached its zenith in Courbuserian design and post-war urban planning.

The trouble with Courbusier's grand design is its singularly misplaced faith in the capacity of architectonics to uplift, spiritually, morally, and materially, the human existent: the classic delusion of seeing angels in the architecture. This assumption has a thoroughbred pedigree, stretching back at least to Plato. It is not the intention of this chapter to describe in detail the nature and history of this Platonic tradition, which are covered by this author elsewhere,[15] but there are obvious key landmarks. The Copernican revolution; Kant and the classical empiricists' strenuous efforts to translate the categorical nature of Rationality into a physiological reality (via analogy with the brain's cognitive processes); the development of behaviourist psychology focused on a stimulus–response view of human interaction with environment – are crucial philosophical watersheds. In Pirsig's painfully personal critique, *Zen and the Art of Motor Cycle Maintenance,* the 'Church of Reason' becomes a key metaphor for the individual and collective palsy of western culture.[16] For Heidegger, the roots of western cultural malaise, expressed in our tendency to think and act in 'deficient modes of concern', lie in the bedrock of western philosophy: the Platonic separation between 'form' and 'substance' and the emergence of Rationality as the definitive philosophical construct.[17] What is even more visible is the material legacy of determinism, in the form of almost the entire portfolio of post-war urban construction. Environmental determinism was Rationalism in bricks and motar, with all the attendant political dressing of the philosophical orthodoxy. Because it preached the dogma that poor environments produce poor minds and negative stimuli produce negative responses, it provided a perfect foil for the dominant class's anxieties. Hooked on the stimulus–response syndrome and unshakably convinced that Nirvana could be accomplished through mastery of the material world: through technics; the separation of 'form' from 'substance' and the enslavement of the material by Reason, twentieth-century planners and politicians set out to create a spiritual Heaven on earth with the aid of architectonics.

The tradition permeates prescriptive blueprints about what the city should be. Implicit in Plato's plans for the 'just city', Campanella's plaintive 'city of the sun'; the creeping paternalism of Victorian tied-town philanthropy, which reached its zenith in the contemporary town-planning movement, is an unyielding faith in architectural determinism.

There is no doubt that a substantial part of such urban Utopianism is dedicated to political design.[18] Undercutting Titus Salt's provision of salubrious architecture for the workers is a deep-seated unease about urban insurrection. As Ruth Glass points out, so long as the poor were huddled together in large cities, so long as they shared the stink of degradation, the more fitfully the exploiting classes slept in their beds at night.[19] By providing sanitary housing, paternalists like Leverhulme and Cadbury, along with their institutional successors, could, first, reproduce labour power more efficiently, by improving material conditions for their factory fodder. Second, they could splinter the homogeneity of working-class culture by a process of spatial segregation, thereby neutralizing the potentially fatal fostering of working-class consciousness. Third, they were galvanized by a belief in the spiritual healing powers of Urban Utopia. If the environment and the hereditary fecklessness of the working class were improved, its natural tendency to wallow in the sty would be replaced by Spiritual Salvation. As Victorian solidity passed into twentieth-century Modernism – 'all that is solid melts into air' – the cherished icons remained. Behind Corbusier's unctuous espousal of the architecture of democracy is an incipient totalitarianism which, with its preoccupations with the 'death of the street' and its sanitizing of the ordure of human occupation, finds expression in arid habitats like Brasillia: the artificial heart of Brazil.

Rationalism and riots

During the 1950s, through the influential work of theorists like Newson and Newson, who suggested that poor, working class urban environements created a 'might is right' and 'backs to the wall' syndrome, there was a resurgence of the old fears that had besotted the dominant economic and social elite. Faced with the possibility of some 'unspeakable revolution' in the inner urban swamps it had created, the elite moved to counter that threat. With Reason on its side, the elite mounted a devastating blitzkrieg, razing to the ground the habitats that were responsible for generating dangerous counter-ideologies and engineering an exodus of people from seedy, debilitating (and difficult to police) communities in the inner city to sanitized, edifying (and easier to control) estates.[20]

In the next decade or so it became apparent just how successful the Rationalist crusade had been. First there was the rejection of the symbols of Rationality, epitomized by the demolition of edifices like Pruit-Ighoe. As Charles Jencks observes, this celebrated, award-winning St Louis housing estate contained all the things to which architectural determinism aspired, with: a Purist style; a clean, salubrious hospital metaphor that was meant to instil, by good example, corresponding virtues in the inhabitants. The meaning of that metaphor became clearer on the 15th July 1972 when, vandalized, disfigured, and utterly rejected by the recipients of its gifts, Pruit-Ighoe was atomized by demolition experts called in by the City Council.[21] Despite attempts to adopt a more pragmatic approach, an enthusiastic acceptance of Oscar Newman's 'defensible space' strategy being an obvious example, despite its tendency to shift urban pathologies elsewhere – civic authorities have remained impotent in the face of people's rough treatment of carefully-designed public housing projects.[22]

After the sybolism came the rejection of the Edifice itself. Following the precedent set by American cities previously, Britain discovered urban riots. In Brixton, Southall, Bristol, and Toxteth, the air cracked to the sound of street hostilities, punctuated by carbon-copy rioting in more tranquil backwaters, as spotty blazer-clad youths hurled chunks of masonry at shop windows in suburban malls. Notwithstanding a fairly well-furrowed track record in these matters (the Chartist riots; Peterloo; the played-down continuity of Belfast street warfare), the establishment reacted as if thunderstruck. The nation pondered. In the Street of Shame, the polemic dripped heavily off the presses like hot fondue, as editors scrabbled unashamedly for Belgrano-like hyperbole. Throughout the aftermath of the riots, pundits, planners, politicians, sages, and sociologists strained and squatted over the problem until a vast guano heap of conjecture was generated. It contained the usual elements of the vilification, resentment, and invective that is normally hurled at the city at such moments of crisis. Once again, the city was on trial, accused of failing to deliver Utopia.

In Jonathan Raban's words:

> The city has always been an embodiment of hope and a source of festering quilt; a dream pursued and found vain, wanting and

destructive. Our current mood of revulsion against cities is not new; we have grown used to looking for Utopia only to discover that we have created Hell.[23]

Though *Soft City* was written over a decade ago, before Britain's well-publicized 'urban riots', Raban's observations on the tendency to take for granted the problematic nature of the city, to envisage it as a suitable case for treatment, are still relevant. There exists a vast body of literature on the city as hell, one which simultaneously acknowledges its capacity to soar like an angel. Phrases such as 'cause for concern' and 'urban crisis' reflect this seemingly inescapable preoccupation with its Janus face (and, by implication, the polarized nature of its human creators). The crucial point is that, underlying the problematizing, is an unshakable belief in the resolution of that polarization; in the reconciliation of opposites; in the triumph of light over dark – all via the supremacy of Rationality.

Economic determinism

This reification of Rational Man in Urban Utopia has also been counterpointed by the notion of Economic Determinism. The connection between urbanisation and forms of economic production and organization is of course inescapable. In its clearest expression, the classic Marxist position is re-iterated in, for example, David Harvey's contention that the city is capital made concrete, and that its meaning is fundamentally determined by property relations.[24] For the French school of Urban Sociology, perhaps best expressed in the work of Manuel Castells, the city, in its expression as the local state, has come to represent the front line in the class struggle. The old basis of class stucture, argues Castells, has been displaced into specifically urban struggles. As the state and the local authorities have increasingly stepped in to organize the reproduction of labour power and provide opportunities for the circulation of capital (via, for example, massive housing and infrastructure programmes) so they come to be seen as the visible agencies of social inequality, when they fail to provide the goods and services people need. Where before, the exploited could point only to an amorphous, undifferentiated 'system', they can now blame the local state when it closes down the only primary school within miles or drives a six-lane motorway throughout their allotments. The result of this displacement of the contradictions of capitalism into urban crisis, suggests Castells, is the blurring of class lines, and the formation of a sort of 'urbanteriat', held together by the common bonds of location and exploitation. Result: the formation of squatters associations, the ecology movement, and the onset of demonstrations and riots in the inner cities.[25] Yet other theorists argue that it is precisely this disaggregation of the power relations into the local state, into the city, that has neutralized the revolution.

As we have seen, the emerging structure of the modern city, whilst creating hot-bed conditions for insurrection by concentrating the masses within spatial production loci, also drew its sting by controlling the spatial dynamics of social stratification. It also created an immensely powerful mechanism for anaesthetizing critical ideologies. It managed to do this by harnessing the capacity of the city to act as a vehicle for the transmission of consumption, both of ideas and of artefacts. The city became, in Jonathan Raban's memorable term an 'emporium of styles'.

The shift from production to consumption functions emphasized in Castells' analysis of the modern city is inherent not only within the key structures of political economy. It pervades right down to the actions of individuals. As Harvey argues, the capitalist city provides a new regime of consumption and accumulation which combines spatial dispersal and mobility, and flexibility in labour markets, labour processes, and consumer markets, whilst being tightly controlled by management systems operating powerful information agencies to monitor and respond to markets.[26] The increasing stranglehold imposed by multi-national corporations on consumer patterns, exemplified in Robin Murray's analysis of Benetton, implies a new imperialism of taste.[27] Although Benetton's tacky slogan (the 'United Colours of Benetton') is hardly world domination, it isn't the harmless soft sell the admen want to project. The alarming inroads that intensifying consumption make on people's consciousness have long been established. The attempts of Marcuse and Gramsci to explain the failure of the revolution in terms of the erosion of critical ideology by consumerism (the onset of the age of 'bourgeois hegemony') were unerring.[28] What the modern city has accomplished, with its proliferation of cotton-wool comforters, its increasingly precious exactness of style, its endless boulevards of DIY emporiums and garden centres, could well be expressed in the words of John Fowles: 'the triumph of the eunuch'.[29]

Thomas, in his discussion of the work of a group known as Situationist International, paints a similar picture. The Situationists described the totality of domination by the new type of capitalism as the 'Society of the Spectacle'. As production becomes concentrated within the hands of giant corporations, their control over consumption is steadily increased. At the same time, a process of consumption transformation is taking place, where millions of individual consumer actions are being structured into 'spectacular life styles'. Attention is diverted from the internal contradictions of capitalism into a kaleidoscope of fashions, crazes, movements. This gives the impression of real innovation, whilst its true purpose is to absorb revolutionary proposals and convert them into harmless images.[30]

In this scenario, the nature of citizenship within the modern western metropolis becomes singularly one-dimensional. If some biogeneticist was briefed to produce a humanoid capable of surviving in the hostile terrain of the city of the 1990s, the outcome would be rather less apocalyptic than that which some of our most enduring celluloid images of urban angst suggests. Instead of Mel Gibson and Tina Turner, our urban son of Frankenstein would more likely emerge dressed by Next, fixtured by Conran and life styled by the Saatchis. As post-capitalist organization merges with urban process into the sort of seamless order predicted by writers like Lefebvre, what chance is there for the urban dweller to reach any kind of existential integrity?[31]

In the final analysis, the base line of urbanization is power relations, and no contemporary theoretician has done more to pinpoint the nature of power in Society than Michel Foucault.

The institutionalization of citizenship

Foucault has been called many things, most of them contradictory. He is both Marxist and anti-Marxist; radical and authoritarian; described on the one hand as being 'obsessed with ... totalities [developing them] with sadistic flourishes', and on the other as 'the most creative thinker this century'. Foucault's main theme is the regulation and control of the individual via the institutionalization of power. Like Goffman, Foucault is preoccupied with the historical development of 'total institutions', such as correction houses and hospitals. In keeping with this slant Foucault's interpretation of space, architecture, and urbanization is geared to their function in relation to the imposition of power relations and structures. In an interview with Paul Rainbow, Foucault talks about the 'politicization' of architecture as becoming only truly penetrating in the eighteenth century. Prior to that period, treatises on the art and forms of government contained very little references to arcitecture and space. During the eighteenth century, political treatises became preoccupied with architecture and space, and, more significantly, bracketed these concerns with 'control', particularly in relation to the concept of 'policing'.

For Foucault, the concept of 'police' occupies a special historical category, its meaning signifying a programme of government rationality; a system for the regulation and control of individuals. The city began to serve as a model for such a programme, implying that the regulation of its street patterns, its capacity for 'policing', could be extended throughout the whole state territory. The city thus became a metaphor for territory and how to govern it. The function of architecture and architects within this model was both to impose a detailed set of coercive structures for control (in the construction of institutions) and a generalized set of parameters for the total institutionalization of power relations. Foucault believes, however, that the impact of new technologies in the later capitalist period has diluted the impact of 'architects' in the formation of power relations and structures. The agencies of control in contemporary social life in relation to the appropriation of space are engineers and technicians, epitomized by the 'Ecole des Ponts et Chausées' in France.[32]

Foucault's analysis of the role of architecture, space, and urbanization is a radically different proposition from that embraced by modernism. In its most extreme form, in the great release of energy generated, for example, by Russian constructivism, Tatlin's massive urban sculptures enshrined a genuine belief in the capacity of architectonics to liberate the human species. Similarly, the architecture of the Bauhaus continues a tradition, developed by the Victorian paternalists, of anticipated spiritual re-generation through the mastery of materials and technics.

For Foucault, this kind of script is fantasy. Architectural determinism is fallacious, It cannot succeed. There is nothing inherent in the structure of things to guarantee freedom. Essentially, The guarantee of freedom is freedom. The city, its built form and the practices of those who sculpt that form will largely conspire to impose those rigidities essential for the rationalization of control over individuals. Sometimes, as in Gaudin's design of worker's housing, architecture can create conditions under which the operation of liberating practices can be facilitated a little.

Architecture cannot, however, be liberating in itself. Neither can the operation and the pursuit of Rationality. Yet we remain hooked on Reason and, in its prescriptive form, the idea of Progress. We get obsessed with the idea of the City as the vehicle of Transformation; we brood fretfully over its failure to conform to our recipes for Utopia; we feel assured of the capacity of Rationality to offer solutions to its 'problematic'. Yet, as Jonathan Raban points out: 'We need, more urgently than urban Utopias, to contemplate the nature of citizenship.'[33]

Comedy and praxis

One might be forgiven for coming to the conclusion that citizenship in the modern metropolis is an endless prostration to consumption, but the picture is a little more complex.

There's a story doing the rounds in downtown Liverpool of the hit-and-run docker. Found bleeding and near-comatose by a passerby in a city street one night, the unfortunate victim is consoled by his chance samaritan. Perceiving death to be imminent, the passer-by hurries off to summon ambulance and priest and returns to the victim, stooping down to whisper in his ear. 'Sorry, kiddo', says the samaritan, 'There's not a lot we can do for youse. But there's something really important I've got to ask youse before you go'. The victim stirs mournfully. 'What's that?' he croaks through pain-clenched teeth. 'Can I have yer job?'

In pillaged, emasculated Merseyside, post-Toxteth, post-Heseltine and post-Hatton, the dockyards have gone, along with the jobs and the politicians, but the humour remains constant, like gravediggers' skills. The laconic put-down; the street-cred summation of the mysteries of life is the currency of working-class urban culture. Billy Connolly, professional Glaswegian comic and urban sage maintains that the mainsprings of true humour are found in predominantly working-class urban areas: in Glasgow, Liverpool, Tyneside, and London's East End. On the surface, the punch-lines appear bitter and sterile, born out of deprivation, exploitation and an enduringly pessimistic experience. And so they are. It would be presumptuous to play down the painful realities of unemployment, bad housing, crumbling schools, infested hospitals; the hollow promises of polticians and the platitudes of pundits. Yet it would be just as presumptuous to attribute a crippling negativity to such expressions. The story epitomises not the resigned stoicism of the ox nor the dark cynicism of the gallows but an essentially creative and constructive response to urban realities, one which Arthur Koestler would have appreciated.

In *The Act of Creation,* and later in *The Ghost in the Machine,*[34] Koestler attempts to define, amongst other things, the nature of humour and innovation, the two mechanisms being linked by what he terms the 'ah ha/ha ha' syndrome. At the risk of oversimplifying his imaginative and erudite discourse, the gist of Koestler's analysis is that the inherently restless, volatile, questioning nature of the human condition comes constantly into abrasive contact with the fixed material universe of structures which that species creates. The resultant clash of irresistible force and immovable object is singularly creative. One possible result of the clash is humour; another is innovation, what Koestler terms the Eureka principle; the mainspring of discovery and radical transformation.[35]

According to Koestler, the essence of human behaviour is not so much Pavlov as Alan Bennett. We are not salivating dogs responding as automatons to the sound of the buzzer, but actors and manipulators. And our basic nature is not a slavish adherence to the script but an essential ad-libbing. Koestler's target, at which he aimed his formidable powers of analysis, was the pervading influence of determinism. Understandably, in view of his incarceration in Fascist concentration camps, he raged against those who would reduce the marvellous flexibility of the human condition to slot-machine status, and he vented considerable spleen on those philosophies which supported them. Following the early Gestaltists like Tolman,[36] Koestler removes from the rats the burden of blind subservience to the cage which surrounds them and imposes instead a capacity to manipulate those surroundings, despite their iron constraints. The rats, says Koestler, adopt 'flexible strategies' in response to 'fixed rules'.

In the city, the adoption of such strategies is a statement of everyday life; an essential 'act of creation'. Nowhere are they more resonant than in the marginal areas of large urban conglomerations. In the bidonvilles of Santiago, La Paz and Calcutta, Corbusier's ghost treads gingerly; flits sheepishly past cascades of corrugated iron high-rise; is mocked by the crudity of improvised 'Unité d'habitation'. Compared with the prissiness of Corbusier's grand schemes for the 'architecture of democracy', the audacity of garbage-can bidonville architecture is breathtaking, not least in its unashamed embrace between unbridled poverty and conspicuous consumption. Hey Carlos, wanna hear my new stereo? Hold these wires while I shin up the electricity pylon.

The city cannot deny its roots within the mechanisms which determine modes of economic integration and forms of production. Yet the role ascribed to the human existent withing classic Marxist interpretations of urbanization adopts a singularly deterministic slant: just as debilitating as that espoused by functionalism. As Barratt, the American philosopher, argues: Marxism has no categories for the unique facets of human personality. At the same time, most perspectives which emphasize the plasticity of human experience – its essentially creative nature, its preoccupation with the anxiety of existence – pay scant attention to the critical imperatives of economic formation.[37]

Fixed rules and flexible strategies

One solution to the problem of this dilemma, the clash between structures and existential action is, as we have seen, to adopt the sort of model espoused by Koestler: to interpret human behaviour within the structural form of the city as a continuing interplay between 'fixed rules and flexible strategies'. I believe the nature of this citizenship to be very close to the sort of model described by Foucault. This means an admittedly very strait-jacketed set of fixed rules within which to play out our flexible strategies, but it seems clear that the nature of urbanization is coming more and more to resemble the rationalization of coercive force over the individual. It is a measure of this process of coercion that the roots of British inner-city riots can be traced not only to a facile environmental determinism focused on the part played by bad housing and unemployment but also to the role played by institutional agencies of coercion (the police) in the crushing of alternative urban economies.

As a number of writers of the so-called 'labelling' school of sociology have repeatedly demonstrated, the policeman's lot is constantly to play the role of villain in response to the executive's labelling of what constitutes criminality. Definitions of 'good' and 'bad' are not immutable but vary historically in relation to social, economic, and political influences. The case of laws aimed at curbing the use of drugs is a classic example. At various historical junctures, illegal substances appear and disappear on and off the proscribed list like books in the Vatican library. With monotonous regularity, successive governments access the media and harness it to the law-and-order carriage to create 'folk devils and moral panics'.[38] Inevitably, the police become, to a greater of lesser extent, reluctant instruments in the perpetration of such crusades. On the one hand, pragmatic policing dictates turning a blind eye to a local dealing economy in the interests of social stability. On the other, a sudden shift in the labelling process necessitates an equally violent about face which will more than likely emerge in escalating confrontations and probably riots.

In Handsworth, the mandate given to the police was to crack down on the local drug-based economy which, amplified by a labelling process initiated by the media, was deemed to have become too visibly high profile for comfort. Now it is an entirely reasonable assertion to contend that the police should be in the forefront of a concerted war against narcotics trafficking. But it is also just as reasonable to contend that the development of such an 'alternative' economy can be interpreted in terms of the development of 'liberating structures' designed to encourage similarly liberating practices for those outside the mainstream. In other words, those operating the alternative local economy were adopting, in Koestler's terms, 'flexible strategies' in response to 'fixed rules'. The subtle power structures operating in Handsworth are based on a realistic manipulation of the life chances available to those who are forced to operate outside the mainstream. Riots occur partly as a result of the violent intrusion into that sub-system by society's 'master institutions'. Unlike the classic functionalist argument, which would explain urban rioting in terms of 'anomie' (the attempt by the disadvantaged to realize economic goals denied them by the system), an explanation of urban rioting that is focused on the idea of 'power relations' assumes very little value consensus on the part of groups operating within the urban structure.

We need to recognize this fundamental set of discourses when thinking about the future of our cities. As the pace of technological innovation and diffusion accelerates, so the range of instruments available for the coercion of individuals becomes more diverse. The result for urban citizenship, as Thomas points out, is the subversion of everyday life by capital in its project to create the society of the spectacle and, secondly, the maginalization and impoverishment of large sections of the population for which that society has no use. Thomas, following the arguments of Rustin, goes on to suggest that the pursuit of quality and equality must remain basic to urban society, and that this quality and equality must be enshrined in a legislative framework. The accent here is thus firmly placed on active participation at community level.

The vitality of local institutions and cultures, even in a differentiated society, is critical for forms of social recognition that are within the reach of all citizens, and not just present in the alienated form of national media celebrities.[39]

Future cities

In the face of this complex interplay of forces which shape the destiny of the city, it would be simplistic to talk about the city in terms of a single future. As Jonathan Raban put it:

the city's form is similar to that of the novel and we need the novelist's vision to penetrate it. It is a novel with multiple endings, rooted in the fluidity and flexibility of urban formation, pregnant with the possibilities of many futures, for is not the selling of futures in the literal sense the City's stock in trade?[40]

The accelerating shift in activity from production to marketing, expressed in the increasing ascendancy of financial institutions within the urban economy suggests the wheel coming full circle. There are strong echoes, in the continuing decline of traditional forms of capitalist production, of a return to the city's former parasitic role. The shift in economic formation has been accompanied by the spread and diffusion of new technologies focused on microelectronics. Some observes have interpreted the burgeoning power of information technologies within the urban system as a new phase in the Kondratiev process. A number of functionalist-based theories, developed to explain the effects of such changes on social formation, have emphasized the emergence of an 'information society' based on further specialization of the division of labour. Epitomized by Daniel Bell, such theories assume 'convergence' to be the essential characteristic of a 'post-industrial society' focused on the service industries and channelled through the urban process.[41]

The future envisaged by the post-industrialists is a cosy one. Freed from its crude industrial shackles, elevated by the spread of technical expertise and mass education programmes, society moves from a period racked by archaic class conflicts to a golden age of consensus. The corollary, as portrayed by writers like Ralph Milliband, is much more pessimistic. The pace of technological innovation, far from encouraging a general raising of educational and technical standards, and a corresponding expansion of job opportunities, simply exacerbates a 'de-skilling' process inherent in capitalist enterprise. Post-industrial society, claims Milliband, is a newer and more potent version of the factory system, which appropriated worker's control over the means of production and progressively de-skilled vast sections of society.[42]

Milliband's synopsis raises crucial issues about the role urban formation is increasingly called upon to play in the control of information processes. In Foucault's terms, one might interpret the increasing prominence of City institutions in political, social and life spaces in much the same way as Foucault interpreted the role of 'engineers' in the first half of this century. As the city spreads its tentacles, particularly within the sphere of 'popular capitalism', it provides further opportunities for the rationalization of power over the individual. The spread of interactive communications systems, focused on cable and satellite provision; the installation of remote electronic mail, home banking, and purchasing systems, serves increasingly to 'privatize individuals, isolating them within the minute spatial locus of the home. By contrast, the power of the state and the corporation increases, as the city appropriates functions which before gave individuals at least limited opportunities to indulge in 'liberating practices', via the community and the work-place.

Outside the home, the increasing shrinkage of the production base of the city, accompanied by its increasing concentration in the hands of the state and corporate enterprises, makes it more difficult for alternative economies to flourish. Perhaps the current media hype about city high-flyers snorting coke in the washroom, cutting it with an American Express Gold Card, is no doubt an apt metaphor for the penetration of alternative economies by the urban institution.

The messages sent out by exponents of the new urban wealth signal a radical transformation of the urban economy. The components of this transformation are nowhere better expressed than in the ever increasing list of planning applications submitted to the London Docklands Development Corporation. As developers are handed an increasingly snowier *carte blanche* to transform the skyline into a greyer Kowloon, it becomes more and more obvious that in the city's role as the ever-accommodating purveyor of information, the ever-expanding 'emporium of styles' is outstripping its production base. The plans to substitute what amounts to a gigantic Telecom Gold for what was formerly the City of London are well-advanced. What is less obvious is the way in which these transformations are blurring the boundaries of the city itself. In the final analysis, the name of the game is power relations. If there could be a blueprint for urban survival, its architects ought to be motivated by a concern to create the conditions under which liberating practices might themselves be allowed to flourish.

How this can be achieved is, of course, the big question. The 'two nations – two cities' slogan is just what it is – a slogan. True, there is a rapidly-increasing north–south divide, and this divide is focused on an industrial-service urban dichotomy. But the problem is not simply rooted in simple antidotes like regional funding, it is rooted in power relations. At the ontological level, we are perhaps talking, like Heidegger, of nothing less than the 'dismantling of the entire edifice of western rationalism' which has created our singularly unedifying habitats, and a good dose of intellectual purgative aimed at the 'problem-solving' disciplines of architecture, town planning, and civil engineering is clearly in the frame. In the arena of political economy, it is the institutionalized structure of power relations that stand accused, in terms of both central and local government institutions and their bureaucratization of the individual. Perhaps we are simply re-stating the case for 'community practices' and the restoration of more fluid political structures that are not monopolized by developers, corporate capitalism, and the state apparatchiki. The debate is open; the structures are closed. Meanwhile, if you happen to be walking Merseyside's mean streets, carry a job donor card.

Notes and references

1. This chapter incorporates, in part, the paper entitled 'Everyday life and culture in the city' by Michael Thomas, presented to the 'Future Cities' Conference at Oxford Polytechnic on 23-24 April 1987.
2. Levi-Strauss, C. (1965) *Structural Anthropology*, London.
3. Williams, R. (1974) *Culture and Society*, London.
4. Thomas, M. (1987) op. cit., n. 1.
5. Friedmann, J. (1983) 'Life space and economic space', in D. Seers and K. Ostrom (eds) *The Crisis of European Regimes*, London.
6. Archbishop of Canterbury's Commission (1985) *Faith in the City*, London: Church of England.
7. Relph, E. (1976) *Place and Placelessness*, London: Pion.
8. Buttimer, A. (9176) 'Grasping the dynamism of the life world', *Annals of the Association of American Geographers* 66: 272–92.
9. Tuan, Y.-F. (1972) 'Structuralism, existentialism and environmental perception', *Environment and Behaviour* 4: 319-42.
10. Sartre, J.P. (1960) *Critique de la Raison dialectique*, Paris.
11. Marcel, G. (1950) *The Mystery of Being*, London.

12. Berman, M. (1982) *All that is Solid Melts into Air*, London.
13. Ibid., p. 64.
14. Lukacs, G. (1947) *Goethe and his Age*, London.
15. Cullen, J. and Knox, P. (1982) 'The city, the self and urban society', *Transactions of the Institute of British Geographers* 7: 276–91.
16. Pirsig, R. (1971) *Zen and the Art of Motor Cycle Maintenance*, London.
17. Heidegger, M. (1962) *Being and Time*, London:
18. Cullen, J. and Knox, P. (1981) 'The triumph of the eunuch', *Urban Affairs Quarterly* 17 (2): 149–72.
19. Glass, R. (1968) 'Urban sociology in Britain', in R.E. Pahl (ed.) *Readings in Urban Sociology*, Oxford.
20. Newson, J. and Newson, E. (1965) *Patterns of Infant Care in an Urban Community*, Harmondsworth: Penguin.
21. Jencks, C. (1977) *The Language of Post-Modern Architecture*, London.
22. Newman, O. (1972) *Defensible Space*, New York.
23. Raban, J. (1975) *Soft City*, Harmondsworth: Penguin.
24. Harvey, D. (1973) *Social Justice and the City*, London: Edward Arnold.
25. Castells, M. (1977) *The Urban Question*, London.
26. Harvey, D. (1987) 'Flexible accumulation through urbanisation', paper presented to Yale School of Architecture.
27. Murray, R. (1985) 'Benetton Britain: the new economic order', *Marxism Today* 29: 11.
28. Marcuse, H. (1964) *One Dimensional Man*, London; Gramsci, A. (1971) (trans. by E. Hoare) *Selections from the Prison Notebooks*, London.
29. Fowles, J. (9179) *The Ebony Tower*, Harmondsworth: Penguin.
30. Thomas, op. cit., n. 1.
31. Lefebvre, H. (1972) *La pensée Marxiste et la ville*, Paris.
32. Foucault, M. (1984) 'Space, knowledge and power', in P. Rainbow (ed.) *The Foucault Reader,* Harmondsworth: Penguin.
33. Raban, op. cit., n. 23.
34. Koestler, A. (1967) *The Ghost in the Machine*, London: Hutchinson.
35. Ibid.
36. Tolman, E.C. (1932) *Purposive Behaviour in Men and Animals*, New York.
37. Barrett, W. (1972) *Irrational Man: a study in Existential Philosophy*, London.
38. Rustin, M. (1985) *For a Pluralist Socialism* (1972) London.
39. Thomas, op. cit., n. 1.
40. Raban, op. cit., n. 23.
41. Bell, D. (1973) *The Coming of Post-Industrial Society*, London.
42. Milliband, R. (1969) *The State in Capitalist Society*, London.

Chapter 8

The metabolism of cities

Herbert Girardet

In this Chapter, Herbert Girardet adopts a global view of the future of the city, examining the demands which cities place upon soil fertility and other natural resources and their environmental outputs in the form of solid wastes and air pollutants. He shows that the linear processes by which cities transform environmental resources into waste products is disruptive of the planet's life support systems. As such, a new approach is urgently needed to reorganize the metabolism of cities so that it is more 'circular' and recycles resources to maintain an ecological balance. Girardet lists some of the practical measures which will need to be adopted internationally but should particularly be adopted in the more affluent nations which both cause much of the problem and have the resources to deal with it.

Herbert Girardet graduated from the London School of Economics with a degree in social anthropology. Since 1976 he has specialized in cultural ecology and has written many articles on the human impact on this planet. He has appeared in numerous radio and TV broadcasts in Britain and West Germany. He organized and researched 'Far From Paradise', a seven-part BBC TV series concerned with the history of human impact and the present state of our planet. He co-authored the book of the series. In 1987 he wrote Blueprint for a Green Planet, *with John Seymour, and was consultant on programmes based on the book which were produced for television. He is currently producing 'Jungle Pharmacy' for Central TV and has been commissioned to write a book,* Closing the Circle, *on the long-term ecological consequences of industrial processes.*

Ancient Rome, at the height of its power, obtained much of the grain needed to feed its citizens from North Africa. Its freight ships crisscrossed the Mediterranean laden with the produce of its colonies. As its own land grew tired, and ever more farmers were turned into soldiers, the insatiable appetite of the metropolis could be met only with foodstuffs grown, or robbed, further and further afield.

The role of North Africa as the bread-basket of Rome had profound ecological consequences:

1) As forests were turned into farmland a massive loss of wildlife habitat occurred.

2) Large-scale deforestation resulted in soil erosion and moisture loss from the environment which is still felt today.

3) The export of wheat and other foodstuffs was also an export of soil nutrients, never to be returned. Thus the soil fertility of much of North Africa was shoved through the stomachs of the Romans into the Mediterranean.

Rome, before its decline, reached a population of about 1 million people. At that time it was, by far, the largest – and most powerful – city in the world. Today, just under 2,000 years later, nearly half the world's 5 billion people live in cities; never has urban growth been as rapid as it is today. Everywhere small farmers are leaving – or are forced to leave – the land. Usually relatively self-reliant peasants or herdsmen with a self-interest in caring for the land that feeds them are turned into consumers of cash-crops, as they adopt – or are forced to adopt – their new urban life-style.

We all need food every day, but every meal represents an export of plant nutrients from the land where it was grown, never to be returned. And where does the precious waste end up? Well, in the sea, eventually. This one-way traffic in soil fertility, first practised by the Romans, has now reached global proportions.

In the nineteenth century, when a new world metropolis, London, grew by leaps and bounds, its 'sewage problem' was solved by building an extensive drainage system. The motto was: out of sight, out of mind. As in Rome, the sewage was disposed of into the sea, and not returned to the land. In order to keep Britain's farm land fertile, guano (bird droppings) were shipped over the Atlantic from Chile.

When the guano ran out, scientists came up with artificial fertilizers. Never mind the sewage, they said, we have mineral fertilizers – nitrate, phosphate, potash – in bags. The victory of these mineral fertilizers was overwhelming and, thus, sewage systems in cities all over the world continue being constructed as disposal rather than as recycling systems. Disposal, not recovery, continues to be the brief of most sewage engineers. Thus, much of the fertility of the world's farmland that feeds the teeming billions in the cities ends up in rivers, and finally, in the sea.

Liquid wastes

Because sewage is considered a nuisance, not an asset, it may as well be mixed with whatever else needs to be flushed out – cleaning fluids, disinfectants, chlorinated hydrocarbons, heavy metals, an all the other poisons we now routinely discharge from our households and factories. The Romans didn't do *that,* but we do, and we hardly bat an eyelid. Add a few million gallons of oil every year and you end up with the kind of potent brew that fish now have to cope with in coastal waters world-wide. And, of course, add fertilizers – nitrate, phosphate, potash – from farmland, half of which are not absorbed by the food plants but leached into the ground-water and, eventually, washed out into the sea. And add slurry from our factory farms, much of it originally imported as animal feed from distant lands, and you have another one-way transport of plant nutrients from the farmland to the sea.

In the 1960s and 1970s there was growing concern about the eutrophication of *lakes* in heavily urbanized regions of Europe and North America: that is, loss of oxygen in the surface waters as a result of overfeeding with plant nutrients from sewage, fertilizers and slurry. Lake Erie, in particular, made the headlines. The problems have not really gone away, though some lakes have been improved by the installation of sophisticated sewage works or, even, by pumping oxygen into the water at great expense.

In the 1980s there is growing concern about *costal waters.* The landlocked seas, in particular, such as the Baltic and the Adriatic, are a real worry. Next on the list is the North Sea where eutrophication now occurs every summer in places like the German Byte. Rivers like the Rhine, the Thames, the Elbe, and the Wester all carry huge quantities of plant nutrients with them. (The Rhine alone transports enough nitrates every year potentially to meet the requirements of the whole of Dutch agriculture.) The over-supply of plant nutrients causes the excessive growth of algae and plankton. They are a sort of poisoned bait to the fish because of the ever more varied cocktail of toxins with which they are laced. These are heavily implicated in the rapid increase in fish diseases, notably ulcers and cancers, that have been observed in coastal waters in recent years.

Modern urban metabolism

Contemporary cities have a much more complex metabolism than their ancient predecessors like Babylon, Carthage, Athens or, indeed, Rome. Their impact was largely confined to forests (extraction of timber and firewood), soil (removal of nutrients, erosion, and salination) and water (long range aquaducts, sewage disposal). The archaeologists who excavated these ancient cities did not find any plastics, toxic waste or, indeed, radioactive substances in the rubbish dumps they examined!

In contrast, every inhabitant of a modern western country (typical level of urbanization being 80 to 90 per cent) generates around 2 tons of rubbish per year: 1 ton of domestic refuse and 1 ton of factory waste from the industrial products we all purchase. Future archaeologists investigating the waste dumps of late twentieth-century cities will be astounded at the sheer volume of artefacts, as well as the bizarre mixture of materials, that we saw fit to use and, indeed, to dispose of.

Urban and industrial rubbish dumps piled up over recent decades pose an environmental hazard whose scale is, as yet, inadequately understood. It is becoming quite apparent now that 'ordinary' domestic rubbish is far from harmless. The problems range from seepage of potentially toxic liquids like disinfectants, wood preservatives, cleaning fluids, used motor oil and medicines left in part-filled containers, to corrosion of discarded batteries and the accidental incineration of plastics. Waste dumps invariably give off toxic fumes as they catch fire, which they often do.

Factory wastes, an essential ingredient of our consumer way of life, are often deposited in the same dump as household rubbish and greatly add to its pollution potential. In one area of the USA alone, in New Jersey, where the problem of waste dumps has been investigated quite thoroughly, hundreds of mixed waste dumps have been found to leach all manner of potent poisons into the groundwater. In West Germany similar problems have now been unearthed in many places. In Hamburg the notorious Georgswerder dump leaked a great variety of pesticide residues, heavy metals, solvents, and other toxic factory wastes and is having to be sealed at huge expense.

The Age of Fire

Air pollution, too, is predominantly a problem of modern urban/industrial society. Coal mining, when it got into full swing in Britain, and then in Germany, in the nineteenth century, made available unprecedented amounts of carbon coumpounds for the purposes of combustion. As fire was tamed into motion power it came to replace muscle power in most of its 'heavy duty' applications – traction, transport, farming, and factory production.

Probably the most significant environmental impact of urban/industrial civilization is the large-scale transfer of carbon from geological deposits into the atmosphere, in the form of carbon dioxide. In the last 100 years the CO_2 content of the atmosphere has increased from 265 to 345 ppm, or by 30 per cent. It is going up by 1.5 parts per million every year. That doesn't sound so much, but few atmospheric scientists now doubt the reality of the greenhouse effect and expect dramatic environmental consequences in the next century. At the present time, however, it is the other by-products of combustion which are the most immediate cause for concern, notably sulphur and nitrogen oxides.

Since the early 1980s it has becoming increasingly clear that air pollution is by no means a problem of the past, as had been assumed when the worst city smogs had been tackled after the introduction of the 'clean air acts' in Britain and elsewhere in Europe and America. The combination of the use of smokeless coal by urban households and the construction of new power stations with tall stacks fitted with dust filters was thought to be the solution to the air-pollution problems of the industrialzed countries. But not so.

By the early 1980s the horror stories of dying trees in Germany and Czechoslovakia were beginning to hit the headlines of the international press. Since then, most European countries have reported serious damage to forests, with the statistics showing a further decline every year. Most countries in central Europe concluded by the end of 1987 that over 50 per cent of their trees were sick, or indeed, dying. Virtually everywhere, with the exception of Britain, air pollution is considered as the primary cause of forest decline.

Sulphur dioxide from power station and factory chimneys, as well as nitrogen oxides from these chimneys and from car exhaust pipes, are overwhelmingly implicated as the main culprits. In addition, some 3,000 'new', man-made, gases in trace quantities add to the cocktail of pollutants which is now permanently present in the air we all breathe. All living beings in the Northern hemisphere are now exposed to these to varying degrees.

The new gases range from seemingly harmless and stable compounds to highly phytotoxic chlorinated hydrocarbons. There is growing concern about the synergistic effect of these new substances reacting with each other under varying climatic conditions. Throughout the industrialized world millions of dollars are now spent on experimental research to try to understand the chemistry of trace gases, their reaction with each other, their persistence in the atmosphere, and their impact on the sensitive tissues of living matter.

It is becoming increasingly clear that it is not just trees that are affected by air pollution but that crops are damaged too. For instance, research in Switzerland has shown that low level ozone, generated by reactions between nitrogen oxides, hydrocarbons, and oxygen in the presence of sunlight, causes a reduction in crop yields of up to 10 per cent. Of course, there is no doubt now that ozone is also a major culprit in forest decline.

The beneficial layer of ozone right at the top of the atmosphere, on the other hand, which protects the Earth from excessive exposure to ultraviolet light, is being corroded by another group of man-made gases – CFCs or chlorinated fluoro-carbons – which are still widely used as propellants in spray cans, as foaming agents in polyurethane foams and as coolants in fridges, freezers, and air conditioners. All of these are ingredients of the urban, convenience oriented, life-style that we have come to take for granted.

Third World cities

The phenomenal growth of Third World cities in recent years has led to a pattern of environmental damage similar to that experienced in the industrialized northern hemisphere. This applies to all the types of impact already mentioned in this chapter.

Deforestation in the south is preceding at an unprecedented speed. Tropical forests in Asia, South America, and Africa are under enormous pressure as a result of growing demand for farm land and land for cattle ranching, space for new open-cast mines, and for gigantic hydro-electric schemes to supply the new industries and the expanding cities with electricity.

The Third World countries continue to supply the consumers in the cities of the industrialized nations with raw materials – including timber, ores, oil, and coal. The pressure on their fragile environments as a result of their own urbanization is thus even more dramatic. Tropical forests are now shrinking at a – literally – breathtaking rate with, as yet, uncalculable consequences for the world's climate. Genetic depletion, too, has reached unprecedented levels – with insects, plants, and mammals, never investigated by science, disappearing as the forests go up in smoke or succumb to the chain-saw. And with the forests go the forest cultures: the intricate knowledge of the forest habitat accumulated by jungle dwellers over millennia of experimentation with food and medicinal plants being lost as rapidly as the forests themselves.

The one-way traffic of plant nutrients from rural areas to the new mega-cities like Calcutta, Seoul, Singapore, Mexico City, São Paulo, or Lagos is causing a severe depletion of soil fertility. Ranches established on the thin tropical forest soils of Amazonia, Central America or South East Asia tend to lose their viability within 10 years or so. Soil temperatures rise as the protective forest cover is removed, soil erosion is vastly increased by the same process, and the depletion of plant nutrients (particularly phosphates) as a result of the export of animal carcasses to urban markets, causes a permanent loss of soil productivity.

The coastal waters of Third World countries with rampant urban growth a now visibly laden with soil as a result of inland deforestation. In addition, they are increasingly polluted with both sewage and household/industrial chemicals. Since sophisticated sewage works which can cope with all types of water pollutants are very expensive indeed, it is likely to take a long time before these environmental problems now afflicting Third World cities are likely to be tackled.

However, the very poverty of Third World cities tends to result in a much more frugal use of non-renewable resources. Recycling of metals, paper, and plastics by the poorest of the poor on rubbish tips is a well-established procedure in cities as far apart as Cairo, Calcutta, or Rio de Janeiro. It is unfortunate that sheer poverty, rather than deliberate environmental policy, is presently the main incentive to this husbanding of resources.

The traffic explosion of cities world-wide is, of course, the major reason for unprecedented air pollution problems. Whilst these have been tackled to some extent by cities in rich countries like the USA and Japan, Third World countries simply cannot afford to curb emissions. The permanent smog over Mexico City with its population of now well over 20 million is a case is point. The chronic bronchial problems of a large proportion of its population are a notorious reality.

Closing the circle

The metabolism of modern cities as manifested at present – their throughput of food stuffs, forest products, fossile fuels and mineral resources – is demonstrably disruptive of the planet's life support systems.

The evidence for this statement is now readily available. Nevertheless, global urbanization is, if anything, accelerating. Industrial development and output growth is continuing apace. Less environmentally damaging cultures whose life-styles are based on long-term sustainable use of renewable resources are everywhere under attack. This applies to tribal groups of hunter-gatherers as well as to pastoral nomads and small-scale farmers world-wide. Urbanization in conjunction with the industrialization of agriculture for urban markets are the prime cause.

But, fortunately, growing minorities of city dwellers – even in the Third World – are becoming aware of the boomerang effect of unchecked urban-industrial growth. Self-interest is, obviously, a powerful motivating force for change and, as it is becoming apparent that we are on a collision course with all the life-support systems of this, our home planet, it is clear that all our futures are also at stake. The process of urbanization is likely to continue but how can its profound environmental destructiveness be reversed? If we can find answers to this question we shall be on the right track.

The most profound problem we are up against lies in the linearity of the development process we are engaged in. Nutrients are taken from the land as food is grown, never to be returned. Timber is felled for building materials or pulp and all too often forests are not replenished. Raw materials are extracted, processed, and combined into consumer goods that end up as rubbish which can not be beneficially rearbsorbed into living nature. Fossil fuels in unprecedented quantities are minded or pumped out from rock strata; they are refined and burned and thus released into the atmosphere. All in all, our present urban-industrial civilization is vastly accelerating the process of *entropy* with, as yet, hardly imagined consequences for the future of life on earth.

To undo the damage already done, and, indeed, to prevent further ravages, a great leap of the imagination, a profound act of collective will-power is called for. Of course, the ecology movement has drawn our attention to the issues at stake for some time now and nobody can claim that 'we didn't know'.

Cities are for people – or supposed to be – and all of us have to realize that our future, or, more precisely, that of our children, is at stake. To make the cities (our homes) ecologically viable must thus become our utmost priority. All living beings are profoundly concerned about the future of their own offspring and act accordingly: except, it seems, us – urban man and woman.

It is true that there has been growing concern about the physical fabric and appearance of cities in recent years. The slogan of the 'greening of the cities' has been catching on, but all too often it has mainly meant creating more green spaces and planting more trees just to improve the look of the place. It is, of course, crucially important to create a pleasant, greener urban environment for people to live in. But surely that can only be a start. Much more profound changes in the urban metabolism are required in order to make them ecologically viable, not just environmentally pleasant.

It will be crucially important to reorganize the whole metabolism of cities, the throughput of raw materials, energy, consumer goods, and the generation and treatment of waste from the perspective of long-term ecological viability. We simply cannot afford to continue with a pattern of input and output which makes the routine production of poisonous, life-damaging wastes a 'normal' activity.

This is not the place to go into great technical or organizational detail as regards the reorganization of the urban metabolism. I have attempted some of that in another book.[1] However, it may be useful to end this section by indicating in diagrammatic form how the 'urban metabolism' behaves at present and what a profound re-organization, according to ecological criteria, might seek to achieve (see Fig. 8.1).

The *'linear'* model of production, consumption and disposal, according to which our cities function at present, is not in the least concerned with the ecological viability of cities. Input and output are considered as unrelated. Food, fuels, construction materials, forest products and processed goods come from somewhere, never mind where, and when we are finished with them they are discarded never mind how. This system is profoundly different to nature's own circular *metabolism.* In nature every output is also an input which renews, and thus sustains, life. The urban metabolism is its present form, on the other hand, being linear in character, is profoundly disruptive of natural cycles. It thus accelerates entropy and undermines the dynamic balance of life on earth. As we are approaching the urbanization of the majority of the world population, this trend has massive implications for the well-being of the world's forests, soils, water courses, oceans, and for the composition of the very air we breathe.

Figure 8.1 Present (linear) and future (circular) urban metabolism

(a) *Present linear urban metbolism*

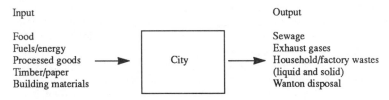

Input
Output

Input		Output
Food		Sewage
Fuels/energy		Exhaust gases
Processed goods	City	Household/factory wastes
Timber/paper		(liquid and solid)
Building materials		Wanton disposal

(b) *Future circular urban metabolism*

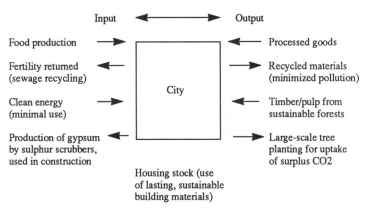

Input		Output
Food production		Processed goods
Fertility returned (sewage recycling)		Recycled materials (minimized pollution)
Clean energy (minimal use)	City	Timber/pulp from sustainable forests
Production of gypsum by sulphur scrubbers, used in construction		Large-scale tree planting for uptake of surplus CO2

Housing stock (use of lasting, sustainable building materials)

Worldwide urbanization can be ecologically viable only if the urban metabolism is designed to be essentially 'circular', (i.e. if it is assured that every output can also be an input). Sewage systems would have to cease being simply disposal systems for that noxious mixture of household and factory wastes. Sewage works would have to be designed to function as fertilizer factories rather than as disposal systems for unwanted, and often toxic, discharges. Liquid chemical wastes from factories would have to be intercepted, rather than released in the somewhat uncontrolled way which is common practice at present. Sooner, rather than later, the routine use of highly toxic materials in factory production would have to be examined.

Household and factory rubbish would have to be regarded as an asset rather than a nuisance. Detailed studies have shown that up to 80 per cent of the rubbish we discard at present could be re-cycled back into useful products. In this and other respects the poor people of the new, giant cities of the Third World have a great deal to teach us. But in the rich countries it is considered by urban authorities not to be economically viable to re-cycle more than a small proportion of our waste. But it is becoming all too clear now that ecological viability is a far more important criterion, as pollution problems are taking on increasingly unmanageable proportions.

The vast energy input required by conurbations is another case in point. It is only too evident now that the generation of CO_2, SO_2, NO_x and hydrocarbons by power stations, factories, household, and vehicles has reached totally unacceptable levels. Energy efficiency and, indeed, the avoidance of energy use must now be considered as policy priorities if further environmental damage by air pollution is to be avoided. This is becoming a particularly pressing issue as Third World coutries are beginning to plan for similar levels of energy use as the rich countries.

Technology to improve energy efficiency has made great strides in recent years. The same goes for 'clean energy technology'. Sulphur rich fumes, for instance, can now be cleaned by scrubbers fitted to power stations. The gypsum produced by injecting lime into the stream of flue gases is, potentially, a most useful building material.

The massive release of CO_2 into the atmosphere as a by-product of combustion can ultimately be absorbed only by tree planting on a huge scale on the barren lands of the earth which have expanded with the growth of cities worldwide. Today we are causing desertification on an unprecedented scale. Who is it who said that deserts are the footsteps of man on earth. Those of urban man in the late twentieth century are vastly larger than those of any of our predecessors. Are we prepared to reforest large parts of the earth and thus to contain deserts while tackling the CO_2 problem we have created at the same time?

If we want to enjoy the benefits of urban life we must also take responsibility for the impact of the urban metabolism on the living fabric of the earth. After all, it simply represents the sum total of our consumption and discharges which are part of our day-to-day way of life. Closing the circle – that is, re-designing the urban metabolism to make it truly compatible with the processes of the living world – is a responsibility we cannot shirk. A barren and poisoned planet is surely not what we wish to leave behind. It is up to all of us to assure that a reversal of current practices is initiated without delay. Re-designing the urban metabolism, as cities are becoming the home of most of us on this planet, is now a key priority.

Note

1. Seymour, John and Girardet, Herbert (1987) *Blueprint for a Green Planet*, London: Dorling & Kindersley.

Chapter 9

Barriers, channels and community control1

John F.C. Turner

The author of this Chapter draws upon a lifetime of work with low-income communities around the world to take up the issue of community participation. His conviction that people themselves are the best judge of what is good for them and that they have successfully taken over major responsibilities for urban planning housing initiatives wherever the state or the market has neglected them, is based upon a much broader view of participation than Rakodi suggested in Chapter 6 planners have so far envisaged. Turner cities the evidence of Lima, Peru to show that in some cities community base organizations (CBOs) and non-governmental organisations (NGOs) have become mainstream suppliers of housing land and builders, and that the onus is now on governments to participate in actions by people rather than the other way round. According to Turner, both CBOs and NGOs have already proved themselves capable of acting as mediators between government and people as well as being community developers in their own right.

Turner is well qualified for his task. He has produced some of the most influential publications on the role of housing in social and economic development and recently co-ordinated the preparation of case studies on community based housing programmes for the Habitat International Coalition.

Mass housing or housing by the masses?

An anecdote from my own past illustrates the difficulty that I think some of us have when trying to explain the understanding that we have acquired. One day many years ago now, when I was in Peru, I was asked by the British Ambassador to take a visiting Minister of State to see some of the unauthorized settlements that local people had built. So I took him up a hillside to have a look over an immense area of building by low-income households. I had assumed that he would be as impressed and as enthusiastic about the capacity that low-income people have, as I was myself. On the contrary, he was quite appalled, shocked, and could not understand my own view at all. And I could not understand his! I realized at that moment, and have been very much aware ever since, that we have a very serious problem of perception. We have a perspective which is different, and not easy to communicate to those who have not shared our advantage of working directly with the people themselves.

I believe that it is not only important to know how much more low-income people do than is done for them, just for one's awareness of the reality of the world, but that we have a great deal to learn – for our use in the urban-industrial world as well. It's not just a question of interest, it's also a question of relevance to our own way of life and our own situations, wherever we may live and work.

We are used to thinking in terms of a public or governmental sector, and a private sector which really combines very different systems. It's essential, to my way of thinking, to differentiate between the private commercial sector, and the private, non-commercial, non-governmental sector. So when we talk about NGOs and CBOs, we are really talking about a sector that is neither commercial nor governmental, and could be termed 'a third system' or 'third sector'. The aim is a new balance between complementary powers, not the hegemony of any one.

My next point is addressed especially to the bilateral assistance policy makers, planners and administrators, and may be of less direct interest to the public in general. It is important to point out that case histories of NGO and CBO action provide many precedents of widely applicable methods, or ways and means of doing things. They are not necessarily valid as models for replication by government agencies or any other kind of organization, commercial or non-governmental. The most significant and encouraging cases are those that show how people can work out their own unique projects and programmes to fit their own needs and priorities – when they have the necessary support of their governments or NGOs and industry. Our search is for the ways and means by which homes and neighbourhoods can be well planned, built and maintained by the masses – the opposite of the failed attempts at mass housing for people by central agencies.

The search therefore, is not for standardized projects and programmes that central agencies can try to replicate. Instead, the realistic search has to be for the ways and means by which governments, non-government organizations, and the building industry can enable people to do well what so may do in any case: the planning, building, and management of their own homes and neighbourhoods at costs both they and society can afford.

There is a bitter end to this well-intentioned but misconceived policy of mass housing for people instead of those that support housing by the masses. Nowhere are the consequences clearer than in Britain. Because all the decisions were in the hands of the professionals and the politicians, who did not even consult with the people they thought they were serving, poor decisions were made: faced with a shortage of skilled labour in Britain following the Second World War, capital-intensive, labour-saving building systems were subsidized and expanded instead of training programmes and the development of the pre-existing and far more appropriate technologies we have now reviewed. These industrialization policies helped sow the seeds of the present harvest of unemployment. Because high-rise building seemed cheaper, seemed to save land, is certainly pofitable for the builders and good for the egos of the architects and engineers, it was strongly encouraged by both the Conservative and Labour governments of the day. If decisions had been shared with those who have to live in and pay for what is designed, it is doubtful if many high-rise blocks would have been built. Many of the high-rise mass housing schemes were poorly designed and badly built, most are hated by their reluctant residents. As a result, the great majority are very badly treated and poorly maintained, sometimes even made uninhabitable by their own residents or, more often, their children. Experts now tell us that more than 1,000 tower blocks built in the 1960s will have to be demolished before the end of the century. Many have been blown up, long before the 60-year loans for their construction have been paid off. And, in case I seem to be putting all the blame on mistaken designs alone, I may add that many low-rise developments that have been imposed on people who have no responsibility for them have also been destroyed.

A word about appropriate technologies. The most simple definition of an appropriate technology is Paul Osborne's: 'a technology that people can appropriate'.[2] That is, that people can take hold of and use. A technology that people cannot use, that makes them dependent on a large organization, is not appropriate for housing and local government. Heavy, capital-intensive tehnologies may be highly appropriate for some large buildings, but not for homes and neighbourhoods.

Alternative ways and means

The precedents that we need to look for are: different ways and means of carrying out the tasks that are common to all participatory projects and programmes: those that involve people and which people can and should share responsibility for community organization, funding, the acquisition of land, local planning and building design, technology choice and acquisition, building, and management and maintenance. There are different ways and means of doing each of these tasks. In my view the experience gained so far confirm three common conclusions.

First, governments which attempt to compensate for the failures of the market to provide the lower-income, or even middle-income, households, must change their priorities: from the provision of centrally supplied housing projects by subsidizing commercial developers, to the enablement of owner-builders, self-managing community-based organizing, and the local governments and enterprises that serve them. The most important supports are those that increase access to affordable and well located land, to secure tenure, basic services, appropriate technologies, to affordable standards and procedures and credit. To use Professor Otto Koenigsberger's words: 'if your government is serious about housing low-income people, then it must not build houses'.[3]

The second conclusion is that the potential of CBOs and NGOs which support the people who build the great majority of homes and neighbourhoods in low-income countries are grossly underestimated and under-used. For instance, according to current statistics, nearly half of all dwellings and neighbourhoods in Lima, Peru (43 per cent) have been built by people and their own local CBOs, some of them with the help of NGOs. The average value of these dwellings at the present time has been estimated at about $23,000 US, or £14,500. That represents about 20 years of most urban Peruvian household's income. So somehow or other these low-income people manage to build houses which, in proportion to their income, are of an extraordinary high standard. They achieve a level of capitalization which would be impossible to achieve through the market or the state, and yet similar evidence can be found in many parts of the Third World.

These facts lead to the third conclusion: that, as the development and implementation of supportive and enabling policies involve changes of relationship between people and government, NGOs as third parties are essential as mediators as well as in their roles as community developers, innovators, and motivators. To quote Dr Arcot Ramachandran's (Executive Director of UNCHS) statement to the UN Commission in Istanbul during 1986, 'The agenda for the next 10 years must be to find the necessary capacities to apply these enabling strategies. We can only give a guarantee of failure for any other kind of strategy.'

A number of practical implications can be derived from these conclusions. These are illustrated in the following figures, though allowance must be made for the limitations of a static, two-dimensional image which oversimplifies the complex reality of any particular case.

Basic tasks and barriers

Figure 9.1 suggests that any significant change in the built environment involves a series of basic tasks in order to overcome actual or potential barriers to any course of action, or programme. No works can be carried out unless the following tasks are successfully carried out:

1. Organizing, by those on whom implementation of the programme depends, and in ways that ensure the required degree of co-operation;
2. Financing, to obtain the necessary services and material resources;
3. Land and acquisition, or obtaining an appropriate form of tenure providing the necessary rights to the use of the property;
4. Planning and the specification of practicable works that can be easily followed or adapted;
5. Acquiring techniques and the necessary tools and materials for the works;
6. Building, by contracted and/or voluntary management and/or labour;
7. Maintenance of the works, if they are not to be lost prematurely.

Figure 9.1: Tasks common to all programmes are barriers

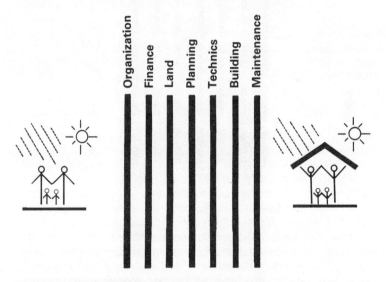

Options for locally self-managed programmes

As suggested in Figure 9.2 there are usually several ways in which each of these tasks can be carried out in most situations. This crude level of generalization ignores the sub-tasks that compose each basic task but it highlights the fact that there are generally many potential courses of action that could lead to a successful conclusion. If, for instance, there are three compatible alternatives for carrying out each of the seven tasks, there would be 2,187 (3^7) possible ways of reaching the goal. And if some of the openings in the barriers provided access for very low-income households (the vital factor which depends on government policy as pointed out below), there would be very few who, supported by an enabling policy, could not meet their basic needs: a residential location convenient to the user's sources of livelihood; a shelter offering privacy and protection with a form of tenure which is secure and/or transferable, allowing the option of either maintaining a tolerable existence or the freedom to pursue opportunties for a better life.

Figure 9.2: Options providing many alternative programmes

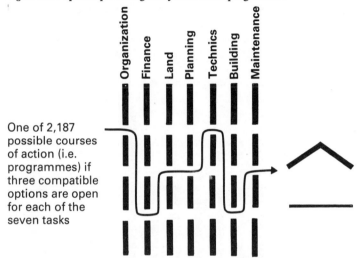

One of 2,187 possible courses of action (i.e. programmes) if three compatible options are open for each of the seven tasks

As frequently observed, remarkably high proportions of low-income populations in low-income economies with flourishing 'informal' economies do find ways of housing themselves satisfactorily. This is largely due to their freedom to ignore most institutional constraints. The lower the income, the greater the importance of a habitat that matches priorities or aspirations. Low-income people have little or no margin for discretionary expenditures, and cannot afford to pay more for transport, either public or private; those dependent on inner-city work often cannot afford the costs of suburban relocation. If their social and economic security depends on the secure tenure of their dwelling, then they cannot afford to mortgage it; so conventional financing is unacceptable for many or most. If their hopes for a better future depend on residential mobility, they cannot risk tying themselves down to a permanent residence, as is often demanded in public housing.

Given the wide range of priorities for specific kinds of location, shelter and tenure, as well as the major changes that commonly take place during the life-cycle of a person or household, the choice necessary to serve a complex and rapidly changing society is enormous. It would be impossible for corporate organizations to attempt to provide such a staggering variety in their programmes, as their economies depend on large-scale, standardized forms and procedures.

The necessity of local knowledge

When decision making is localized, with the people most concerned contributing their own unique local knowledge; when there are sufficient options, and the users are aware of them and can make use of them; then a satisfactory outcome is almost always assured. But if decision making on local programmes is centralized, ignoring local knowledge, it is almost as certain to fail, or else heavy expenditure will be demanded in order to overcome the friction and resistance generated through mismatching supply with demand. This fact is explained in cybernetics by the law of requisite variety as stated by W.R. Ashby: 'If stability (of a system) is to be attained, the variety of the controlling system must be at least as great as the variety of the system to be controlled.' It goes without saying that however simple a dwelling environment may be technically, it is an immensely variable and complex system socially, economically, and spatially.

The implication of this analysis is shown in Figure 9.3. The actual difference and necessary separation of the two kinds of authority and power is based on two complementary kinds of knowledge: the insiders' particular knowledge of their own local situations, expectations and priorities and the outsiders' general knowledge of the overall situation and patterns of change – the connections between local situations which demands the professional distance at which local detail is inevitably lost. It is clear that competent decisions on locally-appropriate programmes depend on those who have to implement, use, manage, and maintain the works to be carried out. It is also obvious that personal and local freedom to make and carry out decisions depends on the appropriate ways and means of carrying out the necessary tasks, a knowledge which the professional consultants should have.

The existence and accessibility of options depend on customs, commerce, and government. Changes essential for the full, orderly use of local resources for community building depend on institutions, which only government can manipulate or legitimize: the structure of authority, the exchange system, and the law and its administration.

People with a strong community base often carry a great deal of authority, as evidenced in the often massive scale of squatter settlements where new openings are made through direct action. The legalization of *de facto* land possession by squatters suggests that this may be the most common way in which effective changes do, in fact, occur. Whether responding to or anticipating popular demand, it is clear that the proper exercise of the state's institutional powers over options for local action differs and is necessarily separate from people's natural authority over the personal and local uses of these options.

Figure 9.3: The complementarity of central and local powers

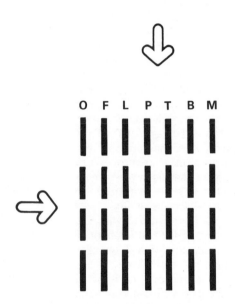

Necessarily central authority with instituitional controls over access to resources and limits to their use

O F L P T B M

Necessarily personal and local authority over personal and local uses of resources for homes and neighbourhoods within authorized limits

The necessity of mediating structures in public policy[4]

These two distinct types of authority are separate but complementary, and negotiation must take place, to avoid conflict and make proper use of resources. Figure 9.4 highlights the vital function of mediating structures in public policy (to borrow the title of the seminal paper by Peter Berger and Richard Neuhaus). Figure 9.4 identifies the three key positions and roles for NGOs and independent specialists in the change-over from supply to support policies:

1. As consultants to central authorities, in their efforts to increase options for local initiative, ensuring that the legislators and administrators concerned are aware of the options that people need, and of the combinations which could be allowed.

2. As consultants to people in planning and implementing their own locally unique programmes, ensuring that they are aware of options and

have access to the knowledge and skills required to combine them into a practical programme, controlled or implemented by themselves.
3. As consultants to both local action groups and central authorities in negotiating agreements on specific programmes.

Figure 9.4: Key roles for the mediators

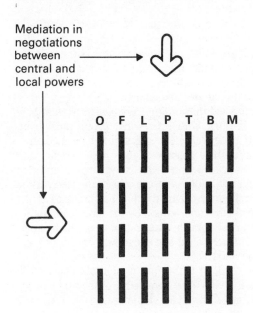

Mediation in negotiations between central and local powers

Assistance to central authorities in the opening of options for locally formulated and self-managed programmes

O F L P T B M

Assistance to self-managing people and their community-based organizations for the formulation and implementation of their own programmes

In all of the above, emphasis is on the necessity for knowledge of actual or potential options. As noted above, possible and desirable combinations and permutations of the options will be limited by their compatibility with each other, with the context and demands. In some contexts, some options are unsuitable. For example, mortgage loans for low-income people in unstable economies would not be viable unless combined with adequate, affordable insurance. Knowledge of possible options is not the only requirement: there must also be an awareness of how they connect with each other and their contexts. With increased access to this general 'knowledge of knowledge', the transfer of decision-making and control over local development from central to local government and community-based organizations will be delayed. This broader, general knowledge is essential to balance and correct the often narrowly sectoral views of the specialists, whose skills are also essential.

Conclusions

The precedents demonstrate how homelessness is most effectively dealt with when large numbers of people build their own heterogeneous communities. This kind of traditional (or what I prefer to call normal) building, generates a wide diversity of activities and demands for local employment as well as providing a wide range of house types, tenures and prices.

Self-managing communities contrast sharply with the centrally administered programmes of conventional housing policies. The ready-to-occupy serviced dwellings, built by government contractors for narrow categories of people, provide little or no construction work for local residents; they are highly standardized and often designed in ways that inhibit or even prohibit mixed uses and tenures.

The case histories summarized in *Building Community*[5] explain how and why so much more is done with less, when people take over, especially when supported by government and assisted by mediating NGOs. The greatest available resource for new home and neighbourhood building is the people who need them, and for improvements and maintenance, those who are already housed. In the United Kingdom this radically different approach is beginning to attract a great deal of attention. Although constrained by the label 'community architecture' this is really part of a much wider movement which shows that we are learning that the same social and economic benefits of local control accrue in our own context.

How well resources are used, or if they are used at all, depends on people's freedom to use their own unique knowledge of their own needs and priorities. Perhaps the most important single reason for involving people directly is that those of us who have to make technical decisions are very much in the air if we ignore the knowledge that people have of their own situations and environments. Much also depends on the choices and decisions people can make from their own experience and with their own skills, time and money, and, of course, on their opportunities to demonstrate their own abilities and commitment. Even when people are materially poor, these resources far outweigh those that the state can acquire in low- and high-income contexts. The good use of land and living space, of materials, of working time and money, all depend as much or even more on local knowledge and personal will than they do on professional expertise, industry, and social institutions.

When large organizations exclude users and residents by monopolizing the production or management of dwellings and related services, they have to replace those personal and local resources that cannot be obtained through market pressures or police powers – and these ways and means of extracting people's contributions also cost time, effort, and money, especially when the contributors are dissatisfied, and therefore reluctant, consumers. What a contrast to the cities that much poorer people build in many Third World countries! Whether rich or poor, healthy people will almost always take care of what they are responsible for. They will usually make the best decisions that their knowledge and experience allows. Experience from all countries, especially from the rich north, east, and west, shows what happens when people are ignored and their resources wasted.

If people are to use and develop their own personal resources in order to make use of material resources, they have to have access to and freedom to use them, of course. The support of local initiative depends most heavily on central government, which has the powers to change the basic institutions controlling access to resources and limits on their uses: the law and its administration, the financial exchange and banking systems, and the structure of central and local government authority. In most cases, the necessary supports for local initiatives are provided through NGOs, either directly or through mediation between local communities and central authorities. NGOs have to work within existing power structures. They have no direct powers to change legislation and very limited financial resources. Nevertheless, the experience gained to date by studies such as that undertaken by Habitat International Coalition show that NGOs have now come to the forefront of policy change despite these limitations.

Notes and references

1. The information on which this chapter draws, was obtained from national and local non-governmental organizations (NGOs) and the community-based organizations (CBOs) whose achievements are presented through the Habitat International Coalition NGO Habitat Project for the International Year of Shelter for the Homeless 1987. The documentation provides a sample of precedents that demonstrate the under-used potential of community-based and non-governmental organizations for human and material development.
   This chapter is a development of the 'Issues and Conclusions' section by Turner, J.F.C. (1988) in Bertha Turner (ed.) *Building Community: A Third World Case Book,* London: Habitat International Coalition. Available from: Building Communities Books, 5 Dryden Street, London, WC2E 9NW.
2. Verbal communication by Paul Osborne, Director of SATIS (Information and Dissemination Service and Information Management System), Netherlands.
3. Statements to participants of the Housing in Development short coures directed by the author (1976-83) at the Development Planning Unit, University College London.
4. Berger, Peter L., and Neuhaus, Richard J. (1977) *To empower people: the role of mediating structures in public policy,* Washington DC: The American Enterprise Institute for Policy Research.
5. See Turner, op. cit., n. 1.

Chapter 10

The politics of sustainable Third World urban development

Tade Akin Aina

The scale of the ecological and social problems which future cities will have to resolve poses a major challenge of political will at local, national and international levels. The political constraints and options applicable to developing countries in their attempts to achieve sustainable development are discussed in the Chapter by Tade Aina. The subject is considered in three parts: an examination of the 'sustainable development' approach; a discussion of the variety of political factors that affect it; and an assessment of the options and prospects for transformation and change beneficial to the majority of urban dwellers. Aina notes the tendency towards authoritarianism and centralization common throughout the Third World, and the concentration of investment and economic opportunities in a few metropolitan centres which this tends to reflect. As he notes, the poor, who are generally excluded from receiving their fair share of resources by such processes, have fortunately been sufficiently resourceful to build much of the cities themselves, putting scarce resources to effective and ingenious use. He concludes by outlining ways in which change can be encouraged by progressive forces within Third World countries and by concerned groups within the First World.

The author lectures at the University of Lagos, Nigeria, and is a Research Fellow of the International Institute for Environment and Development.

Introduction

Available evidence in recent years shows that very few professionals and practitioners of any worth in the field of urban development and welfare, are opposed to a position or vision that sees the desirable future for Third World cities and urban settlements as that of the development of equitable, socially responsive, economically viable and ecologically sustainable settlements.[1] In other words, their position and vision is that of what can be called 'sustainable development'. This is a notion and an emerging approach which captures a gathering world-wide wave of sentiments, concerns, study, political mobilization and organization, around the serious twin issues of the conservation of the environment and the economic development process. But perhaps the most recent popularization of the notion of 'sustainable development' can be found in the recent report of the World Commission on Environment and Development (WCED) titled 'Our Common Future', and known as the 'Brundtland Report' after Mrs Gro Harlem Brundtland, the Prime Minister of Norway, who chaired the Commission.[1]

'Our Common Future' elevated the notion of sustainable development to the level of an operational concept which embodied the principles, ideals, and values which it sees as desirable and necessary if the world is to deal effectively with its problem of the crisis of the environment and the development process. The approach embodied within it is the notion and ideal of a development process that is equitable and socially responsive – in the sense that it recognizes the extensive nature of poverty, deprivation, and inequality in the contemporary world, between and within nations, regions, classes, and communities. It also seriously advocates perception of the world as one integrated ecosystem and advances the need for the economic development process to include as an essential component, the issues of environment and ecology.

In short, there is a convergence in this document of the different strands of arguments which have been in existence in certain circles for several decades. These include the Third World arguments about the inequities of the current world economic system, the failure and irrelevance of the conventional targets and paths of development defined as desirable by the west, the socialist arguments about the inequities and contraditions of a capatalist development process, and, of course, the struggles and arguments of the ecology and conservation movements as to the exhaustible nature of the available resources of the earth, its consequent depletion, deterioration, and degradation.

In dealing with the issues of its concern, the WCED consistently pointed out the importance of policies in bringing about the changes which it recommends and desires. It even provides explicit proposals for institutional and legal changes in attaining environmental protection and sustainable development. But, somehow, the WCED report stopped at a very crucial point, that of the explicit discussion of the variety of specific political factors that either inhibit or facilitate the attainment of the goals of sustainable development, what options there are, and what are their prospects. Yet if there is to be any meaningful and long-lasting transformation of the scale which the Commission desires and/or envisages, it is in the sphere of politics and political struggles at all available levels, that decisive moves must be made.

It is these issues that constitute the main objective of this chapter, which is to examine and discuss the political factors that facilitate or inhibit the attainment of what can be broadly called the sustainable development process in Third World cities and urban settlements. But, first, it is necessary to point out that the national societies covered by what is known as the Third World[3] are extremely complex and varied, both within and between themselves. There is tremendous variation in their history, geography, religion, culture, level of economic development, politics, and urbanization process.[4] Broad generalizations in this context are neither feasible nor helpful. What is required is the extraction and discussion of some of the most commonly recognizable problems. To carry out this task, the rest of this chapter is structured as follows: (a) a brief examination of the 'sustainable development' approach; (b) an examination of the most general outlines of the current urban condition in the Third World; (c) a discussion of the variety of political factors that affect 'sustainable development'; and (d) an examination of the prospects and options for transformation and change beneficial to the majority of urban dwellers.

The 'sustainable development' approach

A brief discussion of this approach is necessary because it is gradually assuming the form of a desirable path or approach to development around which a growing consensus is being built. This requires that its most important elements be isolated and specified. In general, the notion describes a process and an analytical approach, though it has not been expressed within a theoretical framework of any rigour, but is identifiable in a more general, commonsensical fashion. More work seems required in terms of the formalization and systematization of the approach, its central concepts, and their relationship to a theory of the development process. Some evidence of a beginning of these tasks is, however, available.[5] Barbier, for example, has noted that:

> the concept of sustainable economic development is a difficult one to grasp analytically. Given that one is attempting to describe the environmental, economic, and social features of an ongoing process, the difficulty lies in arriving at a universally acceptable definition.[6]

In his paper, Barbier considers that the concept refers to 'any economic activity that raises social welfare with the minimum amount of environmental degradation allowable within given economic, social and technical constraints'.

The WCED document contains a similar definition and identifies what it calls critical objectives for environment and development policies that follow from the concept of sustainable development. These include: reviving growth; changing the quality of growth; meeting the essential needs for jobs, food, energy, water, and sanitation; ensuring a sustainable level of population, conserving and enhancing the resource base, reorientating technology and managing risk; and merging the environment and economics in decision-making. All these objectives point to what appears to be the greatest strength of the sustainable development approach: that is, providing not only a holistic but also an integrated perspective for the analysis, practice, and process of development. As Barbier has pointed out, the concept integrates and maximizes the goals across the biological, resource, social, and economic systems. Sectors of human life and activity cannot therefore be separated in analysis or practice as they are all interrelated and whatever is done in one area/sector has implications for others. In my view, sustainable development is therefore the qualitative and quantitative transformation of the conditions of existence of the majority of a society and the management of that society's resources to the advantage and benefit of the majority of its peoples. It must also be seen within the context of a development paradigm in which human and ecological costs are accorded equal importance with economic costs.

Although the concern here is with Third World cities and urban settlements, the sustainable development approach presupposes that human settlements, whether urban or rural, need to be seen together in terms of the interdependence of the utilization of resources, economic activities, and the overall process of production and consumption. This emphasis on an integrated, holistic approach also emphasizes that Third World cities and urban settlements are now part of the world economic system. They have been incorporated into it along with their national economies, possess functions and roles within it, have definite places within its hierarchy, and are therefore not in any way closed systems. They are, therefore, vulnerable to major political and economic decisions taken by executives in the developed economies of Europe, Japan, and North America (who occupy privileged positions within the world system) with regard to such issues as investments, industrial location, new technologies, credit and flows of finance, trade and tariff issues, armaments and defence issues. Consequently, Third World cities and urban developments are more vulnerable to political, economic and ecological mishaps and disasters – not only from within their national formations and regions, but also from without. It is with these points in mind that the urban condition is best examined.

The urban condition in Third World cities

The current condition and crisis of Third World cities have been the subject of extensive diagnosis and treatment in the literature.[7] Among the main conclusions raised by many observers is that the greatest degradation of the urban environment in the Third World is not merely pollution, erosion, mismanagement of waste, and the depletion and deterioration of resources (which, of course, exist), but rather it is the degraded and immensely impoverished quality of life, particularly for the majority of urban dwellers. Sadly enough, the evidence also points to the increasing incapacity of governments of Third World nations at every level to improve the current conditions, least of all to radically transform them. The reasons for this incapacity range from the limitations imposed by inadequate financial resources emerging from the current world economic crisis, to that of the nature of national and local power relations and the role of vested interests.

Again, there has been no shortage of prescriptions for policies and programmes, institutional and legal changes, that might alleviate, if not transform, these conditions. These have, in fact, often come with the analyses themselves. The problem, however, is that students of the urban condition often avoid in any detail the discussion of the 'politics of urban development and condition', and how the status quo is a product of the ongoing adjustment of the balance of power between different vested interests, classes, and social forces who are often in conflict and in alliance with each other over different issues and at different times. These vested interests are located in both the developed economies and within the nations of the Third World and are active in all aspects of life – commerce, religion, bureaucracy, and the professions collectively. They are often the central obstacle to any movement towards sustainable development of Third World urban settlements. They are, in fact, the agents of the political factors which we now turn to.

Political factors and sustainable development of Third World cities

Three levels of the operation of political factors which affect the sustainable development of Third World cities and urban settlements are identifiable. These are: the global/transnational level; the national level; and the local or grass-roots level. It should be pointed out, however, that these levels are not only sites from which actions emanate but also within which effects are felt. The same forces and vested interests can therefore be seen in operation simultaneously at all levels along with the effect of their action.

Political factors at global/trans-national level

These will include what goes on within the world economic system, particularly within its decisive institutions such as the International Monetary Fund, the World Bank, and similar institutions. Decisions made at this level tend to be decisive for Third World nations. Some of these are based on the defined economic interests of strategic groups, classes, and vested interests in the 'First World', and the perceptions and roles of professionals (particularly with regard to the prevalence of certain orthodoxies in the professions, i.e. monetarism in economics). The recent economic crisis in the Third World, and the role of the trans-national institutions in this, has raised politcal factors to a very significant role.

International relations and world power politics issues are also central at this level. Here, we are referring to a vast network of institutions, relationships, and alliances, and to cultural and racial ties between nations. This can be seen in terms of the activities of power blocs such as the East and West, and the role of their organizations such as the North Atlantic Treaty Organisation (NATO) and the Warsaw pact nations. Closely related to this, it the role of the regional, pan-continental trans-national bodies such as the Economic Community of West African States (ECOWAS), the Organization of Latin American States, the Commonwealth, etc. Within each of these, alliances are made that provide benefits and advantages to whole countries, and strategic groups and classes within them, either in terms of commodity prices, labour mobility, currency exchange rates, investment flows, or technology, trans-national conflicts and the supply of arms are yet other critical factors. The Third World today is a centre of endless conflicts and wars within and between nations. The supply of weapons often come from external sources, so their support is necessary for increasing domestic tension or prolonging the conflicts.

The current experiences of certain countries in Central America and the southern African region confirm the extent to which these conflicts are dependent on trans-national and global politics. Of course, the implications for domestic pursuit of sustainable development are that the cities of such countries are turned into vast refugee camps for the victims of the conflicts, while the battle fronts and the countryside not only suffer social and cultural upheavals, but are also subjected to ecological disruption, resulting in drought, famine, and the deaths of millions.

Several elements come into the politics which operate at this level. First, there is the struggles between different vested interests in the first world (Europe, the US, etc.). These include groups such as industrialists, farmers, trade unions, the churches, charities, higher educational institutions, and aid agencies.

All these interest groups tend to be well organized and concerned with the sectoral benefits to the groups they represent, both locally and abroad. In the context of electoral politics, they are often the repository of powerful lobbies backed with finance and, in some cases, research.

These groups often attempt to, and do, influence their own governments, their national public opinion, and even the position of strategic individuals and officials in important global institutions and multi-lateral agencies. What goes on at this level of political action cannot be ignored in terms of their implications for the sustainable development of Third World urban settlements.

Political factors at the national central level in the Third World

It is impossible to discuss the politics of the Third World in any detail here. This is because of the immense variety and complexity of these societies. However, certain broad features are of importance in the understanding of the obstacles to, and prospects for sustainable development in Third World urban settlements. These will include: (1) the feature of inequality in these societies; (2) the features of unsustainable economic and social development paths; and (3) the character of the State and politics in the Third World.

Inequality

A common feature of several contemporary Third World nations is the nature and extent of social and economic inequality. Apart from a handful of countries whose political economies are deliberately structured to cope with this problem, most of them manifest extreme inequality inherited either from the traditional or/and the colonial past, but which has worsened with the growth of economic development and the modernization process.[8]

Most Third World nations are class-based societies in which the majority of the population are very poor and underprivileged. Class relations and the nature of class conflicts and struggles vary, depending on the specific history, culture, and politics of the country, and the level and type of its economic development. The aspects of greatest significance to human settlements revolve around access to certain strategic resources and basic needs. Some of the resources and needs include: land on which to build adequate shelter; stable livelihood; education; health; water and other services, such as roads and drainage.

Unfortunately, the control of all these often lies in the hands of the Third World elites. Dominant classes, such as landowners, employers, professional groups, wealthy traders, and manufacturers, at one time or the other, hold interests contradictory with those of the poor majority over issues of reform or transformation. They utilize the powers and resources of the state to benefit themselves through the provision of subsidized housing, services and infrastructures to those areas or settlements where they live, yet deny these facilities to low-income settlements.

Unsustainable economic and social development processes

The current crisis of development in the Third World, complicated by the world economic recession and the recent increase in ecological disasters, indicate the bankruptcy of the development paths, which most nations have pursued so far. These are in the main 'unsustainable'. The economic and social development of Third World countries is, apart from a few exceptions, one of dismal failure. But the possibilities of significant changes are commonly tied to changes in the structure of the world system discussed above. It is these, along with the character of domestic politics and the State that determine the choice of development paths, and such choices in themselves define what happens to, and in, urban settlements.

The character of the state and politics in the Third World

This is a subject that has received attention from numerous writers.[9] What emerges inlcudes the following main features. The first has to do with the centrality of the State in Third World formations: that is, the State's role as perhaps the most central institution in national development. The second feature is that, broadly, the State is seen as the main institution of social and economic reproduction. Third is that it is often the forum for clas interaction.[10]

It is in relation to the nature of the State that the character of politics in many Third World societies take its form. Domestic elites and classes, and vested interests from the urbanized countries are often central in this. But it is the complex way in which the various forces and interests interact which gives shape to the specific forms taken by the highly complex and varied character of Third World politics. Prominent among the features that characterize Third World politics is the prevalence of authoritarian and/or non-electoral, non-parliamentary forms of governments. These vary extensively, from absolute monarchies to military rule, and various forms of party systems. The important feature here is either the overt marginalization of the majority of the populace through the denial of participation in electoral politics, political debates, local administration, and the possession of dissenting viewpoints, or their covert marginalization through a ritual of formal electoral politics which either has no meaning in terms of effective participation, or in other cases is only a fraudulent means of legitimizing unpopular and unrepresentative regimes.

A related feature of the tendency towards authoritarianism is the factor of increasing centralization of decisions, concentration of power, and the phenomenon of personal rule. Centralization occurs in terms of the location and source of the major decisions and activities of government. In many Third World countries these are in the centre, which is often the capital city. This, of course, is often a primate city within which there is intense concentration of economic, political, administrative, and cultural activities. Other urban areas and rural settlements are also deprived. Centralization and concentration exists in terms of activities and access to services and resources. In the process of government it leads to the irrelevance of lower levels of administration such as state, regional and provincial governments, and municipal administrations. These are either starved of resources or have to approach the centre for every need. This is often made easier if patron–client linkages exist between strategic individuals and groups, both within the centre and the other areas. It is this element that fuels and reinforces the phenomenon of 'personal rule' – the domination at an individual, direct level of a central authoritarian political figure.[11] In such contexts, the marginalization of the majority is nearly complete. Political participation here is built on patron–client relations, the building up of a cult of the personality, or mobilization around ideological issues such as religion, ethnicity and/or race. Corruption of persons, political parties and groups through graft, bribery and nepotism is also rampant. Behind these is the use, or constant threat, of repression. For the poor, the options range from some form of incorporation through local barons in the patron–client networks, studied apathy and distance from the elites, or a resort to sporadic displays of violence. All these have been effectively documented.[12] They hinder the attainment of 'sustainable development' through the prevention of meaningful and popularly acceptable change. Furthermore, it is at this point that all the other various issues, such as policies and legislation, could be resolved. But the elite's control of the State and their definition of politics often constitute significant constraints. In the end, these conditions create more problems than they resolve, as they encourage the populace to consider violence as the main instrument of change.

Political factors at the local and grass-roots level

These have two dimensions, namely those of government and those of communities. The effects of structural inequality and the character of the State and politics affect the local/grass-roots level in terms of the denial of representation, growth of repression, and denial of access to essential resources and services. It is at this level, particularly among the poor, that the combination of all the features mentioned above manifest themselves in poverty, ill health, bad nutrition, inadequate or non-existent shelter, low and irregular incomes, illiteracy, etc. Although the poor are victims, wherever they may be located, urban conditions aggravate and complicate their circumstances.

An important aspect of the grass-roots level is that the institutions which are meant to guarantee local administration and the delivery of local services are often powerless, in the sense that they are short of funds, qualified manpower, equipment, and other resources they need to be effective.[13] In some cases, their legal status and relationship to other tiers of government are ambiguous and sometimes, when these are clear, they exist as mere formalities, since power is not decentralized.

Fortunately, the local level is extremely resilient in using gaps in the State. In urban settlements, this is manifested in the prevalance of a wide range of activities which, though defined as 'illegal' by the State are considered by the poor as 'normal'.[14] Throughout the Third World, they increasingly build most of the urban settlements and ensure that these are liveable within their own means. They are also involved in their settlements by providing their infrastructure, despite conflict with governments who impose laws and standards that are unrealistic and often hostile.[15] But since a forcible return of the people to the rural areas is impossible, the future of the ever-increasing number of urban dwellers remains in the urban areas. And it is in these that options and solutions must be found.

Options and prospects

It is, perhaps, necessary to state here that options are never neutral. The choice of policy options involves political decisions determined by the structure of power relations and the configuration of social forces. Options are therefore affected by the limitations imposed by the structure in which the actors are operating, and the amount of space for action that they are permitted. Thus, no matter how analytically rational they are, options are in the end determined by effective struggles between concrete groups emphasizing their own vested interests. In the context of the attainment of sustainable development in Third World urban settlements, our earlier discussions point at the need for any improvement to be based on struggles at every level. What most analysts broadly recommend involves a combination of the rational planning of urban centres, along with the provision of basic needs and control of resources and interaction with the environment.

However, the current economic crisis imposes extra constraints on the capacity of Third World governments to provide essential services to low-income settlements. What is more, many Third World nations are immersed in structural adjustment programmes, imposed upon them by the World Bank/International Monetary Fund, and are obliged to curtail public expenditure.[16] It is therefore the ordinary people of these societies who are presently providing their own needs in terms of shelter and infrastructure. What the politics of transforming or improving their conditions imply include stategies for providing access to employment, with adequate incomes, land for building their shelter on dry and safe terrain, and cheap sources of building materials. The removal of obstacles facing the poor is also necessary. These range from legislation, building codes, and norms covering building forms, to land use and economic activities. The removal of such obstacles promises to release people's hidden energies and their commitment to the attainment of sustainable development. This process has both its domestic and external features and it involves both a top-down approach and a bottom-up approach.

Political activity by adherents of sustainable development in the First World could be useful, through mounting pressures on their governments and these agencies to either lift obstacles in the way of Third World nations or enhance their access to the resources that lead to sustainable development. These kinds of activity would be useful in the resolution of the current debt crisis and the trade problems these nations face. The same could be done for other issues such as industrial and nuclear pollution, maritime problems, and defence and armaments issues. The domestic features are those that are directly affected by either the top-down or bottom-up approaches. The former refers to the imposition of political changes instituted by the national elites. This is unlikely to elicit the commitment of the masses towards the changes necessary for sustainable development.

The bottom-up approach is a more people-centred approach, since it involves the political mobilization of ordinary people. It also involves a process of education (not formal, but political) as to their rights, duties, and obligations towards the environment in which they live. The elites are not excluded from this process, but in this case they come as participants and students ready to learn as well as teach. In this context, participation is defined not only as involvement through consultation and elections, but rather as the yielding of the direct control of decision-making in urban settlements to the communities who live in them. This will first involve ensuring the provision of certain basic needs and rights, such as the right to adequate shelter and livelihood. It is only through this provision of a material stake in their environment that the commitment of the poor majority can be attained.

But what are the prospects of the bottom-up approach in the real world of urban settlements? What makes one believe that land-owners, professionals, politicians, and other vested interests will give up their priviledges and rights? Well, no analyst can offer a general prescription for the Third World as a whole. It depends on individual communities to work out their political tactics for dealing with their domestic dominant interests which they know best. Some communities and nations have already started, others still have far to go. What can be done on the global scale is to build coalitions among groups engaged in these kinds of struggles, to share experiences, knowledge, and support. Above all, the existence of basic human rights such as the rights to political participation, the right to adequate shelter and livelihood, and the freedom of movement in the pursuit of legitimate goals should never be compromized. For it is from them that the basic steps of use struggle for sustainable development in both rural and urban settlements can be taken.

Acknowledgements

The author gratefully acknowledges the hospitality and support of the Human Settlements' Programme of the International Institute for Environment and Development, London, during the period in which this paper was produced. He is particularly grateful to Julie Davila, Czech Conroy, and Ed Barbier, all of the same Institute, for their comments during the preparation of the paper.

Notes and references

1. Apart from evidence from the literature, this was the consensus expressed at three major international conferences on housing and human settlements issues in 1986–7. These conferences are: the International African Institute's seminar *'Housing the Urban Poor in Africa'*, held in London in November 1986; the NGOs' global seminar forum on 'Shelter', held in Limuru and Nairobi, Kenya, in late March and early April 1987; and the 'Only One Earth' forum sponsored by the René Dubois Centre, New York, in April 1987.
2. See: The World Commission on Environment and Development (1987) *Our Common Future*, Oxford; Oxford University Press.
3. I use the notion 'Third World' here, in preference to other terms such as 'developing', 'underdeveloped', 'industrializing', in that it was a term coined by the peoples of the Third World themselves, and it characterizes correctly. See Worsley Peter, (1984) *The Three Worlds: Culture and World Development*, London, Weidenfeld & Nicolson; and Harris Nigel, (1987) *The End of the Third World*, Harmondsworth: Penguin.
4. It is this diversity that had led authors like Nigel Harris (op. cit., n. 3) to proclaim 'the end of the Third World'!
5. See, for instance, contributions such as: Biswas, M.R, and Biswas, A.K. (1984) 'Complementarity between environment and development process', *Environmental Conservation* 11 (1) Spring: 35–43; Cadwell, Lynton K. (1984) 'Political aspects of ecologically sustainable development' *Environmental Conservation* 11 (4) Winter: 299–307; Barbier, E.B. (1987) 'The concept of sustainable economic development', *Environmental Conservation* 14 No (3) Autumn. Also, most recently, Redcliff, Michael

(1987) *Sustainable Development: Exploring the Contraditions*, Methuen: London and New York.

6. Barbier op. cit., n. 5.

7. For some of the more recent examinations of the urban condition in the Third World, see: Mabogunje, A.L. (1980) *The Development Process: A Spatial Perspective,* London: Hutchinson University Library for Africa; Hardoy, J.E. and Satterthwaite, D. (1984) 'Third World cities and the environment of poverty', *Geoforum* 15 (3): 307–33; Newland, K. (1980) *City Limits: Emerging Constraints on Urban Growth,* World Watch Paper 38, August; Stren, Richard (1986) 'Urban Housing in Africa since Independence – Itinerary of a Problem', Paper presented at the International African Institute Conference on 'Housing the Urban poor in Africa', London, November, Armstrong, W. and McGee, T.G. (1985) *Theatres of Accumulation: Studies in Asian and Latin American Urbanisations,* London, Methuen; Roberts, Bryan (1978) *Cities of Peasants – The Political Economy of Urbanization in the Third World,* London: Edward Arnold.

8. See: Harrison, Paul (1982) *Inside the Third World,* Harmondsworth: Penguin Books.

9. See: For instance Radkodi, C. (1986) 'State and class in Africa: case for extending analyses of the form and functions of the national state in the urban local state', *Environment and Planning: Society and Space* 1 (4): 419–46; Stren, R, (1985) 'The State and urban society in East Africa', *Project Ecoville Working Paper,* no. 18, March; and Goulborne, H. (ed.) (1977) Politics and the State in the Third World, London: Macmillan.

10. These conceptions of the State come from two different sources, namely: Ziemann, W. and Lanzendorfer, M. (1977) 'The State In Peripheral Societies', *Socialist Register;* Forrest, T. (1977) 'Notes on the political economy of State intervention in Nigeria', *IDS Bulletin* 9 (1) July Institute of Development Studies, University of Sussex.

11. For an 'anatomy of personal rule' in the African context, see: Sandbrook, Richard (1985) *The Politics of Africa's Economic Stagnation,* African Society Today Series, Cambridge: Cambridge University Press.

12. See ibid. for illustrations of the African experience.

13. For discussions of the problems and constraints of the local administration, in this context, see: Richard Stren, 'Local government and the administration of urban services in Africa' and Carole Rakodi (1986) op. cit., n. 9. Also see the journal, *Planning and Administration* 12 (2) Autumn which focused on local administration in Latin America.

14. On the nature of the illegality issue, see the discussion by McAuslan, P. (1985) *Urban Land and Shelter for the Poor,* London; Earthscan/IIED Books. Also see: Hardoy, J. and Satterthwaite, D. (1987) 'The legal and illegal city', in *Shelter, Settlement and Development,* L. Rodwin (ed.) Boston: Allen & Unwin.

15. Evictions and demolitions are an ever-present possibility for the urban poor once they are defined as occupying illegal plots or having built illegally. Several things motivate governments towards demolitions and evictions – an interesting example, presented at the global NGO seminar

in Limuru, Kenya, was the case of several communities in Seoul, South Korea, who faced evictions and demolitions all because the government wanted to beautify Seoul for its hosting of the 1988 Olympics. The Limuru seminar, in fact, explicitly condemned demolitions and evictions in its resolutions.

16. For a more detailed discussion of this, see the various papers, particularly that of John Loxley, in P. Lawrence (ed.) (1986) *World Recession and the Food Crisis in Africa,* London: James Currey Press.

Additional reading

Acharaya, S.N. (1981) 'Perspectives and problems of development in sub-Saharan Africa,' *World Development* 9 pp. 109-147.

D. Aradeon, Aina, Tade Akin and Umo, Joe (1986) 'South-west Nigeria', in J.E. Hardoy and D. Satterthwaite (eds) *Small and Intermediate Urban Centres: Their Role in National and Regional Development in the Third World,* London, Hodder & Stoughton.

Bienen, Henry (1984) 'Urbanisation and Third World stability' *World Development* 12: 661–91.

Brown, Lester R. and Jacobson, J.L. (1987) 'The future of urbanisation: facing ecological and economic constraints' World watch paper May 77, Washington DC: World Watch Institute. The Economist (1986) 'The anatomy of cities', The Economist, Dec. 20.

Hardoy, J.E. and Satterthwaite, D. (1981) Shelter: Need and Response, London: IIED/John Wiley & Sons.

Hardoy, J.E. and Satterhwaite, D. (1981) 'Shelter infrastructure and services in Third World cities', *Habitat International* 10 (3): 245–284.

Paul Harrison (1983) The Third World Tomorrow, Harmondsworth Pengiun.

Newland, K. (1979) *Global Employment and Economic Justice: The Policy Challenge,* World Watch paper no. 28, April, Washington DC: World Watch Institute.

O'Connor, Anthony (1988) The African City, London: Hutchinson.

Renaud, Bertrand (1981) *National Urbanisation Policy in Developing Countries,* World Bank/Oxford University Press.

Richards, P.J. and Thomson, A.M. (eds) (1981) *Basic needs and the Urban Poor,* an ILO-WEP study, London: Croom Helm.

Richard Sandbrook, *The Politics of Basic Needs in Africa: Urban Aspects of Assaulting Poverty in Africa,* London: Heinemann. 1982.

Townroe, Peter M. (1984) 'The changing economic environment for spatial policies in the Third World,' *Geoforum* 15 (3): 335.

The World Bank (1981) 'The challenge of urban youth: responding to growing problems', *The Urban Edge* 5 (3), April.

(1985) 'A fresh look at urban employment', *The Urban Edge* 9 (8) Sept./Oct.

(1986) *Poverty in Latin america: The Impact of Depression,* World Bank.

Chapter 11

Increasing technological choice in Third World settlements[1]

George McRobie

One of the keys to strengthening the control of Third World city dwellers over their lives is to increase the range of technologies available to them for building and servicing their neighbourhoods. This subject is addressed by George McRobie, one of the original founders, with Fritz Schumacher, of the Intermediate Technology Development Group. McRobie is unashamedly opposed to the continued growth of large Third World cities (let alone to the very large ones), and argues that they have become huge 'energy sinks' with ever increasing demands for food and energy which cannot be sustained. He puts his faith in the prospects for the future development of smaller settlements which are closely related to the rural areas, claiming that the costs of creating the number of new workplaces required by the end of the century can be more economically provided in such settlements than in large cities, thereby reducing the need for rural–urban migration. McRobie concludes by stating that experience during the last 25 years has succeeded in creating more appropriate technologies which are now readily available across the board, and that aid-giving and international agencies should urgently develop the means of putting them into place. McRobie is the author of Small is Possible, *a sequel to* Small is Beautiful.*

For the past 40 years the rate of city growth in developing countries has been explosive. Even if allowance is made for a reduction in previous estimates of future urban growth rates in accordance with the evidence presented by Hardoy and Satterthwaite in Chapter 3, it is clear that both metropolitan and secondary urban centres will expand considerably during the remainder of the century in numerical if not percentage terms. On this basis, the number of people living in cities within the rest of the century will continue to expand rapidly. Most of this expansion will be in the Third World, where the annual urban growth rate is 3.5 per cent, more than triple that in rich countries.

Cities have played a major and indispensable role in human history, as regional and national centres of culture and learning, of government, manufacture, and commerce. But to perform these essential functions effectively – to complement and supplement their rural hinterlands – cities do not have to be huge. For centuries they made their unique contribution to mankind as settlements of seldom more than 100,000 inhabitants (and it could be argued that, in terms of human ecology, 100,000 is just about the right size for a city).

Very large cities are a relatively recent phenomenon, which is closely associated with the era of cheap oil. In the Third World they are the result of rural–urban migration and of natural increase within the cities. As might be expected, migrants mostly comprise the younger and more fertile; accordingly, by the 1980s, about 60 per cent of the rise in the city populations was owing to natural increase, 40 per cent to migration. But the numbers of people migrating to the cities shows no sign of falling.

The phenomenal growth of Third World cities represents the disastrous failure of conventional development programmes and policies during the past 40 years. The transfer of large-scale capital and energy-intensive technologies from the rich countries to the cities of the Third World has concentrated 'development' in these cities; and most developing country governments have displayed a strong urban bias in allocating industrial investment and providing services such as education and health, electricity, water, and transport. Only about 20 per cent of national budgets typically go to the rural sector – where about 70 per cent of the world's population still lives. Thus, the giant city has become a monstrosity, offering a wretched, inhuman existence for its shanty-town poor while it swells the shanty-town population by competing its rural hinterland out of existence. Rural slums create urban slums.

But will the huge Third World cities continue to grow apace? Are the predictions about cities of 15, 20, 30 million people realistic? It seems increasingly unlikely. Already the costs of mushrooming cities are becoming insupportable. There is, first, the food problem. A city of, say, 20 million inhabitants presupposes that 20 million people outside the city are producing twice as much food as they themselves need: otherwise the country and the city depend upon imports. Already, today, most countries are food importers. Only North America, Europe, Australia, and New Zealand are exporters, as Table 11.1 shows.

First, the exporting countries are those that are most dependent upon oil and oil-based chemicals to produce their agricultural surpluses. In other words, their agricultural systems are not sustainable beyond a few decades to come. Poor countries can only rely at their peril on distant, increasingly expensive, and non-sustainable sources of food for their cities. The prospects are, of course, not much brighter for poor countries that are adopting oil-intensive forms of agriculture in their efforts to gain food security. A leading authority on world food, M.S. Swaminathan, recently stated: 'The global food scenario is one of hope on the production front. However it is one of despair both in the field of equitable distribution and sustainability of the production pathways adopted.'[2]

Table 11.1: The changing pattern of world trade, 1950–86

	1950	1960	1970	1980	1986
N. America	+23	+39	+56	+131	+102
Latin America	+ 1	0	+ 4	+ 10	- 4
W. Europe	-22	-25	-30	- 16	- 14
E. Europe and Soviet Union	0	0	0	- 46	- 37
Africa	0	- 2	- 5	- 15	- 22
Asia	- 6	-17	-37	- 63	- 73
Australia and New Zealand	+ 3	+ 6	+12	+ 20	+ 20

Source: Worldwatch Institute Paper 77, Washington DC, May 1987.

Second, predictions about continued massive urbanization assume that there will be enough energy to sustain it. In energy terms, the huge city is a huge energy sink: energy (now mostly oil) is needed to produce, transport and process food, to provide fuel, housing, transport, water, sewage, and waste disposal services. As the oil era draws to a close, to be replaced by solar-based renewable forms of energy, the giant city becomes less and less sustainable. Simply to use such energy – direct solar, wind, water, biomass – effectively, future communities must be smaller and more widely distributed.

Third, there is the environmental impact of massive ubanization. There is the damage to human health caused by increasingly polluted air and water. There is also the growth of an urban mentality that regards the rural environment – the air, land, water and, indeed, people, of the city's hinterland – as infinitely exploitable to serve the city.

Finally, predictions of boundless city growth assume that the city can provide work and income for its vastly increased population. This is a totally baseless assumption. A prodigious numer of new work-places is needed in developing countries between now and the year 2000. To be provided in anything like sufficient numbers, these work-places must be capital-saving and labour-intensive; and if massive unemployment and disruption is to be averted, the bulk of the work-places will have to be provided in rural areas or smaller urban centres where the majority of people live. The day of favouring capital-intensive city-based technologies is over. The massive urbanization of Third World countries is, therefore, on a collision course with emerging realities of food and energy supply, with the environment, and above all with the urgent need to create millions of new work-places and step up food production on a sustainable basis.

It is only by creating new economic opportunities through major programmes, bringing industry into the rural areas and smaller urban centres, that the flight of the rural poor into cities can be arrested and a more sustainable rural–urban pattern of development created. And the creation of new workplaces on anything like the scale required demands, in turn, the development and introduction of technologies appropriate to the needs and resources of the rural poor.

The critical role of technology in economic development was first brought into focus by E.F. Schumacher in the early 1960s.[3] He argued that the large-scale, capital- and energy-intensive technologies of the rich countries would do more to exacerbate than to solve the problems of the poor countries. In 1965, a few of us helped him to start the Intermediate Technology Group in London. Our starting point was that mass unemployment and under-employment, rural misery, and mass migration to the cities could be averted only by creating new work-places in the rural areas themselves; that these work-places must be low-cost, so that they can be created in very large numbers without calling for impossible levels of savings or imports; that production methods and associated services must be kept relatively simple, and that production should be largely from local material for local use.

At first, and for several years, the concept of intermediate – or as it is now generally known, appropriate – technology was by no means welcomed by the aid and development establishment in both rich and poor countries. But today, some 20 years on, the conventional strategy of development, based on large-scale capital-intensive industries, is being increasingly challenged by development economists and planners. Many large industries introduced into poor countries – mostly into their cities – have proved to be very inefficient, kept going only by protection and subsidies. They did not generate the hoped-for surpluses, and did nothing to raise the living standards of the rural and urban poor. It is being recognized that small-scale, localized industry and agriculture can be very efficient, providing new work-places at low cost, and cutting down on transport; and that this is the only effective way of distributing incomes. But it is still true that in most developing countries (and all rich countries) government policies favour the city against the village and small town, the big enterprise against the small, the rich against the poor.

Because most poor people in the world make a living by working on small farms, in small family businesses, or as artisans, technologies appropriate to their needs and resources will generally be small, relatively simple, inexpensive and (to be sustainable) non-violent towards people and the environment. There is now a network of organizations around the world with a significant capacity for developing and helping to introduce appropriate technologies. In the industrialized countries there are the pioneer organizations, ITDG, VITA, Brace Research, more recently joined by AT International in the USA, TOOL in Holland, GATE in Germany, SKAT in Switzerland, GRET in France, and IDRC in Canada. The official aid agencies in Norway, Italy and, Japan are others now taking an active interest in appropriate technology. The ILO and UNICEF are two international agencies that are very active in this field. In the developing countries there are dozens of appropriate technology organizations, ranging from technical research and development groups at one end of the spectrum to information-networking teams at the other.

Thus, over a wide range of human activities, especially those relating to basic human needs, technology choices are now becoming increasingly available. Small-scale, low-cost technologies now exist in agricultural equipment and food processing, water supply, building materials, textiles, energy, transport, and over a wide range of small-scale manufacturing. What is now beyond question is that technology choices can be created right across the board. It should be one of the most urgent tasks on the agenda of aid-giving governments and international agencies to ensure that, at the very least, technologies enabling a basic-needs strategy to be implemented should be readily available to the governments and people of developing countries.

International experience of appropriate technology during the past 20 years has conclusively proved that it offers an efficient, cost-effective alternative to conventional, largely ineffective, aid and development programmes. What is now needed is a major expansion of the work pioneered by voluntary agencies during the past two decades: research and development, field testing and demonstration of appropriate technologies, supported by education and training programmes for field workers and administrators; the creation of local credit and other facilites enabling the rural poor to own and operate small enterprises; and the removal of institutional and administrative barriers to the spread of appropriate technologies through the market.

There is nothing inevitable about runaway city growth and rural impoverishment and decay in the Third World. These are symptoms of a distorted and unequal pattern of development, largely attributable to the wholesale transfer, into the cities of poor countries, of inappropriate rich-country technologies and their supporting institutions. The problems created by monster cities cannot be solved in the cities. Rural industrialization through appropriate technology offers a practical alternative, and an affordable and sustainable strategy of development.

Notes and references

1. Sources drawn upon for this chapter include the following: Ghosh, Pradip (ed.) (1984) *Urban Development in the Third World,* Westport, Conn:

Greenwood Press. (See, especially, the chapters by Michael Todaro, Lester Brown, and George Beier.); Brown, Lester and Jacobson, Jodi (1987) 'The future of urbanisation: facing the ecological and economic constraints', Worldwatch Paper 77, May, Washington DC: Worldwatch Institute; Newland, Kathleen (1980) 'City limits: emerging constraints', Worldwatch Paper 38, August, Washington DC: Worldwatch Institute; Stewart, Frances (ed.) (1987) *Macro Policies for Appropriate Technology in Developing countries,* Boulder, Colo: Westview Press.

2. Swaminathan, M.S. (1987) 'The emerging global agricultural scenario', *Royal Society of Arts Journal,* London, November.

3. For a detailed review of these ideas, see McRobie, George (1981) *Small is Possible,* London: Jonathan Cape.

Chapter 12

Controlled Third World decentralization: a tale of two countries

Charles L. Choguill

In Chapters 3 and 11, particular emphasis was placed on the increasingly rapid growth of secondary and plan for it. Two attempts to achieve a more dispersed pattern of urbanization are reviewed in this Chapter by Charles Choguill. After an initial discussion of international experience concerning the development of small towns in the Third World, the author describes and compares the cases of Malaysia and Tanzania. Although they represent two very different economic and political systems, both countries have adopted positive strategies aimed at creating rural-based settlements through the building of new towns. Choguill demonstrates, however, that despite the considerable effort and cost of the programmes, and the undoubted benefits of improved services that they have provided, they have been less successful in creating real jobs and, therefore, in achieving significant reductions in rural–urban migration. This conclusion does not, however, automatically negate the benefits of dispersed urbanization as advocated by McRobie. But, as Choguill stresses, it reminds us how little we know of the dynamics of small-town growth impact.

The author is director of the Centre for Development Planning Studies at the University of Sheffield and Head of Department of Town and Regional Planning. He has carried out studies for the Asian Development Bank and other international agencies.

As a result of the rapid growth of large cities in the Third World and the subsequent problems which have resulted, such as poor housing, congestion, high rates of unemployment and property, many analysts have in recent years begun to examine the potential that exists for development based upon smaller towns within a country. The argument for small towns is itself a simple one. At present, migrants from rural areas and small towns flock to the large urban areas because they feel that economic opportunities are greater in these locations and because they feel that their children will receive better educations in the cities than in the countryside.[1] If better opportunities to meet these objectives can be provided in the small towns, it is argued, then migration flows might well be reduced, thereby protecting the big cities from the serious problems that arise as a result of this migration. Furthermore, if the economies and service levels provided in small towns can be developed, such places might be expected to improve the urban hierarchies which exist in Third World nations, alleviate the inherent problems with primate cities and provide a much more efficient urban–rural interface which might improve the state of agricultural production in such countries.

Before these issues can be examined, however, some consideration of definitions of small towns must be made. The whole idea of defining urbanization within a Third World context is far more complex than might be expected, as, even in the largest of cities, there is not necessarily a clear-cut differentiation of land use between urban and agricultural functions. In large Asian cities, rice paddies sometimes are found remarkably close to the centre of urban areas. In a number of southern African cities, urban residents fully expect to grow at least a fraction of the food that they will consume. As a result, levels of urbanization even in major urban areas seem to be on a continuum between the purely urban and the purely rural. This point complicates the derivation of hard and fast definitions.

The same ambiguity exists at the lower end of the urban hierarchy, as it is sometimes difficult to distinguish when urban landscapes give way to villages and hence to small towns. Such definitions, therefore, take on an element of arbitrariness and those adopted here are no different. It would have been reasonable, however, to suggest that small towns are those places with an urban population of less than 25,000 population and which fulfil some of the more conventional 'urban' functions, such as serving as a marketing, retail, local administration and/or transportation centre. The minimum size of this settlement is even more difficult to determine but, for practical purposes, a lower floor of 1,000 population might be specified as the dividing line between very small towns and villages.

The role of small towns

In recent years, a number of analysts have examined the role that small towns by this definition tend to fulfil. Based on evidence of small towns from India, World Bank Studies, Africa, and Latin America, Rondinelli argues that small towns and cities in developing countries can and do perform a wide variety of social, economic, and service functions that are important to regional and national development.[2]

The contribution that such small towns can make can be divided along an activity line. Lombardo in his study of small towns in

Honduras and Bolivia found that towns within the range of 10,000 to 12,000 population provide health, educational, and commercial services. These towns are important as transport and distribution centres and as markets for agricultural products grown in the surrounding rural areas.[3]

One argument in favour of devoting more development resources to small towns is that they could provide intervening opportunities to rural migrants and thereby act as a countervailing force to reduce migration movements to larger cities. Sibbing's (1984) analysis of migration and employment patterns in twenty-two towns of Minas Gerais, Brazil, shows the potential of smaller towns in retaining such migrants.[4] Fuller's study of migrants' own evaluation of the quality of life in smaller urban centres in north-east Thailand found that migrants, even recent migrants, were quite satisfied with the quality of life found in the smaller urban environments and 'these results encourage optimism about the ability of smaller urban centres in Thailand to retain migrants'.[5]

Small towns also appear to offer a satisfactory location for at least some kinds of industrial developments. Ho studied rural industries in South Korea and Taiwan and found that small towns, in addition to supporting resource processing activities, also provided locations for small market-oriented industries such as the producers of animal feed, ice manufacturing factories, clay building products, earthenware and hand tool producers, and makers of concrete products.[6]

The most important role of such small towns is undoubtedly their link with agriculture. One aspect of this is the distribution of agricultural produce through periodic markets. In Chinchero, Peru, periodic markets were the most important outlets for goods and services.[7] In Kafanchan, Nigeria, local demand had reached a scale where it could support a daily market. Commerce was centred around this market and some permanent retail stores and service enterprises such as bars and lodging houses had also developed.[8] Many large periodic markets may not operate in individual small towns but may act as a nucleus around small village settlements. In Grand Bassam, Ivory Coast, Miracle and Miracle found that at least 112 different commodities and a great number of services were provided in the markets, and that the village hinterlands were very large.[9]

Other studies, however, have identified the failure of small towns to contribute and generate and development process. Singh and Shahi's study of small towns of Gujarat State in India, which is based on population as an index of functional performance, conclude that towns with less than 20,000 population are less effective in generating activity than intermediate and large cities, despite efforts by central and state government to foster their developments.[10] Similarly, Laghouat in his study of Moroccan small towns found that the economic relationship between small towns and their hinterlands was more indirect than direct and that there was no systematic correlation between the size or density, of small towns and the rural populations of their hinterlands, nor between the real or potential wealth of a region and its small towns.[11]

At this stage, it would seem beneficial to examine in somewhat more detail the experience of two countries where small town development has been central to national planning. The objective of this examination will be to determine what urban services can most readily be provided at this level and whether such provision has an effect upon established rural-to-urban migration flows. This in turn will give some measure of evaluation into the expectations which many expect to result from government investment in such small towns. The two cases examined will be the towns established under one of the Malaysian regional development programmes and the results of the *ujamaa* villagization programme in Tanzania.

Small town development in Malaysia

Within the context of Malaysian development policy and the constraints of Malaysia's new economic policy – a policy designed to distribute the benefits of development across all ethnic groups within the country, urbanization is seen as a natural component of the type of regional development programmes which have been developed. A key element of this programme has been the development of Malaysia's resource frontiers. The method used to achieve this has involved the creation of regional development authorities which are given control over a relatively large area of land and are then responsible for the preparation of a plan to exploit this area's resources and for the implementation of this plan. Although the primary strategy for development is based on agriculture, 'rural urbanization' is an important component of the plans. This policy is based upon the realization that most of the poorer members of Malay society live in rural areas and that urban incomes and living standards are higher than in rural areas.

One such regional development authority, Lembaga Kemajuan Trengganu Tengah (KETENGAH) was established in Trengganu State in north-eastern Malaysia. Upon establishment, KETENGAH entered into a contract with British consultants to prepare a master plan to guide the development of the region.[12] The approach used by the master planning team was to view Trengganu Tengah as an isolated region and then to suggest development steps which might be implemented with respect to agricultural development, forestry, industrial development, and the establishment of settlements, including infrastructure and housing. Various agricultural targets were set for major crops. Resource-based industries were scheduled to provide primary processing for agricultural and timber output from the region. Based upon the assumption that agricultural workers on the region's agricultural estates would be living in new townships, population projections were prepared, transportation systems were planned, and urban infrastructure was scheduled.

Five centralized settlements were included for construction in the first phase of the project. Although a number of subsidies were included for various elements of the township plans to make them more appealing to agricultural estate workers, in fact the growth of the centralized settlements disappointed the planners. The aggregate projection of the population of the five centralized settlements was for 54,139 inhabitants by 1983 whereas the actual populations achieved by the towns was 12,492, only 23.1 per cent of the projection.[13] Although there was variation among the achievements of the five, one, Al Muktafi Billah Shah, which had been envisaged as the administrative centre for the region, achieved only 10.4 per cent of its projected population, while the most successful, Ketengah Jaya, achieved only 45.4 per cent of its target.

As a result of this poor record, infrastructural schemes which were actually constructed, such as the centralized water system, were left with large quantities of oversupply. A large number of houses were built which remained unoccupied. From a financial vantage point, the cost per inhabitant of infrastructure far exceeded the most pessimistic expectations of those who planned the communities.

A number of factors have been suggested for the reason why the urban populations in this particular project did not meet expected targets. Some of these reasons were specific to the geographical location of KETENGAH. After the master planning report was completed, oil and gas were discovered off the coast of Trengganu State and the construction phase of this exploitation undoubtedly attracted unskilled labour that might otherwise have settled in the region.

However, other factors were of a more general nature. Although primary employment opportunity in agriculture and other resource-based activities was established successfully, secondary employment did not evolve as expected because of locational disadvantages *vis-à-vis* national markets but also because of the small size of the towns.

The agricultural land tenure system also had a detrimental effect. Competing agricultural development schemes in the region, such as the Federal Land Development Authority, gave actual title to lands farmed to its participants, whereas the KETENGAH scheme was based on waged work on estates.[14] Undoubtedly this has reduced the attraction of the scheme, regardless of the quality of housing infrastructure, health services, and commercial facilities which were provided.

The *ujamaa* village scheme in Tanzania

At the time of Tanzanian independence in 1961, more than half of the nation's rural population lived in small scattered and shifting homestead groupings. Permanent settlements had been encouraged by the colonial powers if they produced crops such as coffee, tea, sisal, and cotton which contributed to exports, while other settlements were largely ignored. From the very beginning, government strategy was aimed at overcoming this legacy. The policy chosen to realize this included the linking of the benefits of low-level urbanization with certain traditional concepts of self-help with respect to the creation of a technologically advanced, agriculturally-oriented economic base.

A plan was prepared to launch sixty-nine model villages during the period 1964 to 1969 relying upon a two-step process: the 'transformation approach' and the 'improvement approach'. In the first stage, new village settlements were created which were expected to employ modern agricultural methods financed by the state. In the second phase, the community development effort was to take place through mass education which was designed to change traditional attitudes.

The results of this early planning were not altogether successful as a result of organizational, co-ordination, and financial constraints.[15] Nevertheless, with the Arusha Declaration in 1967, the objectives of socialism and self-reliance were reiterated. A key element of this policy was the continued emphasis upon *ujamaa* villages as a rural settlement policy with the specific objectives of increasing economies of scale, raising labour productivity through emphasis upon collective rather than individual efforts, improving the rate of innovation within the villages, the pursuit of equality among participants, the promotion of social welfare through further improvements in education and health facilities, and the achievement of self-reliance.

Despite a large increase in the number of such villages from 809 in 1969 to 5,556 in 1973, problems remained.[16] Farmers gave private efforts priority over communal approaches which led to the continuation of a class system within the villages and resulted in a decrease in food production between 1969 and 1974 by more than 50 per cent.[17] Even with a presidential decree in 1976 that everyone must live in a village, the organizational constraints remained which undermined their chances of success.

Despite the problems that have accompanied the *ujamaa* programme, there is evidence that improvement has occurred for at least a part of the rural population. As Shayo notes, by 1980 72 per cent of the village had co-operative shops, 35 per cent had dispensaries, 92 per cent had primary schools, and 38 per cent had clean water supplies.[18] The goal of universal education had virtually been reached by 1981.[19] Further, much of the rural population had been incorporated into the village decision-making process.[20]

The problems which remained, however, were serious ones. These were concentrated on areas where scarce resources could have been expected to make a difference and where complex resource requirements were important. The situation of piped portable water is thought to have deteriorated since 1970.[21] The villages still lack the necessary transport linkages which could effectively tie them together into an integrated urban system.[22] Perhaps most serious of all, the advances expected to take place, with respect to development of the agricultural economic base, have not taken place.

Conclusions

From the Malaysian and Tanzanian experience, the importance of the establishment of a sound and viable economic base appears to be important. In Tanzania, the deficiencies within the sphere of agriculture have had a negative impact upon success, while in the Malaysian towns, although agricultural targets were met, the expected secondary activities did not develop. Certainly, both cases reveal the importance of national agricultural policy upon the success or failure of such small towns.

The cases reveal that extending at least some urban services to such small towns is primarily a matter of spending resources and applying technology. Yet the provision of health and education facilities alone do not stem the tide of migration to large cities. In other words, jobs and employment opportunities remain the major magnets of migration and these have been achieved more successfully in large rather than small towns. Certainly in neither country have small towns led to a significant reduction in such migration flows.

Both cases reveal how very little we actually know about the dynamics of small town growth, about local decision-making and about what people really want in their towns. It is apparent that there is a pressing need for long-term empirical research on the economic base of small towns and the constraints which limit that base. Until we come to terms with these issues, it seems unlikely that small towns will prosper and hence provide the counter-balance that is required to the slums, squatters, and congestion that exist in the big cities.

Notes and references

1. See, for example, Todaro, Michael P. (1981) Economic Development in the Third World, 2nd edn, Ch. 9, New York: Longman; and Roussel, O.L. (1970) 'Measuring rural–urban drift in developing countries: suggested method', *International Labour Review* 101, March.
2. Rondinelli, D.A. (1985) *Applied Methods of Regional Analysis: The Spatial Dimension of Development Policy,* p. 20, Boulder, Colorado: West View Press Inc.
3. Lombardo, Joseph F., Jr (1982) 'Introduction to the human settlements system in Honduras', unpublished report to US Agency for International Development, Tegucigalpa, Honduras.
4. Sibbing, G. (1984) 'Migration, employment and development: on the role of small towns in the state of Minas Gerais (Brazil)', in H.D. Kammeier and P.J. Swan (eds), *Equity and Growth? Planning Perspectives for Small Towns in Developing Countries,* pp. 78–88, Bangkok: AIT Press.
5. Fuller, T.D. (1981) 'Migrants' evaluations of the quality of urban life in north east Thailand', *Journal of Developing Areas* 16 (1) October: 101.
6. Ho, Sam P.S. (1980) 'Small-scale enterprises in Korea and Taiwan', World Bank Staff Working Paper no. 384, Washington, DC.
7. Fabregat, C. Esteva 'A market in Chinchero, Cuzzo', *Ameario Indigenista* 30 (December): 213–54.
8. Hasnerz, Ulf (1979) 'Town and country in southern Zaria: a view from Kafanchan', in A. Southall (ed.), *Small Urban Centres in Rural Development in Africa,* African-Studies Program, University of Wisconsin, Madison.
9. Miracle, M.P. and Miracle, D.S. (1979) 'Commercial links between Grand Bassam, Ivory Coast and rural populations in West Africa', in A. Southall (ed.) op. cit. n. 8.
10. Singh, R.B. and Shahi, V.P. (1984) 'Place of small towns in the urban system of Gujarat, India', in H.D. Kammeier and P.J. Swan (eds) op. cit. n. 4.
11. Laghouat, M.M. (1984) 'Moroccan small towns in theorty and reality', pp. 593–605 in H.D. Kammeier and P.J. Swan (eds) op. cit. n. 4.
12. Hunting Technical Services Ltd, with Shankland Cox Partnership, *Trengganu Tengah: Regional Planning and Development Study,* November 1974.
13. Interpolated from ibid., vol. 1, table 1.12.
14. The Federal Land Development Authority is a Malaysian government corporation which undertakes land development on a co-operative basis. It clears jungle, plants crops, creates nucleated suttlements, and then trains its project participants in the skills required to succeed in agriculture. See Laquian, A.A. (1982) 'Planned population redistribution: Lessons from Indonesia and Malaysia', *Habitat International* 6 (1/2): 39–52; and Hashim, Alladin (1979) 'Land development under FELDA: some socio-economic aspects', in B. Abdul Rahim Makhzani (ed.), *Rural Development in South East Asia,* pp. 63–79, New Delhi: Vikas.
15. Mushi, Samuel S. (1981) 'Community development in Tanzania', in Ronald Dore and Zoe Mars (eds), *Community Development,* p. 158, London: Croom Helm.

16. ibid., p. 171.
17. Yeager, Rodger *Tanzania: An African Experiment,* p. 81, Boulder, Colorado: Westview Press.
18. Shayo, Stan A. (1985) 'The ujamaa framework in the rural development of Tanzania', *Beitrage trop. Landwirtsch Veterinarmed.* 23: 238.
19. Putterman, Louis (1984) 'The planned co-operative community in a developing country: the case of Tanzania', *Journal of Rural Cooperation* 12 (1/2): 61.
20. Maeda, J.H.J. and Bagachwa, M.S.D. (1981) 'Rural development: policies and perspective in Tanzania', in R.P. Misra (eds), *Rural Development: National Policies and Experiences,* p. 335 Singapore: Maruzen Asia for UN Centre for Regional Development.
21. Louis Putterman, op. cit. n. 19, p. 62.
22. Rondinelli, Dennis A. (1983) 'Decentralisation of development administration in East Africa', in G. Shabbir Cheema and Dennis A. Rondinelli (eds), *Decentralisation and Development,* p. 114, Beverly Hills: Sage Books.

Chapter 13

Development through partnership: the Orangi project in Karachi

Arif Hasan

In this final Chapter, Arif Hasan provides evidence which hopefully offers an example of how many of the issues addressed in previous chapters can be resolved, both in First and Third Worlds. His case study of the Organi project in Karachi, Pakistan, has shown how a poor community in a Third World urban slum has been transformed by the efforts of the people themselves, supported by a committed community organization able both to offer social support and technical advice and act as an intermediary between the community and the city's administration. The value of this project is that it amply demonstrates the practical application of the economic, social, political, and environmental concerns of the other contributors, under conditions where any hope of a better future was previously thought to be minimal. If, therefore, success can be achieved despite all the constraints applicable in Karachi, what can inhibit the prospects for other more advantaged cities?

The author is a consultant architect based in Karachi and has been co-ordinating efforts on the Orangi project as part of a non-governmental organization. He has also researched and published papers on other aspects of urban development in Pakistan.

The Orangi Pilot Project (OPP) was commenced in 1980, as a result of an understanding between Akhtar Hameed Khan, a renowned Pakistani social scientist, who is now the Director of the Project, and Aga Hasan Abadi, the President of the Bank of Credit and Commerce International (BCCI), which provides funds for the Project.

Karachi is Pakistan's largest city and its only port. It has a population of over 7.5 million. Approximately 40 per cent of this population lives in squatter colonies. Orangi township, situated on the Orangi table-land west of the city centre, is the largest of such colonies. Half of this township falls within the target area of the Orangi Pilot Project (OPP). This project area consists of about 4000 acres, contains 3181 lanes and 43,424 housing units. Except for a recently installed water supply system through stand posts, and the on-going Low Cost Sanitation Programme of the OPP (begun in 1980), urban services in this area are non existent. The most pressing need of the squatter colonies, or 'katchi abadis' as they are called, is some form of sanitation, especially related to the disposal of excreta and waste water.

There are two major problems in providing a sanitation system to the squatter colonies. First, the local authorities do not have the necessary finances for constructing a sewerage system. Where international finance is available, the problem of repayment arises. Even if repayment were not a problem, international loans can only deal with a small part of an immense problem. This can be appreciated by the fact that there are over 500 squatter colonies in Karachi alone, housing over 4 million people. Moreover, over 20,000 units are added to Karachi's housing stock every year through the illegal subdivision of state land. Second, the cost of urban services as developed by the local authorities are five times the actual cost of labour and materials required for such development. Users in squatter colonies cannot afford to pay these charges in one go, as do their counterparts in Karachi's more affluent areas. Furthermore, experience has shown that it is impossible to recover development expenditure from low-income users in instalments. It is for this reason that the government's Katchi Abadi (Squatter Settlements) Improvement and Regularization Programme could regularize only 18,000 houses out of over 223,000 during the plan period 1974 to 1985.

Keeping the two above factors in view, the Low Cost Sanitation Programme of the OPP aimed from the very beginning at discovering alternative sources of finance for development. This could only come from within the community and had to be available before the development work was undertaken. An alternative method of implementation of development was also necessary. This method, if it was to succeed, was to be low cost and should not exceed the actual costs of materials and labour required for development. To achieve the above objectives it was necessary to study the sociology, technology, and economics of the people's solutions to the sanitation problem, and see if the OPP could build on them.

Before the OPP's Low Cost Sanitation Programme was commenced, the majority of the people of Orangi used bucket latrines which a scavenger – at 15 rupees per month – would empty out every fourth or fifth day, very often into the unpaved lane. The more affluent houses constructed soakpits which would fill up after a few years, and did not solve the waste water problem. Some people had also laid sewerage line from their houses to the nearest natural creek or 'nullah'. These lines were normally defective, and as there was no communal effort, one found many parallel lines in one lane. However, in spite of these shortcomings this system cleared the streets of both excreta and waste water, and if properly laid, no recurring expenditure was required to maintain it. The people also had a preference for an undergoing system, and the OPP felt that if the right kind of technical support and tools could be provided, and if the lane residents could be organized and trained to use them, then a sewerage system financed and constructed by the people could be developed in Orangi.

Three concepts are central to the understanding of the Sanitation Programme of the OPP, First, community participation; second, modification in standard engineering technology and implementation procedures to make them compatible with the concept of community participation; third, that in the process of organization and participation in development, changes are bound to occur in the community. These changes will result in re-defining relations with the local government, with the OPP and with the scope of future development work undertaken.

The first step towards building up a sewerage system therefore was the creation of community organizations. The 'lane', which in Orangi consists of about 20 to 30 houses, was made the unit of organization. This was because it was a small unit and would as such be cohesive, and as a result there would be no problem of mistrust involved between the members. In addition, the traditional Orangi leadership which functioned at neighbourhood level, would not feel threatened if the programme was limited to one lane at a time, and at that initial stage the OPP was not in a position to antagonize anybody. An underground sewerage system is a complex affair, and developing one lane at a time without a master plan was considered by planners to be an invitation to disaster. However, because of innovation and modification to engineering practice, no disaster took place.

The methodology for developing lane organizations consisted of four stages. First, the OPP social organizers, who are paid employees of the OPP, would hold meetings in the lanes, and with the help of slides, models and pamphlets, explain the programme to the people along with its economic and health benefits. They would explain that the Karachi Development Authority (KDA), or the Karachi Municipal Corporation (KMC), do not lay sewerage lines free of cost, and that their charges could not be afforded by the lane residents. The motivators would tell the people that if they formed an organization in which the whole lane participated, the the OPP would give them assistance. In the second stage, the organization was born and chose its lane manager, who, on behalf of the lane, formally asked for assistance. In the third stage, the OPP technical staff surveyed the lane, established bench marks, prepared plans and estimates (of both labour and materials) and handed over this data to the lane managers. Lastly, the lane managers collected the money from the people and called meetings to sort out any sociological problems involved in the work. The OPP staff provided supervision. At no time, however, does the OPP handle the money of the people. Studies of sociological and technical problems, and the way in which the lane organizations have dealt with them, have been prepared by OPP staff, and some have been published in *Orangi,* a magazine published by the OPP.

As no central supervising and controlling agency was looking after the work being done, and as people in many cases worked themselves, the only way of guaranteeing the quality of work was by educating the people. However, people who are financing and managing the work themselves cannot be forced to listen to advice, and their confidence in the OPP could only develop over a 'prolonged association'. As such, certain substandard work was done in the lanes by the people, and in mid-1982 there was a lull in the programme. As a result, an evaluation of the concept, design and implementation procedure of the project became necessary.

As a result of the evaluation, research was carried out to identify causes for substandard work and simplify standard engineering designs. The results of this research were taken to the people through a massive extension effort, and hundreds of meetings were held. As a result, the people learnt about mixing concrete and curing it, and about the proper manner of making inverts to manholes. Masons were also trained in the OPP sanitation technology and their addresses given to the lanes that applied for assistance. This extension effort led to great improvement in the standard of work, and more and more lanes applied for assistance. As the lane was the unit of organization, initially only those lanes which were near a natural creek or 'nullah', or those which could drain into such 'nullahs' easily, asked for assistance. It was feared by the OPP advisors that the programme would end here, unless lanes away from the 'nullahs' came together to construct secondary drains.

To promote the concept of secondary drains, the OPP carried out a physical survey of Orangi. The unit of the survey was the circle of each elected KMC councillor. Architecture and engineering students carried out this survey, showing land use, slope of the land the number of lanes in a councillor's circle, etc. After 30 to 40 students had moved through Orangi, talking to the people and involving them in their work, Orangi became a changed place. People interacted with the students and the concept of secondary drains registered in the people's minds. In addition, the concept of development through community participation went back to the professional universities and colleges, and their involvement with Orangi is growing as a result.

The results of the survey of each circle were compiled along with literature regarding the programme, and given to the councillor of each area. In motivation meetings the people were informed of this, and they started to pressurize their councillors to take an interest in the secondary drains. This resulted in a large number of neighbourhood lane organizations coming together and asking the OPP for technical assistance for construction of secondary drains. As such, this problem, too, was overcome. The OPP no longer needs to motivate the people. Because of the demonstration effect, lanes now organize themselves and contact the OPP for technical assistance, and the OPP organizers find themselves more and more involved in technical supervision rather than organization. Recently the OPP has expanded its area of operation and is responding to requests from those areas of Orangi that were not parts of its original target area.

Major changes have also taken place in the relationship of the Orangi councillors and the KMC as a result of the OPP programme. Councillors get grant in aid from the KMC for certain development projects in their areas which they have to identify. As per KMC regulations, this aid can only be utilized for the construction of roads, or for the construction of open surface drains for storm water. In November 1984, the people of Orangi Sector 5 forced their councillor to use this finance to construct an underground sewer. They initially also insisted that they should be allowed to use this money themselves, and that no KMC contractor should be used for development purposes. However, this was not agreed to, and a contractor was employed according to KMC regulations. The people supervised his work, and as they were now well versed in sanitation technology, did not permit any substandard work to be done. They also insisted, and got their councillor to agree to getting the OPP to design and supervise the construction work on the drain. Since then, the OPP finds itself identifying locations of secondary drains for the councillors in Orangi, designing and supervising works being financed by the KMC, in addition to helping lanes construct their primary drains. The OPP it seems has become a research and extension agency for the KMC councillors.

Out of a total of 3,181 lanes in the OPP's part of Orangi, over 2,267 (or 34,856 houses out of 43,424) had, by September 1988, already built their sewerage system. Over 173 secondary drains had been constructed; 135 financed by the lane residents and 38 by the KMC. The people have invested Rs 26,991,950 (US$ 1,686,996) in this effort whereas the OPPs investment in research and extension has been about Rs 1,500,000 (US$ 93,750), inclusive of capital expenditure for tools, shuttering, and vehicles. The local bodies would have spend US$ 8,434,980 on this work. In addition, the OPP social organizers, the lane managers, and those who participated in the development work are emerging as an alternative leadership to the traditional one, which consists mainly of the land grabbers and subdividers who created Orangi and exploited the people ever since. One of the social organizers of the OPP was elected councillor in the last election, and two others participated in them.

Two other low income areas in Karachi, Masoom Colony and Baba Island, have used the extension services of the OPP for constructing their sewerage systems through community participation and finance. Requests for assistance have also been received from large villages in the rural areas. In addition, the Aga Khan Medical University and the Department of Architecture, DCET, Karachi, have associated their courses with the programme.

A major environmental and social change has also taken place in Orangi. The lanes which have a sewerage system are now cleaner and healthier. The people here have also undertaken an improvement of their houses, and the value of property has gone up considerably. A survey reports that quarrels related to sanitation which were common in the pre-OPP programme days have now disappeared, and there is more social harmony. Systems for financing, operating and maintaining the sewerage lines have also been developed by the residents. On a base established by the Programme, the OPP is carrying out a Housing Programme, Women's Welfare Programme, and a programme for Women's Work Centres. In addition, a programme for garbage collection and disposal is in the experimental stage. All these programmes are based on the research and extension method and aim at finding alternatives to the failure of government policies in these spheres.

The OPP's Sanitation Programme has shown that the unequal political relationship between government agencies and the poor, which results in the further deprivation and exploitation of their areas, can be changed through a development strategy in which they participate and finance, providing that in so doing they replace some of the functions of those agencies. However, it remains to be seen whether the OPP model can, under the present political conditions in Pakistan, be integrated into the government's development policies for low-income urban areas.

Conclusions and new beginnings

David Cadman and Geoffrey Payne

As we indicated in the Preface, this book grew out of a concern, prompted by the New Economics Foundation, to develop an agenda of relevant issues shaping the future of cities. This concern coincided with the European Year of the Environment and the International Year of Shelter for the Homeless which both raised public awareness of the need to improve urban living and working conditions and to address major ecological, political, social and economic problems. In our Introduction, and in chapters throughout the book, we have challenged current assumptions regarding the 'economic imperative' and argued the case for an approach which takes other aspects into account. This has been based on two major concerns.

First, we believe that the very notion of development in its widest sense has been subverted, and consequently debased, by a preoccupation with growth, as though it were not a means to an end (greater welfare and well-being in a safer world), but an end in itself. This preoccupation with growth has created unprecedented affluence for a relative few, but left hundreds of millions to exist in relative or absolute poverty. Even for the fortunate minority, it is questionable whether their sense of welfare, well-being or safety have increased in proportion to their affluence. Furthermore, growth without international and national redistribution can only increase the alienation and desperation of those excluded from its benefits, creating a dangerous legacy for the future. As the traditional focus of such concentrations of economic growth, cities throughout the world encapsulate these extremes of wealth and exclusion and all evidence suggests that their social fabric is in urgent need of repair.

A second and even more compelling force to the 'economic imperative' is now emerging in the natural environment surrounding cities. The rate at which industrial and human wastes and pollution are poisoning our land, air, and seas is increasing much faster than nature's ability to cope. At present, responsibility for such negligence lies mainly in the affluent industrialized countries and the multinational corporations operating in the Third World. They commonly evade their social and environmental responsibilities by claiming a 'lack of evidence' regarding the consequences of their actions for fear of reducing profits. Unless pressure is effectively mounted, however, the long-term costs to all of us could well prove catastrophic and it will be too late to reverse the trend by the time such conclusive evidence is available.

Even within its own terms, therefore, the drive for economic growth has not yielded a corresponding improvement in the quality of life and the comforts made available are exacting a price which, like a credit card statement, has yet to be realized. The 'new economics' approach advanced in this book is inevitably incomplete, but it does emphasize the need for those involved in shaping the future of cities to balance three primary elements; social needs, ecological balance, and economic sustainability. The first requires a concern for the whole population, the second for other species and the environment on which we all depend and, finally, a longer term view of economic benefits than is currently expected.

In the previous pages, we have sought to show how these issues affect and are affected by cities at present and what it is likely to mean for cities in the future. In our discussions of current trends, Chapters 1–4 examined aspects of mainstream ideas on cities. Hay set the scene by describing the forces which have shaped cities in Europe and North America during the nineteenth and twentieth centuries and pointing out the role of technology in their growth and decline. He forecast a continuing trend of suburbanization for the more mobile sections of the population, the emergence of new forms of manufacturing and communications industries with new locational preferences, and a modified service sector role for 'traditional cities'.

In Chapter 2, Begg and Moore looked forward to identify the direction these forces are taking us. Relating their analysis to western Europe and North America, they emphasized the importance of 'tradeables' or exports in securing urban economic survival and concluded, with Hay, that there is not going to be a significant return of conventional manufacturing activity to the urban core. Whilst some urban renewal may be generated by a change in residential preferences, they believe this will not be evenly distributed and predict chillingly that 'in managing balanced decline ... casualties are to be expected'.

In Chapter 3, Hardoy and Satterthwaite concluded that the growth patterns of future Third World cities are likely to be more varied and unpredictable than has been assumed so far. In particular, it would seem that: national urban growth rates are closely related to economic growth rates; the share of very large cities is generally decreasing relative to some smaller cities; the reduced growth rates of very large cities appear to owe little to explicit government policies to restrict growth; the central areas of major cities are commonly losing populations to peripheral areas, creating multi-urban regions and reducing the distinction between 'urban' and 'rural'.

This blurring of rural–urban characteristics, and the existence of extensive urban poverty in the cities of both First and Third worlds, suggests that, in future, resources need to be allocated on a social rather than a spatial basis. It also suggests that concentrating efforts on managing the balanced growth of rapidly expanding secondary cities makes far more sense than attempting to discourage migration to the major cities. In her review of urban management in the Third World, Rakodi identified three main options: strengthening existing administrative systems, community organizations, or the private sector. She showed how the ways in which each option has been put into practice has restricted their potential and argued that these constraints can best be overcome by creating a more harmonious and complementary relationship between public, private, and community organizations than exists at present. This could be considerably enhanced through a strengthening of the resource base and levels of autonomy of urban and municipal government; the establishment of more modest standards and simpler administrative procedures; greater flexibility in negotiating with private developers; and a willingness to consult fully with local community groups. Such measures would go a long way to meeting basic social needs and ensuring the economic sustainability of Third World cities; the question of ecological balance is likely to prove more intransigent, however, and is discussed separately below.

The contributors to Part II then examined a range of alternative views which may shape the future of cities in both the First and Third World. Robertson's scenario of collapse, hyper-expansion, or 'business as usual' drew upon the concerns explored in Part I to propose a fourth option the 'sane, humane and ecological' alternative which emphasizes greater self-reliance at both urban and personal levels. This emphasis upon the quality of life in which trends in technology are related to changes in personal attitudes, work, and life-style and the possibilities of a New Economics, set the tone for exploring specific aspects in later chapters.

In a British context, Holmes and Steeley introduced the concept of the 'spread city' akin to Ebenezer Howard's vision of the 'social city' and consisting of a network of well managed and planned, but self-contained, cities, combining the best of urban and rural life. In a change of focus from the city to the citizen, Cullen questioned the primacy of conventional rationalism in general and economic rationalism in particular. He posited a clash between city structures and existential action and argued that the future of the city must be about the ways in which power relationships are resolved.

Returning to the larger scale, Girardet examined the demands which cities place upon soil fertility and other natural resources and their environmental output in the form of solid wastes and air pollutants. He showed how the linear processes by which cities transform environmental resources into waste products is disruptive of the planet's life-support systems and argued the case for a more circular approach which recycles resources to maintain an ecological balance. He listed some of the practical measures which will need to be adopted internationally, but particularly in the more affluent countries which cause most of the problem and have the resources to deal with it. In Third World countries, a start could also be made by reducing vehicular exhaust and industrial emissions, and sewage treatment (in the form of bio-gas plants) could turn human wastes into a useful product with social, economic and environmental benefits. This is because soil fertility would be maintained or improved at modest costs, and the incomes and social status of those directly involved – currently the lowest in society – could be considerably enhanced.

Returning to the issue of addressing basic social needs, our Introduction drew attention to Max Neef's distinction between 'needs' and 'satisfiers'. In his discussion on community control over future cities, Turner demonstrated that, in many cities, non-governmental and community-based organizations have already shown that they are more socially responsive and efficient in satisfying a wider range of needs then either the public or formal private sectors, despite widespread neglect and even hostility. In some Third World cities they have become the major single channel for providing land, housing, and services. As such, they represent a far more potent force than Rakodi suggests planners presently appreciate and one which is applicable as much in the First as in the Third World.

Progress on any of these fronts poses a major challenge of political will. In countries where public pressures exert direct control over government policies and priorities, such progress is likely to be greater than in those where government is more insulated. In his wide-ranging assessment of political constraints and options for achieving sustainable urban development, Aina notes the tendency towards authoritarianism and centralization common throughout the Third World and the concentration of power and resources in the few metropolitan centres it has produced. Against this, however, he notes that the poor have fortunately demonstrated sufficient energy and resourcefulness to build much of the cities themselves, and concludes with suggestions as to how progressive forces within the Third World can effect change and how concerned groups within the First World can support this. By asserting that political structures are not immutable and outlining options which anyone concerned can pursue, Aina provides a practical agenda for progressive action by individuals as well as organized groups.

As Girardet emphasized in Chapter 8, industrialization has exacted a heavy price on soil fertility and the pollution of our air and seas. A significant proportion of people live in daily threat of their health, and even lives, to produce goods and services which they can never hope to enjoy themselves. Conversely, as McRobie pointed out in Chapter 11, a wide range of more socially, ecologically, and economically appropriate technologies now exist which can benefit a far wider range of people with the necessities for a healthy life. Most have been tested in practice and provide a basis for addressing all the major issues of social needs, ecological balance, and economic sustainability with which this book is concerned.

These trends and forecasts provide us with some ideas of the changes likely to affect cities as we enter the twenty-first century. In addition, by inference, they give us an indication of the likely physical form of future cities. What does this mean for the social and personal dimension alluded to in our Introduction? We began the book with a discussion of inner-city problems in Britain and went on to examine the broader perspectives of cities in very different contexts. The need to recognize the personal dimension provides another possible interpretation of the term 'inner city' as one which signifies individual perceptions and levels of personal fulfilment. Such a term is analogous to the concepts of intuitive creativity discussed in books such as *The Inner Game of Tennis* and those relating to the complementary functions of the left and right sides of the human brain.[1]

These ideas are based upon a conviction that the intuitive modes of thinking and acting which are developed in the right side of the human brain have been suppressed by acquired, or even imposed, notions of order and control developed in the left side of the brain. If the analogy is applied to our attempts to understand and manage cities, it suggests that we have become far too dependent upon negative or passive control mechanisms, which have suppressed innovative, flexible, and locally generated initiatives. Evidence in support of this view can be found in both urban planning theory and practice. Until relatively recently, for example, theory became almost totally dominated by quantitative concepts of systems theory and econometric modelling, and still draws heavily upon the materialist philosophies of Karl Marx or Adam Smith. Since the real world is too complex for either of these theories to explain or predict, urban theory has tended to become moribund. However, new ideas and practical developments are now beginning to emerge in isolated pockets around the world, and some are being connected to each other and to mainstream theory and policy, too, from an increasingly coherent, alternative perspective.

These ideas are based upon a view of planning that is parallel to that advanced for economics by Fritz Schumacher.[2] The notion of planning 'as if people mattered' is, in effect, turning on its head, the conventional view of planning as the preserve of professionals and administrators, in order to demonstrate that the most satisfying and environmentally sustainable developments can be achieved where communities, particularly at a local level, have far greater influence. Ironically, it may be that, in this respect, the economic problems which have beset cities in Third World countries during the last 40 years or so, provide at least a pointer to the future of cities elsewhere. The combined efforts of ordinary, often poor and unskilled, people to organize housing construction and neighbourhood planning, as described by Turner in Chapter 9, have generated a sense of community and personal fulfilment often lacking in the more affluent cities and suburbs of the First World.

This does not mean that governments can abrogate their responsibilities for the provision of basic services, affordable land, materials, finance, and so on. It does, however, pose the question, in both the First and Third Worlds, of whether governments and professionals engaged in urban development have been doing those things which are most needed and for which they are most suited. In many First World countries, the present tendency is for market forces to determine where, and even how, one lives. For most people, social or personal preferences feature well down the list. Although Third World urban land markets can be even more regressive, the large numbers excluded from them have generated whole sub-markets outside the formal market mechanisms, which more accurately reflect the social and personal needs of residents than those pre-planned by professionals.

In the past, these initiatives commonly took the form of squatting or of informal settlements. More recently, however, they have been supplanted by illegal private-sector developers who operate for profit. In many cases, these have removed the cushion against market forces provided by the earlier processes, though many have responded to the economic, if not the personal or cultural, needs of their clientele. In other cases, examples abound of community-based initiatives in the development of new settlements which still provide creative outlets for the personal dimension. As Hasan has shown in Chapter 13, various non-governmental organizations have also become involved in helping such communities optimize their physical, socio-economic and personal needs in upgrading their local environment – a process matched in the First World by the growing interest in 'community architecture' projects.

Most of these successes in community-based housing and neighbourhood development have so far been achieved despite, rather than because of, government action. They serve to demonstrate, however, the vast reservoirs of talent and energy waiting to be tapped for initiatives that create the kinds of cities that people want, rather than the kind that even well-intentioned professionals want for them.

What is needed is simply the opportunity. Third World opportunities have generally arisen by default, through the inability of governmental institutions to control the way cities evolve. Institutions in the First World have had an additional hundred years to refine the means of controlling such processes. Consequently, community-based initiatives in Britain, for example, have had to struggle hard to overcome bureaucratic hostility and inertia. Is it possible, therefore, that the Third World, with its experience in managing with inadequate resources, has lessons to teach the First World in realizing the creative energies of ordinary people, and transforming cities in the process?

How can the profession of planning, and the process of urban renewal, be developed 'as if people mattered'? The current chasm between planners and planned has led to an international loss of public confidence in architects, planners, and developers. This has, in turn, generated self-doubt amongst the professions – not just as a result of past failures but in terms of what should be done in the future. Such self-doubt is, however, a pre-condition for developing new professional and institutional roles and, therefore, represents an opportunity. What is now needed is to formulate new roles for professionals and governments to plan and manage future cities.

For central government agencies, this will entail concentrating upon a limited number of critical components and making greater use of indirect levers to stimulate development by others. The primary objective of policy should be to ensure the the evolution of vigorous, pluralistic land and property markets, enabling scarce public resources to be targeted to those groups in the greatest need. To achieve this, greater flexibility will be required in initial standards of development, especially in the Third World but also in other contexts. At the same time, public agencies would benefit from a more rigorous management of their resources and from being more sensitive to the ways in which such resources are perceived in the voluntary and private sectors.

One area in which higher standards will be increasingly required concerns the ecological impact of future cities. The recent flood disasters in Rio de Janeiro, and more recently in Bangladesh amply testify to the impact of deforestation and soil erosion. Air pollution in Mexico City and water pollution in major rivers, such as the Nile and Ganges, all create massive health problems, reduce life expectancy, and impede economic development. And those of us who live in First

World cities like London can testify to the increasingly disturbing impact of traffic noise, pollution, and congestion. As Girardet has shown, there is a major role for governments to play in educating public opinion and safeguarding the environment on a long-term basis. A further role for central government agencies is to reduce the time-lag between the successful completion of innovative developments and their incorporation into the mainstream of public policy and practice. This would go a long way to accelerating the process of public learning and reduce the tendency to 're-invent the wheel'.

One of the most important tasks which central governments need to undertake, however, is to hand over more power to lower levels of government, particularly at city level. The lack – or erosion – of local democracy means that nobody is accountable to a city's population or enjoys a popular mandate for local policies. Metropolitan and municipal governments cannot be expected to manage the physical or economic development of their cities if they do not enjoy popular support. The reinforcement of this tier of government will not be productive, however, unless its energies are directed at tasks which are consistent with needs, resources, and powers. Squaring this circle will involve very hard choices and, in particular, learning to work with a wide range of other actors such as the voluntary sector, private developers, local communities, and landowners. For many professionals, it will mean rethinking the habits and assumptions of a lifetime and working with local communities on equal terms rather than as 'experts' since, after all, local people will invariably know more about their particular neighbourhood than outsiders, whatever their technical skills. The pioneering work of people like Tony Gibson in Britain[3] and numerous community activists in the Third World, have indicated some of the skills which will be required. What is needed is first of all a willingness to change direction and then the patience and humility to acquire the necessary skills.

As this book goes to press, concern over the environment and wider socio-economic issues are rapidly moving up the agenda of political priorities in many countries. We therefore concluded the contributions with two case studies which attempt to address social, economic, and environmental issues in a sustainable way. In the first, Choguill illustrated the attempts at urban decentralization pursued by Malaysia and Tanzania. He demonstrated that, despite considerable effort and expense – and the undoubted benefits of improved services which they have provided – they have been less successful in creating real jobs, and therefore less successful in reducing rural–urban migration, than had been envisaged.

Whilst this experience does not negate the benefits of dispersed urbanization as advocated by McRobie, it does suggest that such programmes need to be more selective and pragmatic. In the final chapter,

Hasan showed how a poor community in a Third World city was able to transform a major slum with the support of a committed community-based organization acting as a mediator between them and the city administration. Experience from many other countries supports the view that this provides a feasible – perhaps the *only* – option for harnessing the human and material resources desirable to satisfy social needs on a long-term basis, without destroying the environment in the process.

From such conclusions, how can we move to a new beginning? What role or roles are suggested for the state, professionals, and citizens? The first step is to insist that any approach to planning or building cities respects the three basic elements identified throughout the book: social needs; ecological balance; and economic sustainability. To achieve one at the expense of the others cannot be regarded as progress. To each and every decision that has to be made in any city, therefore, the wider social, environmental, and economic factors need to be assessed individually and collectively. A non-polluting and inexpensive technology addressing basic social needs will, on this basis, be preferable to one which yields high profits but incurs significant social or environmental costs. Quantifying the pros and cons will not be easy, and such difficulties will inevitably be used to gain support by those pursuing regressive proposals.

The application of comprehensive environmental impact analysis, together with social impact studies would help to provide a more rigorous basis for evaluating the consequences of new policies or development proposals. Such technical expertise will be of little use under conditions where, in the final analysis, decisions are made and resources allocated on short-term political considerations from the centre. Addressing this issue is, of course, the central one in any developmental process and options open to either professionals, individuals, and non-governmental organizations vary considerably in the degree of influence which they wield. Increasing public awareness and concern has to be a precondition for such participatory influence, however, and this book will have served its purpose if it contributes in some small way to that enormous task.

Notes and references

1. Gallwey, W.T. (1979) *The Inner Game of Tennis,* New York: Bantam Books; and Edwards, Betty (1979) *Drawing on the Right Side of the Brain,* London: Fontana/Collins.
2. Schumacher, E.F. (9173) *Small is Beautiful: A Study of Economics as if People Mattered,* London: Blond and Briggs.
3. Gibson, Tony (1984) *Counterweight: the Neighbourhood Option,* London: Town & Country Planning Association.

Index

Abidjan, Ivory Coast 91, 116, 122
acid rain 174
Act of Creation 163
Adjusted National Product (ANP) 25–6
Ado Ekiti, Nigeria 98
administration: 1st World 10, 38; 3rd World 111–24, 229; see also community, government, local government, private sector
Adriatic 172
Africa 84, 85, 87, 89, 91-3, 103, 112, 213: environmental damage 170–1, 175
Aga Khan Medical University, Karachi 226
ageing population, Europe 45, 61–3, 66, 70, 136, 139–40
agriculture: alternative future 131, 132, 133, 143–4, 147; environmental damage 143, 176; industrial 139; technological development 39, 47, 62, 207–8, 209, 210; 3rd World 77, 88, 90, 91, 94, small town development 213, 214, 215, 216, 217, 218, technology 207–8, 209, 210
aid agencies 97, 102, 103, 209–10
Aids 128
air pollution 173–4, 179, 230, 233
Akron, Ohio 48
Alexander, C. 18
Al Muktafi Billah Shah, Malaysia 216
Algeria 93
alternative future 30, 176–80

Amazon 175
America see North America
apartheid 93
appropriate technology 206, 209–10, 231
architecture: coercive structure 161–2; community 232; determinism 16, 17–18, 23, 30, 157, 158, 162
Argentina 83, 86
arms supply 197
Arusha Declaration (1976) 217
Asansol, India 88
Ashby, W.R. 187
Asia: deforestation, 175; management 116; rural–urban division 213; urban change 84, 85, 87–8, 92, 93, 96–7, 99, 100, 103
Athens 7, 12, 47, 65, 71
Atlanta 71
Aurangabad, India 88
Australia, food exporter 207, 208
authoritarianism, 3rd World 192, 199, 200, 230
Aviles, Spain 48

Baba Island, Karachi 226
baby bulge 46
Babylon 12
Baltic 172
Baltimore 59, 65
Bangalore, India 88, 95
Bangkok 96, 112, 117, 122
Bangladesh 88, 98, 233
barangays, Manila 118

Barbier, E.B. 194, 195
Barratt, W. 164
Bauhaus 162
behavioural psychology 156
Beijing 88, 99
Belfast 46, 48, 71, 158
Belgium 43, 48, 71
Bell, D. 166
Belo Horizonte, Brazil 86
Benetton 160
Bennett, A. 163
Berman, M. 155–6
Berry, B. 42
Beyond the Stable State, D. Schon 5
Bilbao 48, 65
biotechnology 62, 132, 133
Birmingham 40, 68
birth rate 45
Bissau, Guinea Bissau 81
black economy 47
Blake, W. 13
Bochum, FRG 48, 71
Bolivia 164, 213–4
Bombay 11, 88, 89, 99, 112, 121
Bordeaux 71
Boston, Massachusetts 65, 130
Boswell, J. 12–13
Bradbury, K.L. 49
Bradford 9, 10
Brasilia 157
Brazil 79, 83, 86, 157, 214: Rio de
    Janeiro 83, 86, 99, 176, 233; São
    Paulo 81, 83, 85, 96, 97, 99, 175
Bremen 71
Bristol 66, 158
Brixton riots 1, 2, 158
Broadwater Farm riots 2
Brundtland Report 193, 194–5
Brussels 71
budgeting procedures 115, 116
Buenos Aires 83, 86
Buffalo 65
*Building Community: A Third World
    Case Book*, B. Turner 190
Burma 81, 88, 97
business services, 1st World 68
Buttimer, A. 154

Cadbury, G. 157
Cairo 5, 91, 93, 176
Calcutta 9, 88, 89, 98, 100, 101, 164:
    environmental damage 175, 176;
    management 112, 116, 119, 122,
    123
California 96
Cambridge, England 66
Campana, Argentina 86
Cannery, San Francisco 130
Canter, D. 20
capitalism 153, 154, 166, 167, 193:
    economic determinism 159, 160,
    161; investment 28
car ownership 40
carbon dioxide 173, 178, 179
Caribbean 83, 84, 85
Castells, M. 159, 160
Central African Republic 92
Central America 197; *see also*
    Mexico
centralization: 1st World 37, 42, 43,
    44, 51, Britain 1, 2; 3rd World,
    208, power 112, 123, 192, 199, 230
CFCs *see* chlorinated fluoro-carbons
Chad 79, 92
Charleroi, Belgium 43, 48, 71
Chicago 64
Chile 83, 164
China 79, 84, 85, 87, 88, 89, 91, 95,
    97, 99
Chinchero, Peru 214
chlorinated fluoro-carbons 174
citizenship 153–6, 162, 229
city farms 131, 147
City in History, The, L. Mumford 3, 4,
    5, 6, 8, 10
City of London 167–8
City Perceived, The, A. Lees 12
class, social: effect on population
    distribution 41, 45, 47, 51; 3rd
    World 198, 199, 217
Clean Air Acts, Britain 174
Cleveland, Ohio 48, 49, 65
coal mining 173
coastal waters, pollution 172, 175
Cobbett, W. 13
Colombo 112

colonialism 8–9, 11, 122, 198, 217
Colombia 83
combined heat and power (CHP) 131
COMECON 97
Common Agricultural Policy 144
Commonwealth 197
communications: development of cities,
    1st World 40, 55, future 46, 60, 63,
    67, 68, 141; hyper-expansion
    scenario 130; industries 37, 38, 52,
    167, 228; public transport, 3rd
    World 48–9, 122–3, 218
community 18–19, 30: 1st World
    146–7, 148, 149, 150, 168; 3rd
    World 217, housing 118–19,
    181–91, 185, 186, 201, 202, 232–3,
    235, management 111, 112, 113,
    118–21, 122, 124, 149, 229, 230,
    234, 235, Orangi project, sanitation
    221–24, politics 200–1, 202–3;
    architecture 190, 232; base
    organizations (CBOs) 181, 182,
    184; employment 26–7; future
    scenario 131, 167; investment in 29
commuter 137
computer technology 63
congestion 47, 49
conservation *see* environment
Conservative governments 49–50
Constantinople 7, 8
consumption 158, 160, 166, 195
contraction: 1st World 6–9; 3rd World 9
Covent Garden 130
Cooper, C. 22
Copenhagen 46, 59
Le Corbusier 16, 156, 157, 164
core regions 87, 89, 91
corruption, 3rd World 200
cost recovery 117
counter-urbanization 100–1, 102
cotton trade, Britain 11
Countryside 137, 149
Countryside Policy Review Panel 144
Coventry 9, 10
crime, physical environment 16
Cuba 87, 91, 94
Cuernavaca, Mexico 86
culture 65, 142, 154, 175

Czechoslovakia 174
Dar es Salaam, Tanzania 91, 95, 98
Dawdle Report, 1944 19
death rate, Europe 45
decentralization 14–15: 1st World 11,
    37, 43, 44, 45, 46, 47–8, 51,
    Britain 40–1; 3rd World 12, 89,
    100, 102, 212–8; future scenarios
    127, 130, 132
Defensible Space, O. Newman 16, 158
deforestation 171, 175, 176, 178, 233
demography: 1st World 9, 12, 45,
    46–7, 55, 60–1, 70, Britain 39, 66,
    136, 139–40; 3rd World 5, 112
Denmark 43, 46, 59
'dependent urbanization' 11
Derby 67
desertification 179
determinism: architectural 16, 17–18,
    23, 30, 157, 158, 162; economic
    15, 55, 159–60; environmental 16,
    17, 21, 156–7, 164–5
Detroit 48
de-urbanization policy, China 89, 91
    see also decentralization
development authorities, 3rd World
    112, 113
Dhaka, 9, 79, 82
Dickens, C. 13
Divis Flats, Belfast 147
divorce, Britain 136, 140
Docklands Scheme, London 69, 167–8
Doncaster 43
Dortmund 48, 65
Drabble, M. 14
drought 128
drugs 165
Duisburg 48, 65, 71
Durkheim, E. 153
Durgapur, India 88
Dusseldorf 65, 71

ecology *see* environment
Economic Community of West
    African State (ECOWAS) 197
economics 227–8: 1st World 10, 11,
    54, 55–6, determinants of function
    56–61, future developments and

implications 61–64, future of
urban systems 64–8, 70–2, future
in Britain 66–70; 3rd World 94,
95–6, 101, 102, 114, 193, 199,
Africa 92, 93, 112; alternatives,
economic sustainability, New
Economics 23–30, 130–1, 134,
227, 228, 231, 235; economic
determinism 15, 25, 159–61;
'economic space' 154
education 202, 217, 218, 224, 234
Egypt 5, 91, 93, 176, 233
Ekins, P. 23
El Salvador 119
Elbe 172
elderly 45, 61–2, 66, 70, 136, 139–40
electronics industry 62–3, 68
employment: 1st World 140–2; 3rd
World 94, 208, 209, small towns
216, 218
Endell, A. 13
energy: conservation 131, 177, 178,
179, third world 206, 208, 209;
forecasting compared
demographic forecasting 98–9,
199; sources 59, 69
engineering industry, Britain 68
Enterprise Zones, Britain 69
Enugu, Nigeria 122
environment 208, 227–8, 231: 1st
World 143, 145–7, 150, 233–4,
cause of decentralization 47, 48, 49;
3rd World 103, 175–6, 199, 227–8,
230, 233; air pollution 173–4, 179,
230; alternative future 30, 176–80,
sane human and ecological 26, 127,
128, 130–1, 132, 133,134, 229,
sustainable development 193, 194,
195, 196, 199, 202, 235;
appropriate technology 206,
209–10; 'environmental
determinism' 16, 17, 21, 156–7,
164–5; Gross National Product, and
25, 26; history 170–1, psychology
20; waste disposal 116, 122, 172–3,
176–7, 178–9, 227, 230; water
pollution 171–2, 175, 178–9, 230;
see also soil fertility

equity 142
Essen 43, 48
ethical investment 29
Ethical Investment Research and
Information Service 29
Eureka principle, Koestler 163
Europe: colonial power 11; economic
function of cities 56–61; future 54,
61–6, 70–2; effect on 3rd World
195; food exporter 207, 208; urban
development 5, 10, 37–8, 42–3,
45–51, 228; *see also* Belgium,
Denmark, Federal Republic of
Germany, France, Great Britain,
Greece, Italy, Netherlands,
Portugal, Spain
European Economic Community 67,
97
European Year of the Environment
227
eutrophication 172
exurbanization 37, 42, 47, 52

'Faith in the City', Archbishop of
Canterbury study group 154
famine 128
Faneuil Hall, Boston 130
farming *see* agriculture
Faust 152, 155–6
Federal Organization, work 141
Federal Republic of Germany 43,
46–7, 48, 55, 59, 173: future 64,
65, 71
female workforce, Europe 46–7, 140
fertilizers 171, 172
financial: market 5, 28; schemes, 3rd
World 222, 223, 225; services
63–4, 67, 96
First World: impact on 3rd World,
97–8, 175, 195, 197–8, 227–8,
230, colonialism 8–9, 11, 122,
198, 217; lessons from 3rd World
233; urban change, compared 3rd
World 92, 100–1
Florence 9, 10
fluid waste 171–2
food supply: 1st World 143–4, 147; 3rd
World 101, 103, 114, 206, 207, 208

forecasting trends 97–103, 99, 138–9
Foucault, M. 152, 161–2, 164, 167
Fowles, J. 160
France 43, 48, 51, 71: Great Britain, compared 69; Paris 13, 64, 65, 69
Frankfurt 64
Friedmann, J. 154
Fuller, T.D. 214
Functional Urban Regions (FURs) 37, 42–5
Future Work, J. Robertson 26

Ganges 233
Ganz, A. 43
garden cities, Britain 148
Garden Cities of Tomorrow, E. Howard 148
Genoa 48, 65
gentrification 59–60, 65
Georgswerder dump 173
German Byte 172
Germany *see* Federal Republic of Germany
Gershuny, J.I. 140
Ghana 92
Ghost in the Machine, The, A. Koestler 163
Gibson, T. 234
Gijon, Spain 48
Gilbert, A. 121
Glasgow 43, 48, 163: future 65, 67, 68, 71; history 40
Glass, R. 157
government 233, 234, 235: 1st World 51, 150; 3rd World 112, 114, 116, 117, 187, 196, 199–200, urban changes 94–6, 97, 101–2, 103; intervention in privatization 123; intervention in self help 118–9; urban bias 207, 209
Gramsci, A. 160
Grand Bassam, Ivory Coast 214
grass roots politics, 3rd World 200–1
Great Britain: air pollution 173–4; central government 51; city contrasts 1–3, 4; colonial power 11; demographic trends 46–7, 136, 139–40; future 130, 143, 162–3,

168, 229, economics 55, 58, 59, 66–70, 71, farming 143–4, responsibility for 145–6, 147, 148, South East 142, 144–5, 149–50; housing 183, 190; riots 1, 2, 158, 164–5; shareholding 27–8; statistics 43; urban development 14, 40–42, 46, 48, 49, 231, 233, until 20th century 9, 10–11, 39–40; *see also* London
Greece 46, 51: Athens 7, 12, 47, 65, 71
Green, K.C. 117
green belt policy, Britain 41, 58, 69
greenhouse effect 173
Grenoble 71
Gross Domestic Product 58
Gross National Product 25, 26
Groundwork Foundation 146–7
growth rates, urban 3rd World 76, 93, 206, 207; *see also* centralization
Guadalajara 87
Guinea Bissau 81
Gujarat, India 214
gypsum, energy technology 179

Habitat International Coalition 191
Haiti 81
Halifax, UK 43
Hall, P. 102
Hamburg 173
Handsworth 2, 165
Handy, C. 140–1, 149
Hardy, T. 10
Harvey, D. 159, 160
Havana 87
health 26, 176, 208, 217, 218, 231, 233
Heidegger, M. 156, 168
Henri, A. 14
Herbert, G. 19
Hesse, H. 22–3
high rise housing, Britain 183
historical perspective 6–15
home ownership, 1st World 60
Honduras 216
Hong Kong 90, 96
House as Symbol of Self, The, C. Cooper 22

housing: 1st World 16, 47, 60, 147,
183, 190, 201, 202, Britain 58,
165, 183; 3rd World 94, 97, 123,
community organizations 118–21,
181–91, 185, 186, 230, 232–3;
International Year of Shelter for
the Homeless 227
Houston 71
Howard, E. 16, 18–20, 23, 136, 148,
229
Human-scale Economics, M. Neef 24,
29
Hyderabad 88, 120, 121
hydrocarbons 174, 178
hypermarket 137

Ibadan, Nigeria 122
Illich, I. 141
Image of the City, The, K. Lynch 20
immigration: Asia 88; Latin America
83, 86
India: community organization 120;
decentralization 214; 'dependent
urbanization' 11; pollution 233;
urban change 77, 87, 88–9, 95; *see
also* Bombay, Calcutta
individual responsibility 145, 149,
230, 231
Indonesia 90–1, 117, 118, 120
industry: 1st World 10, 37, 38, 42, 43,
45, 48, 52, Britain 9, 10–11, 14,
39–40, 41, Industrial Revolution
10–11, 14, 39–40, 59; 3rd World
86, 88–9, 92, 93, 95, 114, 209,
rural 90–1, small town 214,
215–6; *see also* manufacturing
industries
information *see* statistics
information technology 62, 63, 130,
132, 133, 166: Britain 41, 42, 130
infrastructure 47, 48, 121, 216
inner city: problems, Britain 41, 231;
renewal 58, 66, 70,
Inner Game of Tennis, The, W.T.
Gallwey 231
Inner Urban Areas Act (1978) 1
institutionalization, citizenship 161–2
Intermediate Technology

Development Group 206, 210; *see
also* appropriate technology
international loans to 3rd World 222
International Monetary Fund 196, 201
International Year of Shelter for the
Homeless vii, 227
investment 27–9, 192, 207
Iraq 88
iron and steel production, Britain 40
Italy 9, 10, 48, 51, 65, 71: Rome 3–4,
7–8, 170–1, 172
Ivory Coast 91, 116, 122, 214

Jakarta 80, 112, 117, 118, 120
Japan 64, 96, 101, 142–3, 176, 195
Java 91
Johnson, S. 12
Jos, Nigeria 98
Jung, C.G. 17, 152

Kaduna, Nigeria 122
Kafanchan, Nigeria 214
Kampung Improvement Programme,
Jakarta 117, 118, 120
Kanpur, India 88
Kant, I. 156
Karachi 112, 117, 122, 221–6
Katchi Abadi (Squatter Settlements)
Improvement and Regularization
Programme, Karachi 222–6
Kelantan, Malaysia 90
Kenya, 91, 93, 98, 103, 116, 119
Ketengah Jaya, Malaysia 216
Khartoum 91
Khopoli, India 88
Kinshasa, Zaire 122
Kirby, R. 89
Knight, R. 37, 38
Knulp, H. Hesse 22–3
Koenigsberger, O. 184
Koestler, A. 152, 163–4, 165
Kuala Lumpur 117

La Paz 164
La Plata 86
'labelling' school, sociology 165
labour market 54, 60
Laghouat, M.M. 214–5

Lagos 81, 92, 93, 98, 175
Lahore 8
Lake Erie 172
land ownership, 3rd World 94
land tenure, 3rd World 83, 119, 216
land use, 1st World 62, 69, 148
Latin America 83–7, 84, 85, 89, 92
    93, 121, 175: Organization of
    Latin American States 197
Leeds 68
Lees, A. 12
Leipert, C. 25–6, 29
leisure, future 70, 132, 133, 136, 140,
    141, 146, 149: Britain 67, 68, 69;
    hyper-expansion scenario 127,
    130; retirement population 61
Lembaga Kemajuan Trengganu
    Tengah (KETENGAH) 215–6
Leverhulme, 1st Viscount (W. Lever)
    157
Libya 93
Liège 48, 71
'life space' 154
light industry, Britain 40; *see also*
    manufacturing industries
Lightmoor project 147
Lille 48, 65, 71
Lima 81, 87, 181–2, 184
Liverpool 48, 66: future 68, 69, 71;
    history 10; unemployment 14, 46,
    48, 162–3
Living Cities, C. Mercer 16–17
Living Economy, The, P. Ekins 23–4,
    26, 29
local government 234: 3rd World 112,
    113, 114, 115–17, 123, 124;
    Britain 146, 147
Lombardo, J.F. 213–14
London: City 1, 2–3, 69, 167–8;
    decentralization 12; Docklands
    Scheme 69, 167–8; East End 65,
    163; future 59–60, 64, 65, 69, 71,
    130; history 9, 10, 12–13, 39, 96,
    171; population 12; quality of life
    234; riots 1, 2, 158
Los Angeles–Long Beach 101
Lucknow, India 88
Lusaka 117, 119, 120

Lynch, K. 20

Macaulay, T. 13
McRobie, G. 206
Malaysia 90, 91, 117, 234: small town
    development 212, 215–16, 218
Mali 79
management *see* administration,
    community, government, local
    government, private sector
Managua, Nicaragua 81
Manchester 9, 10, 12, 40, 68
Manila 79, 81, 112, 118, 122
manufacturing industries: 1st World
    45–6, 48, 52, 55, 58–9, 60, future
    54, 62–3, 64–5, 72, 228, Britain
    11, 39–40, 41, 67–8; 3rd World
    83, 88, 112; alternative future 132
Maputo, Mozambique 100
Marcel, G. 154
Marcuse, H. 160
marginalization, 3rd World 199, 200
market forces 24, 50, 149, 232
market towns 41
marketing, future economies 166
Marx, K. 11, 50, 155–6, 159, 161,
    164, 230
Masoom Colony, Karachi 226
Mauritania 90
Mediterranean 45
mega-cities 37
Megalopolis 100, 136, 144, 145
Mercer, C. 16, 17, 20
Mesopotamia 6–7, 9–10
Mexico 83, 84, 85, 86, 87; *see also*
    Mexico City
Mexico City 5, 81, 83, 86–7, 99, 101:
    environmental damage 175, 176,
    233
Middle East 8–9
Middlesbrough 9, 10
migration, population 229, 234: 1st
    World 42, 43, 45, 57–8; 3rd World
    78, 80, 112, 207, small town
    development 212–13, 214; *see
    also* centralization,
    decentralization
Milan 65, 71

military strategy, population
    distribution 95
Milliband, R. 167
Minas Gerais, Brazil 214
Miracle, M.P. and D.S. 214
modernism 153, 156, 157, 162
modernization, 3rd World 198
Mombasa 93
Montevideo 86
Morocco 93, 215
Mortimer, E. 65
movement, population *see* migration
Mozambique 99–100, 119
multinational corporations 96–7, 129,
    160, 227–8
Mumford, L. 3, 4, 6, 19, 148
Munn, J. 146

Nairobi 91, 93, 98, 103: management
    116, 119
Nancy 43
Naples 65, 71
Nasik, India 88
National Product, Britain 39, 40, 41
natural disasters, 3rd World 78
Near East 8–9
Neef, M. 29
neighbourhood 15, 18–20, 23
Nepal 79, 88
Netherlands 42, 43, 48, 49, 51
New Economics Foundation 127,
    134, 227
New Jersey 65, 173
New York City 64, 65, 71
New Zealand, food exporter 207, 208
new-town development 16, 41, 58, 144
Newmark, New Jersey 65
Newcastle 71
Newman, O. 158
Newson, J. and E. 157
Nicaragua 81
Nigeria 77, 98, 116, 117, 122, 214:
    Lagos 81, 90, 93, 98, 175
Nile 233
nitrogen oxides 173, 174, 178
non-governmental organizations
    (NGO's) 181, 182, 184, 188–9,
    188, 190, 191

non-renewable resources 175, 176–7
non-tradeables 54, 56–7, 57, 58, 60,
    70
North America: effect on 3rd World
    195; environmental damage 172,
    173, 176; food exporter 207, 208;
    future 52, 55, 58, 64, 65, 68, 71,
    96, 130; Pruit-Ighoe 158; society
    154; urban development 5, 37, 42,
    43, 45, 46, 48, 228, compared 3rd
    World 101, military expenditure
    95, policy 49, 50, 51
North Atlantic Treaty Organisation
    (NATO) 197
North Korea 90, 91, 95
North Sea 172
North–South divide, Britain 168
Norway 43
Norwich 9, 10
Nouakchott, Mauritania 92

oil 8, 207–8
Organi Pilot Project (OPP), Karachi
    221–26
Organization of Latin American
    States 197
organizational responsibility 145,
    146, 149
Osborne, P. 183
Other Economic Summit 134
Ottoman Empire 8
'Our Common Future', Brundtland
    Report 193, 194–5
'Ownwork', Britain 149
Oyama, Y. 142–3, 150
ozone 174

P'Yongyang area, North Korea 91
Pakistan 9, 79, 81, 88, 226: Karachi
    112, 117, 122, 221–26
Palermo 71
Paris 13, 64, 65, 69
participation, community 113–14,
    118–21, 124; *see also* community
part-time work, future 141–42
Peking 88, 99
Perry, C. 19
personal perspective 15, 20–3

Index

Peru 77, 81, 87, 181–82, 184, 214
Philippines 88, 119
physical environment, city 15, 16–18,
  23
Pittsburg 48, 65, 71
planning 232, 233, 235
Plymouth, Britain 67
polarization reversal 86, 89
police 2, 131, 165
policy 233, 235: 1st World 49–52,
  59–60, 66, 72, Britain 69
Policy for the Inner Cities (1977),
  DOE 1
politics, 3rd World 92, 94, 231:
  sustainable development 192–203
pollution 171–72, 178–9, 229: 1st
  World 47, 49, 173–4, 233; 3rd
  World 175, 176, 230, 231; and
  GNP 25
population change *see* demography
Port au Prince 81
Portugal 46
post industrial 149
poverty 2, 5–6, 16, 111–12, 229
prediction of trends 97–103, 99, 138–9
private sector 232, 233, 234: 3rd
  World 111, 113, 122–3, 124, 229,
  230
production 158, 160, 166, 195
Professional Organization, work 141
project oriented approach, 3rd World
  112, 117, 123
protectionism, 1st World 97
proto-scenes 143
Pruit-Ighoe, St. Louis 158
Psychology of Place, The, D. Canter
  20
public transport 48–9, 122–3, 218
Puebla, Mexico 86

Queretaro, Mexico 86

Raban, J. 158–9, 160, 162, 166
railways, Britain 40
Ramachandran, A. 184
Rangoon 81
recycling 131, 176, 178, 179
refugees 78, 100, 197

regional: centres 1st World 67, 70;
  policy 49, 50, 51
Relph, E. 154
renewable resources 176
research technology, 1st World 64
residential preferences, 1st World 54,
  57, 60, 61, 65, 70, 228: Britain
  40–1; compared 3rd world 92, 101
resource accounting 26
retirement population 61–2, 66, 70
reurbanization, Europe 43–4
revenue generation 115
Rhine 172
Rio de Janeiro 83, 86, 99, 176, 233
riots 1–2, 6, 158, 160, 164–5
Robertson, J. 149–50
Roman Empire 7
Rome 3–4, 7–8, 170–1, 172
Rondinelli, D.A. 213
Rosario, Argentina 86
Rotterdam 48
Roubaix, France 65
Rousseau, J.J. 12
rural: 3rd World 5, 6, 80, 90–1, 94,
  207, 209–10; land use 62, 69;
  urban values 11–12, 15; *see also*
  urban–rural realtionship
Rural Rides, W. Cobbett 13
'rust belt' 46

Saarbrücken 48
St. Étienne 48
St. Louis 65, 71, 158
San Francisco 130
San Lorenzo, Argentina 86
San Nicolas, Argentina 86
Sane Alternative, The, J. Robertson
  127
sanitation, Orangi Project 221–26
Santiago 164
São Paulo 81, 83, 86, 96, 97, 99, 175
satellite towns, 1st World 11, 58, 66
Saudi Arabia 88, 117
Schumacher, E.F. 156, 209, 232
scrubbers, energy technology 179
secondary cities 228, 229
self-build housing 184
self-employment, future 141

244

self-help 112, 113, 118–21, 122, 124, 217
self-sufficiency, Britain 145–6, 149
Seoul 88, 96, 99, 175
service industries 166: 1st World 11, 46, 51, 52, 54, 55, 59, 60, 65, 72, Britain 39, 41, 42, 48, 68; 3rd World 112
sewage 171–72, 175, 178, 230
sex ratios, 3rd World, 93
Shahi, V.P. 214
Shamrock Organization, work 141
Shanghai 79, 88, 89, 99
shareholding, Britain 27–8
Shayo, S.A. 218
Sheffield 68
Singapore 90, 96–7, 175
Singh, R.B. 214
single parent families, Britain 140
Situationist International 160
Sivaramakrishnan, K.C. 117
slums, 3rd World 207
Small is Positive, G. McRobie 206
small towns, 3rd World 212–18
'social city', E. Howard 16, 18–20, 23, 136, 148, 229
social indicators 26
social investment 28–9
social problems 17, 66: riots 1–2, 6, 158, 160, 164–5
social provision 228, 235: Britain 41; 3rd World 101–2, 199
socialism 193
Soft City, J. Raban 21–2, 159
soil fertility and erosion 143, 170, 171, 175, 176, 230, 231, 233
solar energy 208
South Africa 93, 99–100, 197
South Korea 79, 88, 95, 214: Seoul 88, 96, 99, 175
Southall, London 158
Southampton 67, 68, 69
Southey, R. 13
Spain 43, 46, 48, 51, 65
special projects, 3rd World 116–17, 123–4
spiritual needs, New Economics 30
'Spread City', South East Britain 136, 144–5, 147, 148, 150

squatters, 3rd world 187–8, 221, 222, 232
Sri Lanka 112
statistics: availability of, 1st World 43, 3rd World 75, 76–7, 79, 80, 82, 88; forecasting trends 97–8, 138–9
steam power, Britain 39–40
Stren, R. 116, 122
surburbanization 40, 42, 43, 47, 52, 228
Sudan 91
sulphur 173, 174, 178
Sunderland 43, 48
Surabaja, Indonesia 90
sustainable development, 3rd World 192–203: 'living' 137, 142, 145
Swaminathan, M.S. 208
Swansea 67
Sweden 43

Taiwan 90, 214
Tanzania 92, 94, 98, 116, 234: small town development 212, 215, 217–18
Tatlin, V.Y. 162
technology 165–6, 167, 235; 1st World 38–9, 55, 59, 228, future 61, 62–3, 64, 70, 140, Britain 67; 3rd World 206–10, 223, 224; biotechnology 62, 132, 133; environmental 179, 206, 209–10, 231; hyperexpansionist scenario 26, 127, 129–31; *see also* information technology
Tess of the d'Urbervilles, T. Hardy 10
textile industry, Britain 9, 40
Thailand 90, 96, 112, 117, 122, 214
Thames 172
The Other Economic Summit (TOES) (1984) 23, 27, 28
theories, development 231–32
Third World relationship to First: *see* First World
Thomas, M. 154, 166
Timeless Way of Building, C. Alexander 18
Tokyo 64, 101, 142

Toluca, Mexico 86
Tonnies, F. 153
Torino, Italy 48
Tourcoing, France 65
tourism: 1st World 59, 64, 67, 130, 132; 3rd World 96
toxic waste 173, 178–9
Toxeth, Liverpool 1, 2, 158
trade 207, 208: 1st World 10, 59, 63–4, 67
tradeables 54, 56, 57, 58–9, 60: future 65, 66, 67, 68, 72, 228
traditional cities 37, 38, 45, 48, 61, 65, 228: US 51, 52
transport *see* communications
Tuan, Y.F. 154
Tunisia 93
Turkey 7, 8, 9
Tyneside 163

ujamaa programme, Tanzania 215, 217–8
unemployment 16: 1st World 46, 47, 49, Britain 48, 69, 162–3, 165; future scenarios, 128
United Kingdom *see* Great Britain
United Nations: Population Division 99–100, 101; predictions 76, 78
upgrading 120, 121
urban areas compared cities, 3rd World 76, 77, 78, 82
urban–rural relationship 131–32: 1st World 137, 148, 149; 3rd World 77–8, 102–3, 212–3, 229
urban sprawl, 1st World 136, 144, 145: fringe 137
urbanization: 1st World 10, Japan 140; 3rd World 75–6, 133, 176, 'dependent urbanization' 11; *see also* centralization
Uruguay 83, 86

Valenciennes, France 43, 48, 65
Van den Berg, L. 43, 45, 49, 50
vandalism, physical environment 16

Vaughan, R. 13
Voltaire 12
voluntary sector 233
Von Thunen 21

Ward, P. 121
Warka, Mesopotamia 6–7, 9–10
wars, 3rd World 197
Warsaw pact 197
waste disposal 116, 122, 172–3, 176–7, 178–9, 227, 230
water: pollution 171–72, 175, 178–9, 230; supply, 3rd World 117, 122, 218, 221–26
wealth distribution 142
Weber, M. 153
West Midlands 48
Wester River 172
'Westgate' housing project, America 16
Whitlock, B. 13–14
Williams, R. 153
win-win situations 149
women: programmes, 3rd World 226; working, 46–7, 140
Wordsworth, W. 13
work, lifestyle patterns, future of 26–7: *see also* employment
World Bank 120, 133, 196, 201
World Commission on Environment and Development (WCED) 193, 194–5
World economic system 196–8
world market, effect on 3rd World 63–4, 96, 97
world trade *see* trade

Yokohama 101
Yorkshire 68

Zaire 92, 122
Zambia 117, 119, 120
Zarate, Argentina 86
Zen and the Art of Motor Cycle Maintenance, R. Pirsig 156
Zola, E. 13